PAYING FOR THE PAST

PAYING FOR THE PAST

The Case Against Prior Record Sentence Enhancements

Richard S. Frase and Julian V. Roberts

OXFORD
UNIVERSITY PRESS

OXFORD
UNIVERSITY PRESS

Oxford University Press is a department of the University of Oxford. It furthers the University's objective of excellence in research, scholarship, and education by publishing worldwide. Oxford is a registered trade mark of Oxford University Press in the UK and certain other countries.

Published in the United States of America by Oxford University Press
198 Madison Avenue, New York, NY 10016, United States of America.

Library of Congress Cataloging-in-Publication Data
Names: Frase, Richard S., author. | Roberts, Julian V., author.
Title: Paying for the Past : The Case Against Prior Record Sentence Enhancements / Richard S. Frase and Julian V. Roberts.
Description: New York, NY : Oxford University Press, 2020. |
Includes bibliographical references and index.
Identifiers: LCCN 2018058212 | ISBN 9780190254001 (hardcover) |
ISBN 9780190055042 (electronic publication) | ISBN 9780190254018 (UPDF)
Subjects: LCSH: Sentences (Criminal procedure)—Social aspects—United States. |
Recidivists—Legal status, laws, etc.—United States.
Classification: LCC KF9685 .F734 2020 | DDC 345.73/0772—dc23
LC record available at https://lccn.loc.gov/2018058212

SUMMARY OF CONTENTS

CONTENTS

PREFACE

Sentencing enhancements based on the offender's record of prior convictions (or "criminal history") are a feature of all modern sentencing regimes. In many systems—particularly those in the United States—these enhancements have powerful and often undesirable impacts on sentencing outcomes, greatly increasing the severity of punishments and the resultant burdens on strained state budgets and on the lives of offenders, while also undercutting important sentencing principles and limitations. Yet this topic has received little attention from researchers and policymakers—it has simply been assumed that repeat offenders merit greater punishment. Moreover, existing enhancement rules were adopted with very limited research or discussion, and vary widely across systems; they cannot all be equally just and cost-effective. There is widespread agreement that some degree of enhancement for repeat offending is usually appropriate, but much less agreement on how much additional punishment is necessary, or why.

Until very recently, no one had even surveyed different enhancement schemes, and documented the intended and unintended consequences of powerful prior record enhancements. Nor has anyone attempted to devise a principled, evidence-based model to guide researchers, sentencing policymakers, judges, and other practitioners. This book provides such a model, drawing on a comprehensive, multi-year study of existing practices in American jurisdictions employing sentencing guidelines, and on consensus views of the relevant issues. (For further information on prior record enhancement rules and practices in U.S. guidelines systems, and on other aspects of those systems, see Frase et al. 2015; Robina Institute 2018; and Frase 2019.)

Difficult problems of policy and practice abound in this neglected area of sentencing law. Some of these are ethical in nature: Why should an individual's previous criminal acts, for which he has already been punished, increase his punishment for later crimes? Proponents of retributive punishment theories are deeply divided on whether, why, and to what extent a repeat offender deserves more punishment for a new offense than someone without prior convictions who commits the same offense. And although there may be plausible crime control reasons to punish recidivists more severely, those reasons—and any prior-record enhancement formulas based on such reasons—require empirical validation. Yet almost no such research has been conducted. Across the United States, sentencing commissions have routinely imposed additional punishment to reflect prior crimes, without ever conducting validation research, or even explaining to defendants why their prior, previously punished crimes now trigger yet further punishment. This represents a serious failure on the part of the guidelines authorities.

If prior convictions can justify sentencing enhancements, many important questions arise, for example:

- How much weight should a prior record carry in the sentencing equation—as much weight as the seriousness of the current offense being sentenced? Less weight? More weight?
- How much weight should different kinds of prior offending carry, in the prior record formula—should that depend on the seriousness of the prior crime? On the degree of similarity to the current crime? On data correlating patterns of prior offending with recidivism risk?
- Should prior crimes committed when the person was a juvenile count in sentencing proceedings as an adult? If so, which kinds of offenses, and how long should they remain alive for the purposes of subsequent sentencing decisions?
- How long should an adult prior conviction count before it is removed from the offender's record and no longer considered at sentencing for a new crime?
- Even if "look-back" limits are imposed, excluding consideration of convictions entered many years earlier, should further limits be placed on prior record enhancements when sentencing aging offenders, in light of their well-documented declining crime risk?
- How should policymakers and judges respond to data consistently showing that prior record enhancements have a strongly disparate impact on nonwhite offenders?
- Should sentencing judges have discretion to adjust guidelines recommendations and/or customary sentencing norms, to lessen the prior record enhancement problems previously noted, just as they traditionally have power to "depart" based on atypical case-specific *offense* factors?

- Should criminal history enhancements be mitigated when there is evidence that the defendant has made some progress toward desistance, even if he has failed to completely stop offending?

These and many other critical but largely unexamined questions arise from the policy of imposing harsher sentences on defendants with prior convictions. As we shall demonstrate, prior record enhancements generate additional punishment even if the latest conviction occurred years after the most recent prior sentence expired, and even if that conviction was committed in very different circumstances. Moreover, across the United States, the effects of such enhancements are often rigidly formulaic and cumulative, imposing progressively harsher punishments that are unjustifiable in terms of either crime prevention or retribution.

This volume describes the use of prior-record enhancements in U.S. sentencing guidelines systems, exposes the theories underpinning this penal practice, and explores the practical consequences of these enhancements. The reason for the focus on U.S. guidelines is twofold. First, they contain formal rules directing judges to impose specific sentence enhancements based on prior convictions, and the extensive sentencing data available in many of these jurisdictions lay bare the effects that these rules have on actual sentences imposed. Elsewhere, while prior convictions are taken into account, their effects on sentencing are far less transparent. Second, the enhancements are much stronger in the United States than in any other country: repeat offenders in the United States pay a much heavier price for their former crimes.

Here are some examples of the ways that prior record enhancements trigger substantial and very problematic penalty increases in many U.S. guidelines systems:

- A 60-year-old can have his sentence greatly enhanced for offenses committed when he was only 20 (or even younger).
- A single prior offense can move the offender halfway (or more) across the criminal history categories of a sentencing grid.
- A series of nonviolent felonies (thefts for example) can move an individual all the way across the grid.
- Offenders in the highest criminal history category have recommended custody sentences that on average (across all guidelines systems) are about six times longer than sentences for the lowest criminal history category; in some systems the average high-history sentence is over 10 times longer, and for certain types of crime, as much as 100 times longer.

This volume critically examines the two principal rationales for prior-record sentencing enhancements: the repeat offender's assumed higher risk of further offending (the crime control rationale), and his alleged greater culpability (the retributive or Just Deserts rationale). The book also identifies and measures the many negative consequences of substantial prior-record enhancements, which:

- Increase the size and expense of prison populations;
- Undermine the important principle of punishment in proportion to offense severity;
- Increase the need for prison beds to house property and other nonviolent offenders;
- Generate large numbers of aging, low-risk, high-cost prison inmates;
- Contribute to racial disproportionality in prison populations;
- Undermine offenders' efforts to reintegrate into society.

Our central message of the volume is this: *across U.S. guidelines systems (and likely in other jurisdictions as well), repeat offenders are routinely subject to levels of punishment that cannot be justified in terms of the twin rationales for prior record enhancements, risk and retribution, and the adverse impacts that these enhancements produce.* Few would argue that courts should sentence offenders totally blind to their prior criminal histories; treating the first offender as harshly as the multiple recidivist is unfair to the former, and wasteful of scarce public resources. But as this volume will show, the magnitude and rigidity of prior record enhancements in the United States generate criminal penalties that are unnecessarily severe, undeserved, and harmful. The consequence is mass injustice.

ACKNOWLEDGMENTS

The research reported in this volume was conducted over several years and was generously supported by the Robina Institute of Criminal Law and Criminal Justice at the University of Minnesota Law School, and by the Research Support Fund of the Faculty of Law, University of Oxford. We are grateful to the Institute and the University of Oxford for their support. Many colleagues helped us to refine our thinking in this area and make this a better book. We would particularly like to thank Rhys Hester for his contributions to the four chapters of this book that he co-authored, and for his extensive comments on other chapters. Thanks also for the many useful suggestions we have received from Kelly Mitchell, David Boerner, Stephen Chanenson, Alessandro Corda, Jan de Keijser, David Farrington, Melissa Hamilton, James Jacobs, Julia Laskorunsky, Kevin Reitz, Michael Tonry, and Ronald Wright. We are also grateful to participants attending several seminars where these ideas were discussed, including sessions at meetings of the National Association of Sentencing Commissions. Finally, we gratefully acknowledge the contributions to this project of our research associates at the University of Minnesota and in the United Kingdom over the years, especially Lewis Anderson, Jihn Harn, Keir Irwin Rogers, Austin Keller, Haaris Pasha, and Thomas Schram.

R.S.F. and J.V.R.
Minneapolis and Oxford
October 2018

INTRODUCTION

PRIOR RECORD SENTENCING ENHANCEMENTS IN CONTEXT

Sentencing practices and structures vary widely around the world, yet two features are universal. First, the retributive principle of *Proportionality* establishes a correspondence between the severity of punishments and the seriousness of the offense (including the offender's culpability for that crime).[1] According to this principle, the severity of the penalty should progressively increase to match the seriousness of the crime and the offender's level of blameworthiness for the offense.

The second universal sentencing feature concerns the offender's criminal past. Again, whether through statutory provisions, appellate judgments, or formal sentencing guidelines, almost all[2] countries impose harsher sentences upon repeat offenders. This practice is known as the *Recidivist Sentencing Premium, Criminal History Enhancement,* or *Prior Record Enhancement.* (Throughout the remainder of this book, we will sometimes use the abbreviation "PRE" to refer to Prior Record Enhancements and other elevated penalties for repeat offenders.) The recidivist premium typically mandates progressively increasing severity in response to the number and seriousness of the offender's prior crimes, and these enhancements may or may not be subject to capping or other overall limits. A great deal of scholarship on sentencing has accumulated in the post-guidelines era, yet scholars have devoted far more attention to offense seriousness; criminal history has only recently become the focus of sustained examination (see, e.g., Hester et al. 2018; Lippke 2016; Frase et al. 2015; Hamilton 2015; Bagaric 2014a; King 2014; Roberts and Yalincak 2014; Frase 2013a; Tamburrini and Ryberg 2012; Roberts and von Hirsch 2010; Roberts 2008a, b).

Prior record enhancements are important, both by virtue of the volume of individuals affected and the major consequences of these enhancements. The recidivist premium affects the majority of offenders appearing for sentencing. In 2006, in a sample of the 75 largest counties in the United States, over 70 percent of convicted felons had one or more prior convictions, over half had at least one prior felony conviction, and both of these proportions had risen since 1992 (BJS 1995, table 31; BJS 2010, table 15). State-specific data reveal similar patterns. For example, two-thirds of felons sentenced in Minnesota from 2014 to 2016[3] had at least one criminal history point, while only 38 percent did in 1981; moreover, the proportion of Minnesota offenders with significant criminal history scores (4 to 6 or more points) has also grown steadily—from 8 percent in 1981 to almost one-quarter in 2016 (MSGC 2017c, 46). Likewise, most offenders in common law jurisdictions outside of the United States have prior convictions. For example, in England and Wales, 90 percent of offenders sentenced by the courts in 2013 had at least one prior conviction or formal caution, and approximately half had at least 10 prior adjudications (Roberts and Pina-Sanchez 2015, table 9.1).[4] Finally, as we shall document more fully in chapters 5 through 8, the magnitude of criminal history enhancements, and their fiscal costs and other consequences, are substantial.

Notwithstanding the frequency and impact of PREs, surprisingly little attention has been paid to their rationale and justification—*Why, exactly, should we punish recidivists more harshly?* The penologist Nigel Walker referred to prior convictions as "the most obvious example of aggravation" (1985, 44) and more recently Hessick and Hessick (2011, 45–46) described the recidivist sentencing premium as "one punishment issue on which everyone seems to agree." Well, not quite everyone perhaps. As we shall document in chapter 1, there is considerable disagreement among retributive theorists, and a number of them explicitly reject the use of prior convictions at sentencing. But it is certainly true that taking previous convictions into account at sentencing carries great intuitive appeal.[5] Members of the public believe that offenders with previous convictions should be punished more severely, particularly if the prior offenses are the same as the current conviction. This has been demonstrated in empirical investigations in several countries. Thus, when asked to sentence offenders with different criminal histories, the public punishes recidivists more severely than first offenders (see Hester et al. 2018; Roberts and Hough 2011; Roberts 2008a, b). (On the other hand, as we discuss later in this volume, there is also public support for limits on repeat offender enhancements, in particular, for disregarding older priors and juvenile crimes.) Most criminal justice practitioners also share the view that prior convictions are relevant at sentencing, although this consensus breaks down when different groups are asked to conceptualize and quantify the practice.[6] Finally, the rather limited research also suggests that defendants see prior convictions as relevant to the sentencing decision, albeit in ways that differ from the views held by (non-defense) practitioners.[7]

The remainder of this introduction is organized as follows. Part A provides an overall summary of the widely varying PRE rules found in U.S. guidelines systems and in other common law jurisdictions. Part B explores the most widely accepted rationales for these enhancements, laying the foundation for several later chapters examining these issues in more detail. In Part C we address the critical need for, and paucity of, research to validate the choice of prior record formulas and their effectiveness in achieving stated goals and rationales. Part D elaborates on the negative consequences of substantial PREs. Part E summarizes the remaining chapters of the book.

A. Varieties of Prior Record Enhancement (PRE)

Prior convictions affect sentencing in many ways, including: recidivist statutes (the best known of which are the "three-strikes" laws that proliferated in the 1990s, and remain in effect in many jurisdictions), "criminal history" formulas embedded in sentencing guidelines regimes, statutory sentencing provisions that identify priors as an important aggravating factor or create separate "recidivist ranges" or lower penalties for first-time commission of the offense, and appellate judgments. The prevalence of a general rule that prescribes more severe punishments for repeat offenders masks great diversity in theory, prescribed rules, and practice. Variation exists in terms of the *philosophy* justifying record-based sentencing enhancements, the *magnitude* of those enhancements, the specific *dimensions* of a criminal record that are incorporated in criminal history rules, and the *implementation* of those rules by judges and other practitioners.

The most common approach to PRE in other common law jurisdictions such as England and Wales, New Zealand, or Australia involves a general sentencing provision that directs courts to aggravate sentencing to reflect prior convictions (see Appendix B for additional illustrative provisions from common law jurisdictions). For example, in England and Wales, section 143 of the Criminal Justice Act 2003 states that:

> In considering the seriousness of an offense committed by an offender who has one or more previous convictions, the court must treat each previous conviction as an aggravating factor if (in the case of that conviction) the court considers that it can reasonably be so treated having regard, in particular, to:
>
> (a) the nature of the offence to which the conviction relates and its relevance to the current offence, and
>
> (b) the time that has elapsed since the conviction.

In England and other jurisdictions, the degree to which previous convictions aggravate a sentence is a matter for judicial discretion to resolve. One consequence is that while the aggravating effect of a record (or the mitigating effect of a "clean" record) may be clear, there is little clarity regarding the magnitude of the enhancement appropriate for recidivists, or the degree of mitigation appropriate for first offenders. Defendants, their lawyers, sentencing judges, and other interested parties can have little accurate idea of how much additional punishment is imposed upon a defendant as a result of his criminal past. Sentencing statistics are little help in this regard. Some countries publish custody rates or average sentence lengths broken down by categories of criminal history, but these are usually uncorrected for important correlated variables such as crime seriousness, which makes it hard to isolate the effect of previous convictions.[8]

1. *Sentencing in the United States: Exploiting the Natural Laboratory of Penal Practices*

Across the United States, many jurisdictions employ formal, numerical sentencing guidelines that specify the way that prior convictions enhance the sentence and the degree of severity arising from prior convictions.[9] Yet there is wide diversity of PRE application within the U.S. schemes. The evolution of prior record sentencing enhancements has been haphazard, and also parochial in the sense that each guidelines jurisdiction[10] has developed its own PRE practices and policies without any comparative or "best practice" analysis. Providing such an analysis is one of the goals of this volume.[11]

Some guidelines mandate a powerful PRE while others limit the degree of aggravation arising from previous convictions (Frase et al. 2015). Guidelines systems also differ greatly in the ways in which they compute their criminal history scores. Here are two examples. Custody status—whether the offender was on parole or probation or in another designated release or confinement status when she committed her latest offense—is a component of the criminal history score in about two-thirds of guidelines jurisdictions, but not in the others. And while about half of guidelines jurisdictions exclude prior convictions that were entered many years ago, at least for less serious priors, the other half ignore this dimension of criminal history. The existence of explicit counting rules and the wide variation in practice thus creates a natural laboratory for researchers to explore the consequences of record-based sentencing enhancements. In this project we have capitalized on the substantial and transparent variations in the PRE rules contained in guidelines to explore these issues.

If there is one lesson about PREs that emerges from scholarship and research over the past 20 years it is that the issues are more complex than the public, policymakers, or even sentencing commissions often assume. Many earlier approaches to a criminal record as an aggravating factor reflect a simplistic approach by which the assumed risk of re-offending or level of culpability tracks the number of prior convictions. This simplicity is reflected in many guideline structures where each prior felony triggers the same quantum of additional punishment (see Part A.4). In general, a cumulative, monotonic relationship emerges between the number and seriousness of prior convictions and the severity of recommended sentences. This has long been the case: the first version of the Minnesota guidelines manual asserted in 1980 that "severity of sanctions [should] increase in *direct proportion* to increases in the severity of criminal offenses and the severity of criminal histories" (MSGC 1980, 26, emphasis added). Our response is to ask: Why?

2. Counting Prior Crimes: The Criminal History Calculation

This volume explores the variability in the methods and magnitudes of criminal history scoring and resulting sentence enhancements across the United States (see Appendix A for a sampling of American guidelines criminal history provisions). We examine the dimensions of criminal history (such as how long ago the prior conviction was entered, whether the offender was serving a sentence at the time of the current crime, and the degree of similarity between the current and previous convictions) and ask whether these dimensions (and the weight they carry), are theoretically sound and validated by systematic research. In order to ground the discussion, however, it is worth briefly noting here the most common approach across the United States to considering prior convictions, which involves the assignment of criminal history points. These points are then totaled to constitute a criminal history score that generates some degree of sentence enhancement—often additional time in prison.

The following example shows, for a given case in two guidelines states (Minnesota and North Carolina), how the criminal history score is computed in each system and what recommended sentence results from that score. The illustrative case involves a felony—armed robbery—classified by both states in the fourth-highest level of offense severity,[12] with the following potential criminal history components (not all of which are actually counted in both states): a prior felony at the same offense severity level as, and similar in nature to, the current offense; four prior misdemeanor convictions; two prior juvenile court adjudications for felony-level crimes; and custody status (on probation) at the time of the current offense. The points assigned in each state, for each of these potential criminal history components, are shown in table I.1, along with the resulting increases in recommended sentences.[13]

Table I.1. Illustrative guidelines calculations for two states

	Added criminal history points	
	Minnesota	North Carolina
1 prior felony conviction (4th-highest severity level)	1.5	6
Similarity of prior and current felony offenses	0	1
4 prior misdemeanor convictions	1	4
2 prior felony-level juvenile court adjudications	1	0
Custody status (on probation) at time of offense	1	1
Totals	4.5 points	12 points
Recommended minimum sentence	59 months	88 months
Zero-history recommended sentence	32 months	58 months
PRE increase over zero-history sentence	+83%	+52%
Portion of recommended sentence due to PRE	46%	34%

Sources: MSGC 2017a, North Carolina Sentencing and Policy Advisory Commission 2014.

The Minnesota offender has a total criminal history score of 4.5 points (which the guidelines round down to four points); this places him in the third-highest criminal history category, resulting in a recommended minimum sentence of 59 months assuming full credit for good behavior in prison.[14] If he had no criminal history points he would be subject to a recommended minimum sentence of 32 months. As shown in the last two lines of the table, there are several ways to quantify the criminal history enhancement in such a case. One way is to express it as a percentage of the base (zero-history) sentence: the recommended sentence with 4 points is 83 percent longer than the recommended zero-history sentence. Considered from another perspective, when the 4-point offender receives the recommended minimum sentence of 59 months, previous convictions are accounting for almost half of his sentence—the PRE increase of 27 months (from 32 to 59) is 46 percent of the 59-month sentence.

As for the North Carolina offender, his total of 12 points places him in prior record category IV (10–13 points, likewise the third-highest category), giving him a recommended minimum sentence of 88 months (using the midpoint of the applicable range for that cell on the sentencing grid). If his criminal history was zero he would have a recommended minimum sentence of 58 months. The PRE recommended sentence, 88 months, is 52 percent longer than the zero-history sentence, and the PRE increase of 30 months (from 58 to 88) accounts for about one-third of the 88-month sentence.

In the above example, several dimensions of criminal history play a more limited role in one state or the other. In North Carolina, custody status receives only one-sixth of the weight of the prior felony (versus effectively equal weight, in Minnesota), and the two juvenile adjudications add no points in North Carolina. On the other hand, there are no added points for offense similarity in Minnesota. And although prior misdemeanors contributed a slightly higher proportion of the total point score for North Carolina in this example (one-third of total points, versus effectively one-fourth for Minnesota), the contribution of a larger number of misdemeanors would be much higher in North Carolina because there is no upper limit on how many points misdemeanors can add (in Minnesota they usually add at most one point).

3. Equal PRE Increments, as Prior Record Increases

Most grid-based guidelines employ regularly spaced increments in sentence lengths to reflect the offender's prior offending. For example, in North

Carolina, presumptive sentence ranges for felonies increase by a fixed percentage for each prior record level: thus for offense class B1, sentence ranges increase by 15 percent over the previous (i.e., lower) prior record level (North Carolina Sentencing and Policy Advisory Commission 2014). Other schemes adopt a similarly static approach, although not always based upon a percentage increase. In Minnesota, criminal history categories in the main grid increase sentence length by a fixed number of months at each offense severity level (with larger increments at higher severity levels). For example, at level 8 criminal history categories increase by 10 months; at level 11, categories increase by 20 months (MSGC 2017a).

This method is adopted for the sake of consistency of application,[15] but it suffers from the simplifying assumption that the significance of prior crimes is always the same, and therefore the degree of aggravation should be constant. Yet this is a procrustean solution that is the equivalent of creating equally spaced rankings of offense seriousness levels and then forcing all offenses into one of these ranks. It is an oversimplification to consider each prior conviction as having the same risk-predictive weight, or to see each prior conviction as increasing culpability to exactly the same extent—two offenders with the same criminal history score may represent very different levels of risk or blameworthiness. A major goal of this volume is to explore and highlight the complex ways in which prior convictions interact with other offender risk factors; another goal is to question when and to what extent prior convictions increase offender culpability for the current offense.

4. *The Criminal History Assembly Line*

Criminal history calculations in U.S. guidelines systems function like an assembly line with the offender acquiring additional criminal history points for circumstances such as committing the offense while on probation, having a given number of prior felony convictions, and so on. When she reaches the end of the line, her total points convert to a corresponding number of recommended months in prison (if the offense warrants custody). There are many adverse consequences of this mechanistic arrangement. For example, when an offense is committed while on probation, that probation violation may have the same or an even greater punitive weight in the sentencing equation as the prior conviction itself—a Minnesota offender's custody status counts as much as a prior felony of seriousness level 4 or 5, and counts more than a prior conviction at levels 1 to 3. This arrangement also produces a kind of double-counting—a prior conviction and the probation status it generated both contribute to the criminal history score. To take another example: in many guidelines systems an offender's prior crimes can contribute more to his total sentence than the new offense for which he is being sentenced. This is the penal equivalent of the tail wagging the dog—an aggravating factor (prior record), becomes more important than the base offense.

A further difficulty with the formulaic use of PREs in most U.S. guidelines systems is their inflexibility—nothing in the record, and nothing the individual does, can efface or reduce his criminal history points and their impact on sentence severity. A related defect of existing PRE rules is that they either ignore the age of a prior conviction, or else fully count it until, at some point, it suddenly disappears entirely—a clearly continuous variable (time since the previous conviction) becomes dichotomous, resulting in an additional point or not, depending on whether the prior crime is sufficiently remote in time.

The rigid and simplistic use of prior convictions at sentencing in American guidelines systems is anomalous when compared to practices in other common law jurisdictions. As was already noted, almost all countries apply a policy of imposing harsher sentencing for recidivists, but no system outside of the U.S. imposes additional punishment in a directly cumulative way, with each prior conviction carrying a specific quantum of extra time in prison.[16] In the absence of numerical guidelines, courts usually have considerable discretion to interpret and weigh prior convictions as an aggravating circumstance at sentencing, and criminal history is usually an important sentencing consideration. But nowhere does this factor assume the same importance as it does in the United States, where it is often one of two principal axes determining sentence outcomes. (Appendix B provides some typical examples of criminal history enhancement provisions in other common law countries.)

B. Justifying Criminal History Enhancements at Sentencing: Risk or Retribution?

All aggravating factors at sentencing require justification; this is particularly true for criminal history, since it affects a high proportion of offenders appearing for sentence and affects them in very significant ways. People have a right to know why additional punishment is imposed for their previous convictions, especially when prior convictions can result in such a significant increase in the severity of sentence imposed (see chapter 5). There are two principal justifications for criminal history enhancements, one relating to risk, the other to retribution. We shall shortly outline the preventive and retributive justifications but first we briefly note what we term the intuitive rationale.

1. Penal Intuitivism and the Appeal of the Recidivist Premium

Penal Intuitivism connotes an approach to sentencing that privileges lay intuitions as a guide to the distribution of punishment. Some scholars have argued that community views should determine (or shape) sentencing policies and practices, either because these views have normative significance or because aligning sentencing with public opinion will generate greater respect for, and ultimately compliance with, the criminal law (see Robinson 2013, 2014; for contrasting views see Ryberg and Roberts 2014, and Roberts and de Keijser 2014). How are we to explain the strong intuitive appeal of sentencing recidivists more harshly? A number of explanations exist, although their normative value as a justification for the policy is questionable.

One explanation for the mass appeal of punishing repeat offenders more harshly may relate to a widely held expectation that legal punishment should result in desistance. Despite having been punished the offender has failed to "learn his lesson." This failure provokes a punitive response from the court. It is as if the offender, having entered into a contract with the state, which included a covenant to comply with the law, has breached that agreement. Assigning greater blame has intuitive appeal, under these conditions. People may see the offender as willfully defying legal authority, and blame him for this defiance. A related branch of intuitivism echoes the expressive theory of punishment—repeat offenders could be seen as asserting a false moral claim to act without regard to the rights of others or of society (Hampton 1988), a claim that grows more offensive with each additional crime.

Another reason for the intuitive appeal of PREs is that many people make character-based attributions regarding repeat offenders. Indeed, social psychology offers a clear conceptualization of this phenomenon. When the same actions are repeatedly associated with an individual, people attribute the behavior to the person's character rather than environmental influences; as criminal acts accumulate, explanations external to the offender become less plausible while internal explanations become more convincing.[17]

All of these reactions are understandable, but none provides a convincing justification for PREs. First, all persons have a duty to obey the law, and no special contract with the state is agreed to at the time of sentencing. Second, intuitive arguments incorrectly assume that re-offending always reflects a willful decision on the part of the offender, or a recalcitrant attitude toward authority rather than some other motivation. Third, the criminal law punishes behavior not beliefs, conduct not defiant attitudes per se.

2. *The Retributive Rationale*

Some retributive theorists regard prior convictions as irrelevant to the offender's level of culpability for the current offense. Other theorists assert that repeat offenders are, on a number of possible grounds, more blameworthy than first offenders because they have continued to offend after having been subject to legal punishment, or because they are more culpable for having failed to address the causes of their offending (Lee 2010; Roberts 2008a, b). The retributive arguments have been debated energetically in recent years,[18] and are explored in greater depth in chapter 1 of this volume. Whether one accepts the retributive justifications or not, the reality is that many statutes and most guideline schemes reflect or actively promote the view that repeat offenders are more blameworthy and hence deserving of more punishment.

Our own view is that prior convictions do have some bearing on the offender's deserved punishment, but that the typical magnitude of PREs under American sentencing guidelines is much greater than can be justified on retributive principles. More precisely, and as further explained in later chapters, we endorse the following propositions:

1) first offenders are typically less culpable than repeat offenders, so the former deserve substantial sentence mitigation;
2) as repeat offenders continue to offend, their deserved punishment rises only modestly;
3) the magnitude of PRE must be limited so that it does not undercut the important goal (shared by both retributive and utilitarian principles) of making punishment severity proportional to the seriousness of the crime being sentenced;
4) that core proportionality goal means that PRE should never account for more than one-half of the total sentence;
5) in any given case, the PRE component of the sentence must be limited both by retributive principles and by utilitarian efficiency goals—PRE must be *both* deserved and cost-effective in achieving utilitarian goals (of which crime control, discussed in Part B.3, is paramount).

3. The Crime Control Rationale

The more common and, we believe, more compelling justification for PREs is preventive. Utilitarian sentencing philosophies, which aim to prevent crime through deterrence, incapacitation, and/or rehabilitation, consider prior convictions as evidence of the offender's propensity to reoffend. As a general rule, the more serious the prior record, the higher the ascribed risk of re-offending and thus, it is assumed, the greater the need and justification for a more severe sentence. But these are empirical matters, and there is little research to validate either the accuracy with which various prior record scoring systems predict risk, or the crime preventive effectiveness of more severe penalties based on PRE; indeed, the available evidence suggests that increased penalty severity, whether based on prior record or other factors, has little increased crime-control benefit.

The question of whether PREs prevent crime in a cost-effective manner will be explored in later chapters, which critically evaluate the literature on re-offending, desistance, and the marginal benefits of more severe punishment. If prior convictions are only weakly related to subsequent offending,[19] or if more severe punishment has little added crime-control value, then a powerful PRE will result in over-punishment—the offender is punished more severely to incapacitate him or deter him[20] from committing a crime that he would never commit, or that he will commit in any case, or that he will commit *because of* the more severe penalty. This is an example of an excessive (or even counterproductive) PRE. On the other hand, if criminal history is a strong predictor of re-offending, and if more severe punishment will reduce the likelihood of re-offending by this or other repeat offenders, then preventive efficacy is undermined by a sentencing process that is blind to prior convictions (or imposes only a modest prior conviction enhancement). This is an example of insufficient PRE, resulting in the commission of preventable crimes.[21]

Summary

The two primary justifications—retribution and prevention—support different approaches to operationalizing PREs. If preventing crime is the purpose, and if deterrence and incapacitation are the means by which this objective is achieved, sentence severity should escalate in a manner that reflects the increasing risk of re-offending and the effectiveness of greater severity in managing that elevated risk; PRE increases might taper off at higher levels of prior record, if crime-control benefits encounter diminishing returns, but there would be no a priori upper limit on PRE magnitude. On the other hand, if repeat offenders are punished more because they *deserve* more punishment on account of their criminal past, then it is unlikely that optimal PREs will display the same magnitudes and patterns of escalation. In particular: under a retributive rationale there will be a need to cap any record-driven PRE; the seriousness of the current offense must, on any retributive account, take precedence over variables unrelated to crime seriousness. Of course, these two perspectives are not mutually exclusive: repeat offenders may be regarded both as more culpable and as representing a higher risk to reoffend. But in that case, the magnitude and pattern of sentence enhancement must be tailored to respect both retributive principles and demonstrated crime control value.

Whatever the primary or combined justification for PRE, we endorse the well-established principle of parsimony—a punishment should be only as severe as necessary to achieve the goals of sentencing. Applied to the recidivist sentencing premium this means that prior-record-based severity increments should track, as far as possible, the degree of heightened risk or culpability. An enhancement based on a previous conviction that does not increase the offender's degree of risk or blameworthiness violates the parsimony principle that the severity of the sentence should be the least intrusive sanction sufficient to achieve the objectives of sentencing. Similarly, a premium that imposes, say, a 50 percent increase in severity to reflect a minor increase in risk or culpability would also violate the principle.

4. *Statements of Purpose in U.S. Guidelines*

Since the focus of this volume is on U.S. guidelines systems, what can we say about the underlying purposes articulated in those systems? Variation emerges: some guidelines are silent about the justification for sentencing enhancements; others explicitly identify risk and/or retribution (see Roberts 2015b). The U.S. federal guidelines provide the most explicit statement of justification, asserting that prior convictions are relevant to all principal sentencing purposes:

> The Comprehensive Crime Control Act sets forth four purposes of sentencing. (See 18 U.S.C. § 3553(a)(2).) A defendant's record of past criminal conduct is directly relevant to those purposes. A defendant with a record of prior criminal behavior is more culpable than a first offender and thus deserving of greater punishment. General deterrence of criminal conduct dictates that a clear message

> be sent to society that repeated criminal behavior will aggravate the need for punishment with each recurrence. To protect the public from further crimes of the particular defendant, the likelihood of recidivism and future criminal behavior must be considered. Repeated criminal behavior is an indicator of a limited likelihood of successful rehabilitation.[22]

In contrast, the Minnesota guidelines adopted a primarily retributive approach (see Parent 1988 and discussion in Roberts 2019). At the outset of its work the Commission concluded that PRE "can be justified to some extent on desert grounds—offenders simply deserve more punishment if they persist in unlawful activity" (MSGC 1984s, 12). The Commission further noted that its PRE provisions retain utilitarian sentencing goals "somewhat amorphously, but with reduced importance"[23] and added that PRE can serve the goals of incapacitation and rehabilitation (MSGC 1984, 10, 12). In later years the Commission justified its decision to weight prior felony convictions according to their guidelines offense severity level solely on the grounds that "Offenders who have a history of serious felonies are considered more culpable than those offenders whose prior felonies consist primarily of low severity, nonviolent offenses" (MSGC 2017a, cmt. 2.B.103). It is worth noting that whether the commissions based their enhancements on preventive or retributive rationales (or a combination of both), these are affirmations, claims that are never justified by reference to validation data. No Commission has demonstrated that a PRE actually prevents crime effectively. No Commission has ever seriously considered the adverse unintended consequences of record-based enhancements. This volume fills this important void.

C. Validation of Criminal History Enhancements

It is important not only to clearly state the rationale(s) underlying PRE rules (which many commissions have not done), but also to conduct research validating the magnitude and distribution of these enhancements. Validation of the preventive function of PRE is relatively straightforward; the Commission can determine the extent to which any given factor increases the risk-predictive accuracy of the total criminal history score, and can also consult research on the extent to which enhancements based on a higher score prevent crime in a cost-effective manner. Validation for blameworthiness is less obvious, an issue to which we will return later in this volume. To anticipate that discussion however, one possible validation exercise entails public opinion surveys in which respondents are asked to impose sentence and express blame in scenarios that vary according to different criminal history components. For example, if a representative sample of the community regards an offender with a recent conviction as being significantly more culpable than one with an older prior conviction, this may serve to validate and calibrate the retributive rationale for PRE.

As for the preventive rationale, one of the most well-established findings in criminology is that prior offending predicts future crime. The use of a prior record as a proxy for recidivism risk has therefore been validated in general terms. Yet PRE is usually based on a composite score composed of multiple dimensions such as the offender's custody status, number and seriousness of prior adult convictions, juvenile adjudications, and in some systems, how long ago the prior convictions were entered, the similarity of the prior to the current conviction, and various other score components. While the composite index may carry predictive validity, this does not mean that all of its constituent components are risk-related—yet each component triggers greater punishment for the offender. What is needed, then, is validation research on all components of the criminal history score. Such validation should determine whether and to what degree each component improves the risk-predictive accuracy of the total score.

One of the few PRE-and-risk validation exercises was conducted by the U.S. Sentencing Commission.[24] The federal guidelines formerly imposed additional criminal history points to reflect the recency of the latest prior conviction. Specifically, under former section 4A1.1(e) of the Guidelines Manual (USSC 2009), two points were added if the defendant committed the instant offense less than two years following release from confinement on a previous sentence of at least 60 days. As noted in the Commission's validation report (USSC 2010), this provision had remained unchanged since it was included in the 1988 Guidelines Manual, and was justified on the grounds that recency of prior conviction indicates a higher risk of reoffending and also may render the offender more blameworthy—for having reoffended relatively soon after the prior sentence ended. However, based on a study of offenders sentenced in 1992, the Commission concluded that "including recency in the criminal history calculation has minimal predictive power," while requiring almost 1,400 additional prison beds (USSC 2010, 22).[25] In response to this finding the Commission ultimately dropped this element of the criminal history score. This research and its resulting policy change raise a broader question: Do other dimensions of criminal history likewise add little to the predictive power of the criminal history score in many guidelines systems, while requiring substantially more prison beds?

This risk validation research is important, yet insufficient—for PREs to be fully validated, two conditions need fulfilling. First, it is necessary to demonstrate that any given sentencing factor (or dimension of a factor) is predictive of the risk of re-offending. Second, it is necessary to prove that the penal response triggered by the prior conviction will actually reduce the risk of re-offending by this offender or other individuals. We cannot simply assume that, once a given factor is shown to be risk-related, the presence of that factor justifies the imposition of a harsher sentence; we need to know that the increased punishment will in fact reduce future crime, and do so in a cost-effective manner. We also need to be confident that the recidivist sentencing premium is a more effective remedy than other measures. It could very well be the case that the substantial financial resources needed to support longer PRE-based prison terms would have greater crime-preventive benefit—and better protect potential crime victims—if those resources were redirected to other crime control and crime preventive measures. Furthermore, to fully justify any given PRE rule or practice we must be confident that its superior crime control benefits are not outweighed by other, undesirable consequences such those described in the next Part.

Finally, even if an existing or proposed PRE rule has been validated in terms of its crime-preventive accuracy, cost-effectiveness, and balance of desired and undesired consequences, the rule must also be re-examined from time to time. While crime seriousness rankings also need revisiting, at least in light of new crimes created or re-ranked in the interim, it is even more important to revalidate PRE rules, especially those justified on crime control grounds. Our knowledge of how well previous convictions predict future crimes is constantly evolving, and so is our knowledge of how much crime is prevented by more severe penalties, and with what costs and adverse consequences; the weighting and counting of previous convictions should closely reflect the latest research on these matters. Yet despite the steady accretion of such research, the architecture of PREs has been stable[26] over the lifetime of most state guidelines.[27] Commissions have been far too complacent in their acceptance of structures created decades earlier, when far less was known about the effects of punishment on re-offending.

D. Negative Consequences of Substantial Prior Record Sentence Enhancements

Prior record enhancements, even when they are carefully calibrated to reflect crime-preventive benefits and/or increased culpability, may create unintended, adverse consequences. This volume explores the following important adverse impacts of robust PREs.

1. Increasing the Size and Expense of Prison Populations

Even if existing or proposed PREs are shown to be justified on crime-preventive and/or retributive grounds (or if they are assumed to be justified, despite the lack of validation research), there is reason to be concerned about the sheer magnitude and expense of these enhancements. As will be shown in chapter 5, existing PRE rules in most guidelines systems have a dramatic effect on the number of offenders recommended for prison commitment, and on the duration of recommended and imposed prison terms. And as shown in chapter 8, the fiscal impacts of these PRE rules can be equally dramatic. The financial crisis of 2008–2009 led most Western governments to reduce the budgets of all public services—including criminal justice. Money spent on PRE-based prison terms is money that is not available for other pressing public needs, both within and outside the criminal justice system. It is therefore becoming increasingly important to ensure that prison terms are only used when community punishments are clearly inappropriate, and also that prison terms are no longer than necessary to achieve their purposes.

2. Undermining the Important Goal of Punishment in Proportion to Offense Severity

What effect does a robust PRE have upon offense rankings within a guidelines system? Most sentencing guidelines are based on a model of offense-based proportionality: more serious crimes should receive a correspondingly more severe sanction. If prior convictions constitute a significant element of the sentencing equation, the principle of proportionality is undermined. Prior convictions relate to the offender and not the offense; if any variable unrelated to the crime carries significant weight at sentencing, offense-based proportionality will be affected. As we will demonstrate in chapter 6, powerful

PREs result in offenders with lengthy criminal histories receiving longer prison terms than other offenders convicted of much more serious crimes—a serious reversal of offense-based proportionality.

3. *Increasing the Need for Prison Beds to House Property and Other Nonviolent Offenders*

A major goal of some guidelines reforms has been to set priorities in the use of limited and expensive prison beds, and in particular, to ensure that more person offenders and fewer property offenders are committed to prison (see, e.g., MSGC 1980, 15). But since nonviolent offenders generally have longer criminal histories, a robust PRE is likely to shift the balance of prison admissions toward property, drug, and other nonviolent offenders. Again, as will be shown in chapters 6 and 8, the prison-bed and financial impacts of these shifts can be very substantial.

4. *Generating Large Numbers of Aging Prison Inmates*

Since many older offenders have elevated criminal history scores but declining risks of recidivism, PREs tend to increase the numbers of aging, low-risk, high-cost prison inmates. In chapter 6 we present data showing the extent to which robust PREs significantly increase the proportions of aging offenders in prison populations.

5. *Contributing to Racial Disproportionality in Prison Populations*

The use of prior records at sentencing increases the disproportionate numbers of racial minority prisoners, since these offenders tend to have longer criminal histories (Frase 2009; Tonry 2011). In chapter 7 we document the disproportionate impact of PREs on minority defendants. It is well known that African American citizens account for a disproportionate number of prison places and admissions, and we demonstrate that much of this racial disproportionality is a result of PREs—an apparently neutral sentencing variable, criminal history, creates racial disparities.

6. *Undermining Offenders' Efforts to Reintegrate into Society*

As noted above and discussed more fully in chapters 1 and 2, the crime-preventive justification for imposing harsher sentences on recidivists is more compelling than the culpability-based retributive justification. And since research suggests that the marginal deterrent benefits of increased sentence severity are quite limited, incapacitation of higher-risk offenders emerges as the primary justification for PREs. The concept of desistance interacts in complex ways with the recidivist sentencing premium. Desistance is not an all or nothing concept; for many offenders, the journey toward total desistance is interrupted by periodic lapses into criminality. Yet many offenders, including some with substantial records, make significant efforts toward desistance. Imposing enhanced punishment on an offender who has made progress toward desistance may be self-defeating.

First, the extra punishment may be gratuitous; as a result of the individual's efforts, re-offending is now unlikely. Second, the additional punishment—usually more time in prison—may impede the offender's ability to self-reform. For example, a lengthy term of custody—or even a relatively short term—imposed in light of previous convictions may interrupt the person's progress in rebuilding a career or supporting a family. It may also enhance the likelihood of further offending through labeling (see for example, Farrell and Swigert 1978), and by magnifying the employment, housing, and other debilitating collateral consequences of criminal conviction (Jacobs 2015, chapters 13 and 14). It may also further alienate the offender from society because of the perceived unfairness of "double punishment" for the prior offense. Indeed, "double punishment" is an understatement—multiple sentencing hearings will result in an earlier conviction visiting additional punishment on the offender at every subsequent sentencing. Prior convictions thus result in "snowballing" of punishment (Roberts 1997). When applied to custodial sentences, the first offense will, cumulatively, result in a great deal of additional time in prison, as it will trigger more punishment at every subsequent sentencing. For all these reasons, courts need to carefully examine the offender's circumstances and consider any efforts toward desistance prior to imposing a recidivist sentencing premium.

Prior record enhancements adopt a unidimensional strategy to prevent crime: the offender is subject to a more severe punishment in the expectation (more a hope) that he will be deterred from re-offending. A more rounded approach would encourage ex-offenders to actively take steps to address the causes of their offending. One strategy would entail expunging prior convictions more quickly to reward individuals who demonstrate progress toward desistance. Finally, even if the retributive justification for PREs is accepted, efforts to desist offer a rebuttal to the higher level of culpability that is ascribed to the individual because of his lapse into further criminality (see Lee 2010 and Roberts 2008b, 220–22, for discussion).

Summary

All of these adverse effects of PREs need to be weighed against the preventive benefits of these enhancements (as well as their retributive value, if that is deemed important). To date, most of the literature and policy discussion has focused on the assumed crime-preventive benefits of PREs without fully considering the many adverse consequences. Finally, there is also the question of *comparative* cost-effectiveness: Do criminal history enhancements, especially those resulting in longer prison terms, deliver value for money when compared to other risk reduction and crime prevention strategies such as enhanced probation supervision or greater use of risk-needs interventions and programs?

E. Plan of the Volume

Chapter 1 explores the retributive rationales for and limitations on PREs. Many retributive theorists reject all PRE rules, and other theorists support only modest degrees of enhancement, or only support mitigation for first offenders. But even if retribution is not deemed to provide a convincing positive rationale, it must at least place upper limits on the permissible magnitude of PREs. If reducing risk and preventing crime were the only guiding objectives, that would permit punishments far in excess of what is deserved. "three-strikes" laws are good examples of sentencing provisions in which the severity of the sentence greatly exceeds the seriousness of the offense for which the sentence is imposed, but many other PREs can also have this effect. A harsh recidivist sentencing law, or a very powerful PRE, violates offense proportionality in sentencing—the universal feature of sentencing to which we have already alluded.

Chapters 2 to 4 evaluate the evidence that criminal history enhancements prevent crime by repeat offenders. Chapter 2 addresses the relationship between prior convictions and recidivism risk—how well does a higher criminal history score predict future crime, and do all score components improve predictive accuracy? Chapter 3 examines other factors related to recidivism; an offender's risk of re-offending is a complex combination of many variables, and these variables may interact with criminal history. For example, as offenders grow older, they become less likely to reoffend (while the costs to house them, especially medical costs, steadily increase); yet older offenders also have the longest criminal records. These questions pose complex normative and practical challenges for guidelines authorities: Is it fair, or even legal, to allow sentence severity to vary according to demographic risk factors—or even some kinds of criminal history? Chapter 4 builds on the two previous chapters, and poses the bottom-line question: Even if prior record and other factors can be combined in ways that accurately predict recidivism risk, do the resulting sentence enhancements actually reduce crime, and do they do so in a cost-effective manner? There is a substantial empirical literature on the deterrent and incapacitation effects of more severe penalties, but only a limited number of studies have addressed the more focused question of how much crime is prevented by imposing a sentencing premium for previous convictions. We review the existing research, and conclude that sentence enhancements based on prior convictions often far exceed the likely crime-control benefits. Chapter 4 also addresses ethical and legal objections to PREs, even those that are cost-effective in preventing future crimes.

Chapters 5 to 8 assess the costs and undesirable consequences of PREs. The magnitude of these enhancements varies considerably across the United States, and chapter 5 uses several indices to measure their sentence-aggravating power. We show how a more robust PRE increases the number of offenders recommended for and receiving prison terms, while also increasing the duration of their terms. We then review the major variations in how guidelines systems count and weight prior crimes, and show how these variations affect the numbers and types of offenders who end up with high criminal history scores. Chapters 6 and 7 explore other adverse consequences of criminal history enhancements to which we have already referred, namely: undermining offense-based proportionality, interfering with prison-use priorities by increasing the numbers of aging and nonviolent offenders held in prison, and exacerbating racial disparities in sentence outcomes and prison inmate populations. Chapter 8 presents data on the prison bed and fiscal impacts of these adverse consequences, and of PREs generally.

Chapters 9 and 10 focus on several problematic components of criminal history scores: the reach of criminal histories to include even very old convictions; counting of juvenile court adjudications, adult misdemeanor convictions, and the offender's custody status (e.g., on probation) at the time of the offense; the use of patterning rules that enhance sentence severity based on the similarity of past and current offenses; and the heavy upweighting of prior felonies according to their seriousness.

Chapter 11 outlines our model PRE scheme, designed to promote a more rational, parsimonious, and humane consideration of previous convictions at sentencing. Our model includes a set of principles and proposed provisions reflecting what we and other scholars have learned about the justifications for PREs, and their costs, benefits, and adverse consequences.

Appendices A and B provide, respectively, a sampling of PRE provisions in U.S. guidelines systems, and in other common law jurisdictions outside of the United States. In Appendix C we briefly examine several types of offenders that may require greater or lesser penalty severity than are provided under the general principles and procedures of our proposed model.

1 RETRIBUTIVIST PERSPECTIVES ON AN OFFENDER'S CRIMINAL OR CRIME-FREE PAST

Are repeat offenders more culpable and worthy of blame or censure than first offenders? Colloquial references to repeat offenders often invoke quasi-retributive language and concepts; in daily life people talk about recidivists *deserving* more punishment than first offenders. Yet we need to distinguish such casual sentiments from a principled retributive argument. The key questions include the following: Is there a convincing retributive justification for imposing harsher penalties on repeat offenders? If yes, how should penalties for first-time and repeat offenders be arrayed in a way that is consistent with a retributive rationale?

Several U.S. guidelines systems justify their prior record enhancements (PREs) by reference to retribution (Roberts 2015b, table 1.1). The federal guidelines manual provides an explicit justification in terms of culpability when it notes that: "A defendant with a record of prior criminal behavior is more culpable than a first offender and thus deserving of greater punishment" (USSC 2016, chap. 4, pt. A, Introductory Commentary). The U.S. Sentencing Commission may be confident of the criminal history-culpability link but, as discussed further later in this chapter, little consensus exists among retributive scholars regarding this issue; instead, the retributive perspective encompasses several conflicting positions. Some retributivists reject outright the use of prior convictions at sentencing, while others argue that the presence or absence of prior convictions does, in various ways, affect the offender's level of culpability for his current offense.

This chapter evaluates these competing retributive claims. Although views differ, some common positions emerge, and we have incorporated them into our model approach to prior record enhancements. In Part A, we briefly summarize common features of retributive theory generally, and how that theory should be applied to prior record enhancements. Parts B, C, and D then address the three differing approaches taken by retributive theorists: (1) The *exclusionary model* holds that prior convictions should play no role in sentencing for a new offense; (ii) Under theories of *mitigation*, offenders with no prior convictions, or with only a very minor prior record, are deemed to be less blameworthy, or at least entitled to some degree of sympathy; (iii) Under theories of *aggravation*, an offender's blameworthiness and deserved punishment steadily increase, based on the number and seriousness of prior convictions. The latter approach is the one that best describes PRE rules in most guidelines systems in the United States, with one important caveat: there is usually an upper limit or "cap," after which further convictions no longer increase recommended sentence severity.

Our view is a blend of the second and third approaches described in the preceding paragraph. We conclude that there is a solid basis to posit significantly reduced blameworthiness and deserved punishment for first offenders, but that desert then rises only modestly as offenders accumulate more and more prior convictions. We also strongly endorse the widespread practice of "capping" PRE, so that prior convictions do not count more heavily than the seriousness of the conviction offense(s). An upper limit is needed to ensure that offenders are not punished more severely than they deserve, and to avoid undercutting the important goal of maintaining proportionality between sentence severity and the seriousness of the current crime(s). That goal is endorsed by all retributive theorists, including both the stricter and the looser versions described in Part A. Proportionality of punishment severity to offense seriousness is also a central precept of utilitarian and consequentialist punishment theories—penalties that fail to respect at least a rough sense of offense seriousness send confusing and even counterproductive deterrent and norm-reinforcing messages, and are less likely to match punishment costs with crime control benefits (Frase 2008, 2012, 2013).

A. Elements of Retributive Theory Generally, and Its Relation to Prior Record Enhancements

Most desert theorists agree that a person's deserved punishment for an offense depends on two factors: the *harms* caused or risked by the offense, and the offender's individual *culpability* in committing that offense (based on factors such as his or her degree of intent, motives, mental capacity, and role relative to co-offenders) (von Hirsch 1993, 29–33). Most desert-based theories of prior record enhancement have been based on mitigated or enhanced offender culpability; these theories presuppose that variations in offense harm cannot explain or justify such enhancements—the harm to the victim or victims of the current offense (say a burglary) is deemed to be the same regardless of the offender's prior conviction record (Roberts 2010). But as discussed in Part D, a few writers have suggested a harm-based rationale for giving repeat offenders more severe punishment.

It is important to stress that any retributive prior-record enhancement theory, whether based on offender culpability or offense harms, must establish that prior convictions make the offender more blameworthy *for the current offense or offenses being sentenced*. An offender with many prior convictions may be considered more blameworthy in some overall sense, but he cannot now be given more punishment for his prior crimes because he has already been punished for those; imposing added punishment for those earlier crimes, in the current sentencing, would violate constitutional and human rights Double Jeopardy principles (see, e.g., *Witte v. United States* 1995).

One further important variation in desert theory, which has implications for PRE rule drafting, is the difference between stricter and looser conceptions of desert and its role in sentencing. The stricter "defining" (Morris 1982) or "determining" (von Hirsch 2017) theory of desert assumes that assessments of blameworthiness can be made with some precision, at least relative to other crimes and to more and less serious forms of the same crime—what von Hirsch (1985) refers to as "ordinal" desert. On this view, the deserved prison term is either a precise number of years, or it falls within a narrow range of years. Many proponents of this strict version of desert theory further believe that punishment severity should conform closely to (ordinal) desert, even if non-desert sentencing purposes would call for a very different penalty. In contrast, theories of "limiting" retributivism posit either a broader range of deserved (or "not undeserved") punishment for any given case (Morris 1974, 1982; Morris and Tonry 1990; American Law Institute 2003), or an asymmetric approach under which desert—even if it can be defined with some precision—sets firm upper limits on allowable punishment severity with looser limits on required minimum severity (Armstrong 1969; Frase 2013a).

Under strict (defining or determining) desert theories there is little if any room for PRE unless a convincing case can be made that prior convictions increase the offender's deserved punishment for the current crime or crimes being sentenced. Under looser, limiting-retributivist theories, PRE can operate within the broader allowable desert range; increments of punishment within that range may be based on assumed variations in recidivism risk and crime control benefits, without having to be justified by differences in blameworthiness.

In this book, we propose a model PRE regime that we believe is consistent even with a fairly strict version of desert theory. Our model meets stricter desert requirements because of the way we view prior convictions and offender culpability: we posit significantly reduced desert for most first offenders (so the significant sentence mitigations we would allow are deserved); and we advocate only modestly rising PREs for offenders with longer records based on their modestly enhanced desert (which means that these PREs can fit within a fairly narrow desert range across these offenders; of course, our model is even easier to justify under a broader desert-range conception of desert). As will be further discussed in later chapters, the available evidence on recidivism risk and the crime-control benefits of punishment indicates that most first offenders pose significantly lower risk (moreover, many of them will actually be made more crime-prone by severe punishment), whereas recidivism risk and crime-control benefits increase only modestly as offenders acquire longer records. Also, as noted previously, upper limits on PRE are needed to preserve the crime-control benefits associated with offense-proportionate sentences. Thus, even if a looser conception of desert would permit a substantial magnitude of PRE for offenders with many prior convictions, such enhancements should be rejected because they cannot be justified on crime-control and cost-effectiveness grounds.

In the next three Parts we address the three differing approaches to PRE, taken by retributivist writers.

B. The Exclusionary Model

A number of writers who favor a retributive rationale for punishment have taken the view that a prior conviction does not render the offender more culpable for her current offense, and that sentence severity should therefore not be influenced by the offender's criminal record (see Fletcher 1978, 1982; see also Singer 1979; Davis 1985, 1992; Bagaric 2000, 2014a; Duff 2001; Tonry 2010; Corlett 2012; Dagger 2012; Dressler 2015, sec. 6.04; Lippke 2016).

The retributivist objection to the use of previous convictions at sentencing is clear. According to a retributive perspective, legal punishment conveys blame and expresses societal disapprobation—but only for a specific criminal act. Sentence is imposed for a proved offense, without which no legal censure is justified. If this were not the case we would live in a society in which from time to time people were held accountable for their entire lives up to that point. Under a retributive account, the sanction should reflect the seriousness of the crime and the offender's level of culpability in committing the offense for which he is called to account. On this view, previous convictions should play no role—any more than other extralegal considerations that nevertheless may have some intuitive appeal as sentencing factors.[1] As Bagaric observes: "People should be punished only for what they do; not according to the type of people we think they are.... In a community governed by the rule of law... people are judged by their actions not their values or beliefs" (2000, 15; see also Gross 1979; Galligan 1981; Bean 1981; Fox 1994).

Communicative theorists such as Duff (2001) also exclude previous convictions: "The mere fact that an offender now convicted of a crime has a prior criminal record can make no justified difference to his sentence... The fact that this is the offender's twentieth burglary does not justify a harsher punishment than was imposed for the tenth burglary" (167, 169). Davis (1992) takes a similar line: "The principle of just deserts does not allow a criminal to be punished more severely than he deserves for what he did" (132). Tonry describes the desert arguments that have been advanced to justify record-based enhancements as "unpersuasive" (2010, 111), while Bagaric definitively concludes that "all retributive arguments used to justify a retributive enhancement are unsound" (2014a, 383).

While there is clarity to the exclusionary position, we see important reasons to reject this approach. Ignoring criminal history denies the sentencing process an important inquiry into the offender. In particular, the first offender is denied a powerful source of mitigation. She is treated in a way that fails to distinguish her from the multiple recidivist, and this seems inappropriate. First-offender mitigation is a near-universal feature of sentencing that is often explicitly acknowledged in sentencing statutes,[2] and is also apparent in sentencing practice—sentencing statistics reveal that the absence of prior convictions often results in a significantly mitigated sentence (see, e.g., Roberts 2008b, chap. 6). Finally, a wealth of public opinion research demonstrates that most people regard a first offender as deserving of significantly mitigated punishment (Roberts et al. 2009; Roberts and Hough 2011). Although public attitudes do not provide a principled justification for considering priors, they do suggest that a regime that ignored the issue would encounter significant public opposition.

In short, notwithstanding the theoretical purity of the exclusionary perspective, omitting prior convictions entirely from the sentencing equation is so manifestly at odds with current practice, as well as community and professional opinion, that any scheme proposing to eliminate this variable is doomed to be ignored. Indeed, adoption of the exclusionary view might encourage sentencing policymakers and practitioners to ignore desert principles entirely, on the grounds that a key element of the proposed desert account is so strikingly at odds with contemporary public and professional opinion (Frase 2013a). We are therefore disinclined to jettison all retributive justifications for considering an offender's past in mitigation or aggravation.

C. Theories Justifying Sentence Mitigation for Offenders with No Priors, or Only a Few

As was noted in Part B, sentencing mitigation for first offenders finds strong support in sentencing laws, sentencing practices, and public opinion surveys. Such mitigation has also been endorsed by many sentencing theorists (see, e.g., Roberts 2010; Lee 2010). Indeed, O'Neill, Maxfield, and Harer (2004, 246) conclude that "[o]ne note of near concordance regarding the use of criminal history in sentencing is that, all other things being equal, first time offenders are more deserving of lower sentences than repeat offenders." Some theorists would go further, extending a lesser degree of mitigation to offenders with only a minor prior record. Under the theory of "progressive loss of mitigation," widely endorsed in common law systems outside of the United States, mitigation is gradually reduced until, at some point, the repeat offender is held fully culpable and punished accordingly.

Sentence mitigation for first-time and low-record offenders has been defended on the grounds either that such offenders are less culpable and thus deserve mitigation, or because society should recognize the frailty of human nature and show some degree of sympathy toward these offenders.

1. *Diminished Culpability of First Offenders*

A number of rationales have been advanced by those who posit reduced first-offender culpability. One argument is that until he has been arrested, charged, convicted, and sentenced, an offender may reasonably claim that he was not fully aware of the wrongful nature of his conduct. The exculpatory force of this claim will vary depending upon many factors, including the inherent wrongfulness of the crime committed—the illegal nature and the likely harms arising from the offense are obviously clearer for some kinds of offenses than for others. Contact with the criminal justice system and the subsequent exposure to state prosecution and punishment may bring a moral awakening to the offender; in particular, official and unofficial warnings about the wrongfulness of the conduct can affect the offender's level of culpability for subsequent offending, especially when that offending is for the same or a very similar crime for which the offender was previously punished. Consider an offender convicted of importing taxable products without paying the appropriate import duties. If he has been informally warned on one or more occasions by customs officers, and especially if he has been convicted and sanctioned for this crime, these warnings will reasonably aggravate the sentence imposed. Conversely, an individual found guilty of this offense who has never received warnings or been convicted for the crime will be treated less harshly, because he is reasonably deemed less blameworthy.

There are also situations in daily life where we are naturally inclined to express less blame when a person transgresses for the first time. Thus, the speeding driver who recklessly races through crowded streets despite repeated warnings and appeals to slow down from his passengers is more culpable than one who speeds alone. We also tend to give first offenders the benefit of the doubt because we are more willing to accept innocent explanations for the breach—a colleague who thoughtlessly delays the departmental staff meeting for half an hour is blamed less on the first occasion than when it becomes a monthly occurrence. In each case he might have been unavoidably delayed for number of reasons. However, his lack of punctuality on a *third* consecutive occasion is harder to ascribe to transportation delays or to a mechanical breakdown while driving; it would appear to reflect more upon his agency and intentionality, or his culpable indifference to the interests of colleagues.

A related justification invokes a diminished awareness of the full consequences of the crime. A central function of the criminal trial and of the penal communication is to sensitize the defendant to the actual harms caused by his criminal conduct. At trial, the state identifies the exact acts for which the offender is being held accountable; at sentencing, the court calibrates a message of censure appropriate to the seriousness of the conduct and the offender's level of culpability. In addition, when a victim impact statement is filed this may reinforce state censure by highlighting for the offender the effects that his actions have had on the crime victim.[3] Until these communications are received, the offender may claim a degree of diminished awareness of these effects. No such claim may be plausibly made by the recidivist, particularly offenders reconvicted of the very same crime, hence the significant distinction made in many statutes between first and repeat violations of the statute.[4] This account means that if offenders are arrayed along a continuum of prior convictions from none to many, the distinction between first-time and second-time offenders is much more significant than between any adjacent categories of recidivist (see also Bagaric 2014).

The justifications for regarding first offenders as being less blameworthy therefore invoke considerations such as the absence of formal censure and warnings, the greater possibility of innocent explanations for the offense, and incomplete awareness of the consequences of the crime. Repetition of the crime strips the no-prior-censure and limited-awareness-of-harm arguments of plausibility, while also undercutting the likelihood that there are innocent explanations for the transgression.

2. Mitigation as a Concession to Human Frailty

Some retributive scholars defend sentence mitigations for offenders with little or no prior record on grounds other than culpability.[5] Andrew von Hirsch has affirmed an approach to prior convictions that supports multiple, declining mitigations. This model reflects the well-established principle of the *Progressive Loss of Mitigation*, by which mitigation is offered to all first offenders, and then repeatedly extended, albeit to a lesser degree, for some recidivists. Once the offender has accumulated four or five convictions, all mitigation on this account is exhausted and the offender receives the full sentence (which remains at that level for each further offense, with no additional increments in severity). Von Hirsch draws upon everyday moral judgments to justify the need to show understanding, tolerance, and sympathy for "the all-too-human fallibility that can lead to a first offence" (von Hirsch 2017, 75). He further argues that

> Our everyday moral judgments include the notion of a *lapse*. A transgression (even one of a substantial nature) is judged less stringently when it occurs against a background of prior compliance . . . even an ordinarily well-behaved person can have his or her moral inhibitions fail in a moment of weakness or willfulness (von Hirsch 2017, 76).

The distinction between the human-frailty or lapse account advocated by von Hirsch, compared with other accounts, is that von Hirsch decouples the mitigation from any consideration of the offender's culpability (von Hirsch 2010, 11). Under his model, all first-time offenders are accorded mitigation out of recognition that to err is human. In contrast, according to Roberts (2010b), the first offender discount is deserved; the novice offender is *entitled* to mitigation, which is not granted simply out of societal indulgence or sympathy for a lapse from law-abiding conduct. Similarly, the arguments for enhanced punishment for recidivists, discussed in Part D, assume that recidivists deserve additional punishment and that first offenders (or those with fewer priors) deserves less punishment.

3. *Critiques of the Mitigation Justifications for PRE*

The lapse theory has been criticized and rejected by other scholars (e.g., Durham 1987; Bagaric 2014a; Ryberg 2010; Roberts 2010). By drawing upon everyday moral judgments as a justification, the theory invites these views to influence sentencing. This is part of the popular appeal of retributivism in general, which, as Matravers notes, "seeks to capture an intuition that wrongdoers deserve punishment" (2000, 95). Although there is a link to intuitive reactions to wrongdoing, the lapse approach to previous convictions is more complex. It incorporates notions of tolerance for imperfection in human behavior, and a desire to extend leniency on more than a single occasion. This indulgence toward offenders arises in part out of recognition that offending reflects a multiplicity of influences and that many members of society are subject to forces that make compliance with the law more demanding.

But even though the policy of offering mitigation to first offenders carries considerable intuitive appeal, it may be inappropriate to extend this leniency to all crimes. A first offender convicted of a spontaneous and fairly minor assault will receive a significant discount to reflect his previously law-abiding life. He or she may advance the plausible argument that circumstances explain a temporary lapse: "I don't know what came over me—that's not me at all." However, the discount is less plausible when proffered by an offender convicted of an offense that requires a considerable amount of planning, or a spontaneous but very serious crime such as aggravated assault or rape. If the crime has taken weeks or months to plan and has involved multiple preparatory acts, the offender has effectively been engaged in the criminal enterprise for such a period of time that he cannot claim the act was the product of a sudden lapse. Similarly, offering an offender a mitigated punishment because he had not, until this point, ever committed this particular serious crime (for example: child sex abuse), could only bring the sentencing process into disrepute. For this reason, as Ashworth (2005) observes, the progressive loss of mitigation theory should not apply across a wide range of offending, but should be restricted to certain offenses and certain offenders. This is clearly the case in practice, where the first-offender discount carries little weight for the most serious crimes.

The progressive loss of mitigation (PLM) doctrine has also been criticized by desert theorists (e.g., Bagaric 2000, 2001; Ryberg 2004; Roberts 2010). Bagaric (2000) for example argues that this constitutes an unwelcome discretionary intervention into the principles of sentencing. It is also unclear why the mitigation accorded to first offenders, even if justified under a lapse or human frailty theory, should be extended to second and subsequent offenses and only *progressively* withdrawn, rather than offered on only a single occasion. An employee convicted for the first time of defrauding her employer may reasonably ask a sentencing court for a "second chance" on the intuitive grounds that the offense was out of character and reflected a temporary slip, an aberration in a normally law-abiding life. Von Hirsch and Ashworth (2005, 152) describe this as "a moment of unwisdom." It would be a severe judge indeed who would deny some mitigation in response to such an appeal. But if the offense occurs a third and fourth time, the claim for mitigation seems less plausible. Why then does the progressive loss of mitigation extend some mitigation, albeit less, on the second, third, and possibly subsequent occasions?[6]

The progressive nature of the loss of mitigation seems inconsistent with the oft-encountered description of the principle as "a second chance" (Wasik and von Hirsch 1994, 410). Desert theorists offer no precise number of convictions after which the severity of sentence should level off. The nature and seriousness of the offending and the severity of the first sentence should influence the number of convictions that may accumulate before mitigation is lost. A person convicted of robbery and sentenced to custody should be denied further mitigation because he cannot claim the indulgence of the state, having already been censured to such a degree. However, an offender convicted of a minor fraud, and who receives a suspended sentence may more plausibly argue that he had transgressed mildly and the sentence imposed was insufficiently severe to call him fully to account and to make him appreciate the wrongfulness of his conduct.

Von Hirsch (1981) suggests that there is no specific number of repetitions that could be required before the mitigation is exhausted, although the description in one publication suggests a relatively protracted period of withdrawal.[7] Wasik (1987) proposed five as the limit before mitigation is lost: "the crucial point is that after those five convictions, reconviction would not attract greater severity" (118; see also Wasik and Taylor 1991, 28). But only a very credulous judge would accept an argument that the current conviction was out of character when the offender had four previous convictions. In terms of "tolerance for a lapse," it would be a very tolerant court that can still extend some mitigation to an offender with such a number of prior offenses. Ashworth adopts a more conservative (and credible) position that "the third offence may be censured fully" (2005, 188), suggesting the discount is exhausted after two convictions.

Some of the critiques above apply not just to lapse and PLM theories but also to those that posit reduced culpability for offenders with few or no prior convictions. In particular, the existence and extent of reduced culpability would seem to depend on the nature of the current offense—even a first offender may be deemed fully blameworthy (or at least, entitled to only very limited mitigation) if the crime is serious enough and/or required extensive advance planning. Another problem is that reduced culpability theory may lack widespread support from either the general public or legal practitioners;[8] it seems that many people's moral intuitions tell them that a criminal record is a matter of enhanced culpability for repeat offenders (as discussed below), not reduced culpability for first or second offenders (Lee 2009).

On the other hand, any mitigation theory, whether based on reduced culpability, lapse, or PLM, has one important advantage over the PRE rationales discussed below, all of which posit enhanced culpability for second and subsequent crimes. The mitigation approach places a clear upper limit on the severity of penalties given to recidivists, based on desert factors associated with the current offense(s); in contrast, the logic of enhanced-desert theories seems to permit an open-ended escalation of sanction severity. Implicit in mitigation theories is the idea that the seriousness of the current offense sets an upper limit on sanction severity, and this idea finds support in sentencing guidelines systems—all recognize an offense-based "cap" beyond which criminal history no longer raises the recommended sentence (Frase 2013a).

D. Theories Justifying Sentence Aggravation due to Prior Convictions

Unlike the mitigation theories discussed in Part C, a number of PRE rationales assert that an offender's blameworthiness and deserved punishment are enhanced in light of the number and seriousness of his prior convictions.

1. The Recidivist's "Bad Character"

Character-based theories of enhanced punishment for repeat offenders are based on the idea that such offenders have shown themselves, with each additional crime, to be more and more antisocial and indifferent to the rights of others. However, punishing bad character violates the fundamental principle that people are punished for what they have done (and with what intent), not for who or what they are. There are also significant practical problems in applying this approach—how much more blameworthy does the offender become with each additional crime, and is there any upper limit to penalty enhancements under this approach? Character-based theories eventually lead to the conclusion that the offender has forfeited any right to have his punishment limited by retributive, human rights, or other deontological principles. Such an open-ended forfeiture concept may indeed be the core rationale of "three-strikes" and other very severe habitual offender laws, but most retributive scholars strongly oppose such laws.

2. *Heightened Notice of Criminal Prohibitions and/or Defiance of Prior Sanctions*

Another group of theories (summarized in Lee 2009) posits enhanced culpability for offenders who, after receiving formal condemnation of their prior criminal acts, ignore society's general (statutory) and individualized (judicial) warnings, and commit further crime in open defiance of these warnings. Both types of theory (especially notice theories) appear to assume that there was an intervening conviction and sentencing event between the prior and current crimes; however, contemporary prior record enhancement rules often sweep much more broadly than that, including many "prior" crimes that were sentenced after commission of the current offense (Frase 2013a, 2015b). The notice theory may also assume some degree of similarity between prior and current offenses. Again, actual criminal-record enhancement rules are much broader—except for the treatment of traffic crimes (which generally do not enhance non-traffic penalties, and vice versa), enhancement is often based on prior offending of a totally different nature. Moreover, notice theory is unconvincing when applied to very serious crimes, and is also inconsistent with the traditional principle that people are assumed and expected to know what the law prohibits. Finally, the theory does not explain further enhancements of punishment severity for a third, fourth, or subsequent offense.

As for defiance theories, some authors (e.g., von Hirsch 1985, 79–80) have questioned whether such a rationale is acceptable under a legal system in which people are punished for their acts, not their attitudes and thoughts. One possible answer to this criticism would be to invoke an expressive theory (see, e.g., Hampton 1988), according to which offenders are punished to repudiate their false moral claim to act without regard to the rights and interests of others or of society; arguably, such false claims grow more offensive with each additional crime. But again—how much more offensive are they, and is there any upper limit to prior-record enhancement under such a theory?

3. *Recidivism as a Culpable Omission or Culpable Response to State Censure*

Several writers have employed theories of culpable omission to conclude that prior convictions increase an offender's level of culpability. Darcy MacPherson (2002) argues that the recidivist may reasonably be punished more severely for having made a culpable choice not to respond to penal censure.[9] Two restrictions are placed on this culpability-based aggravation. First, in order to preserve offense-based proportionality, MacPherson's model "supports a minor increase in culpability for recidivism" (213), thus suggesting that the increase in punishment severity would be correspondingly modest. The reason for this is that failing to respond appropriately is only a minor element of the offender's overall level of culpability.[10] Second, MacPherson stipulates that the enhancement is restricted to cases where the prior and the current offense are the same.

Youngjae Lee (2009, 2010) advocates a similar approach, arguing that the repeat offender's culpability is enhanced because he has failed to take appropriate action to control his criminal tendencies in light of his earlier crime, conviction, and punishment. The theory assumes that, because of the prior conviction(s), the individual is or ought to be aware of her own heightened risk of offending. From this actual or constructive awareness Lee derives a heightened duty on the part of the offender to rearrange her life in a way that ensures she will avoid further criminality. Bennett (2010) recasts Lee's concept in terms of a communicative theory; on this view, punishment symbolizes how sorry an offender ought to feel because of her offense, and therefore how strong an obligation she has to take steps to ensure that she will not offend again.

Compared to some of the enhanced-desert theories previously discussed, omission theory may better explain rules that progressively escalate sentence severity as the number of prior convictions increases—the duty of the offender to control his criminal tendencies becomes steadily more important and obvious. This theory may also provide a workable formula for determining how much to enhance the repeat offender's sentence, and when to discontinue further enhancement for additional prior convictions. Since the theory blames offenders for failing to address their manifest risk of re-offending, and since risking harm is less culpable than actually causing harm, the added penalty for the former should not exceed the penalty for the latter (see Lee 2010, 67, for further discussion). In practical terms, this would translate into a rule of thumb that prior record, no matter how extensive, should never account for more than half of the offender's total sentence. Stated differently: offenders with the longest records should not receive penalties more than twice as severe as the penalties given to first offenders who commit the same offense (Frase 2013a, 185). As will be discussed in later chapters, we agree with this "doubling" limit, but on different grounds: in order to preserve offense proportionality, an offender's prior convictions should never carry more weight at sentencing than the severity of his current offense.

However, omission theories suffer from some of the defects of the other desert-based rationales previously discussed, in particular: they only explain (or are best at explaining) prior-record enhancements that involve an intervening conviction and sentencing event, and they only (or best) apply to offenders whose past and current crimes are similar, or at least caused by the same criminal impulses (which the offender is then expected to address). In addition, such theories would seem to require courts to engage in difficult assessments of the extent to which the offender tried but was unable to control his criminal tendencies. One can imagine an offender who has made strenuous efforts yet failed to address his offending impulses. Alternatively, offenders may desist for reasons that are external to their efforts to avoid further offending (e.g., aging, or because their criminal associates have been incarcerated). Finally, omission theories punish offenders for failing to act in a way that will prevent further crime; but a core principle of Anglo-American criminal law is that liability based on omission is exceptional, and is only recognized where a legal duty to do the required act has been imposed by law or otherwise clearly established (Tonry 2010, 105–06).

4. The Greater Harms of Crimes Committed by Recidivists

As was noted at the outset, most desert-based theories of prior record enhancement are based on mitigated or enhanced culpability; these theories assume that variations in offense harm cannot explain or justify such enhancements since the harms caused by a crime are the same whether or not it was committed by a recidivist. But some writers have argued that an offender's prior record of crime may affect how we view the seriousness of her most recent criminal acts (Durham 1987; Frase 2010; Tamburrini 2012). The repeat offender's current burglary is perhaps more disturbing, to both the victim and society, in light of—and in proportion to—her prior crimes. We may conclude that this offender poses a heightened threat to all of us, a heightened threat that is roughly proportional to the extent of her prior record. This conclusion makes us fearful, reduces our level of trust in others, and encourages both victims and public officials to take extra precautions against this offender; such precautions incur additional expense, and may entail some loss of freedom or convenience.

One problem in applying this theory is that the supposed greater harms associated with a recidivist's recent crime, described above, may be too speculative to permit a proportionately scaled sentence enhancement. Another problem with the theory is its potential to justify a limitless escalation of sentence severity: our feelings of fear and distrust, and the extra precautions that victims and officials are forced to take, arguably continue and accelerate with increases in the offender's prior record, eventually yielding a penalty far in excess of the seriousness of the actual crime being sentenced. The wider-harm theory does not provide any practical formula for deciding how much to enhance for each additional prior offense, and when to stop adding enhancements.

5. *Reserved Desert, From Prior Sentencing Events*

A few writers have suggested that prior-record enhancements might be justified if the offender did not receive all of his deserved punishment in one or more prior sentencing events; such "reserved" severity would then be available to enhance his deserved punishment for the current crime (Morris 1982, 185; Roberts 1997, 353–54). But this theory finds no support in traditional recidivist enhancement rules—such enhancements have never been scaled to or limited by any such reserved-desert concept; offenders receive prior-record enhancements without regard to the degree of leniency given them in prior cases (Davis 1985, 41). In addition, the theory would sometimes yield perverse results, dictating that offenders who were so culpable that they were fully punished in all prior sentencing events cannot receive any recidivist premium. A reserved-desert theory would also be quite difficult to put into effect and, for both practical and legal reasons, could only operate prospectively (Frase 2010). Courts would have to begin to make express findings of full desert and reserved desert at each sentencing, announcing the reserved part in the form of a suspended sentence. Until this new practice became routine, a later court would have no way to know how much desert was reserved in prior sentencings. Such findings would also be needed in order to avoid Double Jeopardy issues, making clear that later sentence enhancements are not additional punishment for prior crimes; instead, such added punishment would be deemed to have already been imposed, but suspended, for the earlier crimes. And until the new system was fully in place, most "old system" convictions lacking any express finding of reserved desert would have to be ignored.

Conclusions

Where does this review leave us in terms of current retributive theorizing, and what implications does it have for a model PRE scheme? Leaving aside the "Exclusionary" school, we see consensus with regard to the following propositions:

- No retributive account justifies a powerful role for previous convictions as an aggravating factor at sentencing.[11]
- Except for very serious crimes, or those that involve extensive advance planning, offenders convicted for the first time (and, exceptionally, a second time) should receive a significantly reduced punishment, for a number of reasons. Those reasons include not just the consequentialist grounds discussed in the next chapter, but also reduced culpability as a result of never having been subject to state punishment and criminal justice interventions, and never having been called upon to recognize the wrongfulness of the conduct and to avoid repetition. The absence of prior state censure and intervention, and the possibility that the offense was an uncharacteristic lapse, provide powerful—and categorical—rationales for sentence mitigation.
- Some repeat offenders are more culpable for the current crime, yet the aggravation must be limited in scope; the view that prior record enhancements should be modest seems to be one of the points on which all theorists agree (see, e.g., Davis, 1985; Roberts 2008a, b; MacPherson 2002). Such enhancements must also entirely cease to be applied at some point—capped, in other words; continued escalation in punishment severity would eventually eclipse the seriousness of the offense, which on a retributive analysis should remain the primary determinant of sentence severity. Accordingly, the punishment given to repeat offenders for a given crime should not be more than twice as severe as the punishment given to first offenders (except where case-specific aggravating offense facts apply to the recidivist's crime, and/or the first offender benefits from mitigating offense facts).

- Most importantly, the rising culpability of repeat offending should only be a presumption, rebuttable by the offender. In particular, prior-record enhancements should be reduced or eliminated for any offender who has taken steps to correct the causes of his offending.[12]

We conclude that in terms of the foundational justification for taking a prior record into account, the retributive analysis is less compelling than the risk-based rationales to be discussed in the next chapter. For this reason, our primary focus in the rest of this volume is upon the risk-reduction aspects of criminal history enhancements. However, we shall return periodically to the retributive perspective, particularly to ensure that criminal history enhancements do not depart markedly from the requirement of offense-based proportionality found at the heart of all retributive theories.

With respect to the model scheme we develop in this volume, the lessons from the retributive literature seem clear: the model should allow a substantial mitigation for first offenders, and only very modest enhancements thereafter. We view culpability considerations as providing a strong rationale for distinguishing between first and second offenders, but limited support for further repeat-offender enhancements; in addition, offense-based proportionality sets a strict upper limit upon these enhancements, even those that seem strongly grounded in preventive goals.

Our model is designed to be consistent with the view that retributive principles define just punishment within a fairly narrow minimum-to-maximum range. Of course, if one adopts a more flexible, "limiting retributive" model (see, e.g., Morris 1974; Morris and Tonry 1990; Frase 1997; American Law Institute 2003; Frase 2013a), first offenders and repeat offenders may be subject to a broader range of deserved penalties. But even under that model, prior record enhancements must be more limited than they are now, to maintain offense-based sentence proportionality and to avoid imposing punishments that cannot be justified by crime-preventive benefits.

To summarize: an offender's previous convictions do have desert-based consequences for sentencing of his current crime. To ignore prior convictions entirely would result in over-punishment—first offenders do not deserve the same degree of censure and sanction as recidivists (as discussed in the next chapter, these offenders are also usually much less likely to re-offend). Yet the significance of the past can be, and in practice almost always is, overstated. Most sentencing schemes assume that prior convictions reflect enhanced culpability, yet as we have seen, retributive theories fail to convincingly support such a view. Part of the problem appears to be the abiding intuition that repeat offenders deserve harsher treatment. This intuition may spring from an expectation that state punishment should and normally does encourage offender desistance; when reconviction occurs there is then a natural tendency to increase the degree of punishment, based on the offender's obstinate refusal to in fact desist. But this intuition is unrealistic; research on criminal careers, some of which we review in the next two chapters, shows that although most offenders eventually desist, many of them take a while to do so. Desistance from crime, like addiction to drugs and alcohol, is often a relapsing phenomenon in which progress is measured by increasingly long periods of desistance, not by sudden and complete cessation after an initial intervention.

2 PRIOR RECORD AND THE RISK OF RECIDIVISM

Having examined retributive approaches to prior record enhancements we now turn, in this and the next two chapters, to the more common and more convincing justification for recidivist sentencing premiums: crime prevention. As the U.S. Sentencing Commission noted (1986, 126): "crime control arguments provide a stronger justification for using criminal history to adjust sentence."[1] One underlying assumption is that prior convictions provide a useful proxy for recidivism risk, and that assumption is well supported by research, at least as a general proposition. But there is much less research on how well particular prior record formulas predict risk. Moreover, the risk-based crime prevention rationale for prior record enhancements also rests upon a second key assumption: that progressively increasing the severity of punishment for recidivists will prevent further offending in a cost-effective manner. Both assumptions require empirical validation; it cannot simply be assumed (although it often is) that a higher criminal history score indicates higher recidivism risk, and that giving higher-risk offenders substantially more severe penalties is a cost-effective way to control crime.

In this chapter we review the empirical evidence relevant to the first assumption: that prior record, as measured by existing guidelines criminal history scores, is a strong predictor of future offending (we return to this issue in later chapters, examining particular dimensions of prior record). Next, chapter 3 will explore an important related question: Which factors other than criminal history predict higher and lower risk of repeat offending, and how do these factors relate to a prior conviction record? If prior record enhancements are justified primarily by elevated recidivism risk, it is necessary to also consider non-record factors that indicate a higher or lower risk than is predicted by record alone. Chapter 4 then reviews research demonstrating the modest effect that increased sentence severity has in preventing crime. That chapter also notes a number of ethical and legal objections to sentence enhancements based on prior record and/or other risk factors.

Research has repeatedly shown that, in general, repeat offenders have a higher risk of re-offending than first offenders, and that recidivism risk generally rises with increases in the number of prior convictions. Yet we need to answer a number of other questions about the relationship between past and future offending. For example:

- How strong is the relationship between the seriousness of the criminal record and the likelihood of future offending? This is commonly represented by the statistical association between the number of priors and the probability of recidivism.
- Since an offender's prior record (or criminal history score) is a composite of different elements, which components are the strongest predictors of re-offending? Are there any criminal history score components that have little or no added predictive power?
- Are the increments in sentence severity prescribed by grid-based guidelines, across criminal history categories, proportionate to demonstrated increases in recidivism risk? In other words, how closely do prior record enhancements in the guidelines map onto distinctions in offender risk?
- How strong a predictor is criminal history relative to other legally relevant variables (such as current offense seriousness) or demographic variables such as age, gender, or socioeconomic status? Is the relationship between prior offending and re-offending modified by other variables such as offense category, offender age, and gender? For example, is the relationship stronger for certain offenses, or certain age groups of offenders?

The remainder of this chapter is organized as follows. Part A explains why it is so important to examine the extent to which guidelines criminal history scores and score components accurately predict offender recidivism risk. Part B summarizes the ways in which guidelines systems have directly or indirectly incorporated positive and negative risk-related factors into their guidelines. In addition to the number and seriousness of prior convictions, risk factors such as the remoteness in time of a prior conviction, crime-free "gap" periods, and the offender's custody status at the time of the current offense are often included in the guidelines criminal history score. Alternatively, some guidelines systems allow these and other assumed risk factors to be considered as grounds for departure after the recommended sentence has been determined based solely on current offense and prior convictions. Part C summarizes research on the extent to which prior convictions predict re-offending. In Part D we examine the lack of close fit between recidivism risk, as criminal history scores rise, and increments in recommended sentence severity. Part E discusses the problem of enhancing penalties according to a rigid criminal history formula, and argues that judges must be given power to adjust sentences to take into account case-specific variations in risk. Part F briefly outlines our recommendations for research to improve the risk management function of criminal history enhancements.

A. Criminal History and Recidivism Risk: A Critical Policy Issue That Is Ripe for Review

Some sentencing guidelines commissions expressly justify criminal history enhancements in whole or in part on the ground that a more extensive prior conviction record indicates a higher risk of repeat offending (MSGC 1984, 14; USSC 2016b, 5), and most other commissions have probably assumed this to be the case. All commissions have, or could assemble, individual sentencing data that would validate the risk-predictive accuracy of the system's criminal history score and each score component; yet commissions and other researchers have rarely conducted such validation research, either when each system's initial criminal history score was being constructed or at a later point in time.

As discussed in Part C, the widespread assumption that criminal history serves as a proxy for recidivism risk is supported by research showing that, in general, offenders with a more extensive record of prior convictions are more likely to commit further crimes. But considering the wide variations in criminal history scores and other offender factors found in existing guidelines systems, it is implausible to suppose that all existing criminal history scores are equally accurate and efficient in their risk-predictive power. It is far more likely that the criminal history scoring formulas in many guidelines systems include components with little additional risk-predictive value that are unnecessarily enhancing sentences, consuming scarce resources, and burdening offenders and their families. As noted in Part F, this is indeed what the federal, Pennsylvania, and Minnesota sentencing commissions found when they examined the risk-predictive accuracy of components of their criminal history formula. Conversely, there may be score components with strong risk-predictive power that are underweighted in some guidelines systems.

B. How Guidelines Criminal History Rules Have Incorporated Risk Factors

Although existing guidelines systems include very few explicit offender risk factors in their criminal history scoring formulas or other rules, most criminal history score components are at least plausibly related to lower or higher risk of recidivism (however, very few of these factors have actually been empirically shown to predict risk, alone or in combination). Risk-related features of guidelines criminal history scores include the following:

- *Number of convictions.* In most guidelines systems the principal component of the criminal history score is the number of prior adult-court felony convictions, reflecting the assumption (supported by empirical evidence, discussed in Part C) that recidivism risk is positively correlated with the number of prior convictions.
- *Age of convictions.* Some guidelines systems have rules that no longer count convictions entered more than a certain number of years earlier (these are variously known as decay, lapse, washout, or look-back limits; see generally chapter 9). These rules plausibly (but with limited research support) reflect the lower assumed risk-predictive value of very old convictions—such convictions may date from a very different living environment and/or phase of the offender's life, and in any case they reflect the higher propensity to crime found in younger persons. Indeed, such rules are sometimes intended as proxies for current offender age (USSC 2005, 8). As further discussed in chapter 3, advancing age is a well-documented low-risk factor, but one that is seldom recognized in guidelines rules.
- *Crime-free periods.* As is also discussed in chapter 9, some systems have "recent gap" rules that permit older convictions to be excluded if an offender remained crime-free in the community for a substantial period of time immediately preceding the current offense. Such a period of desistance suggests that, despite the offender's relapse in committing the crime for which he is now being sentenced, his criminal career is tapering off and may soon end entirely (see chapter 3 for further discussion of the "age-crime curve" of offending, and individual variations therein). Moreover, there is empirical support for the assumption of lower risk after such a gap in offending.[2] A few jurisdictions apply a different gap rule, under which a prior crime no longer counts if there is a crime-free gap following that offense, even if the current offense was not immediately preceded by such a gap. These "any-gap" rules likewise may reflect an assumption that the

offender currently poses lower risk, since he seems to have been capable of abstaining from crime for an extended period in the past.[3] (However, such an inference seems much less plausible when the crime-free gap in question occurred many years ago.)

- *Juvenile priors*. Almost all guidelines systems include at least some juvenile-court adjudications in the criminal history score (Mitchell 2015b), and this factor finds some support in research on factors predicting recidivism risk and the length of adult criminal careers (see further discussion in chapters 3 and 10). The strongest juvenile-record factor confirmed by research relates to the age of the first recorded delinquency. Yet guidelines criminal history scores include juvenile adjudications without regard to the presence or absence of "early onset"; indeed, some scores exclude the earliest adjudications!
- *Patterning*. Some systems have rules that give more weight to prior crimes that are the same or similar to the current crime or crimes (see chapter 10). Research on criminal careers suggests that such offense patterning is not likely to be a strong predictor of elevated risk, but it remains possible that such patterns can sometimes help to identify professional, career, or persistent offenders who pose an elevated risk.
- *Weighting*. A similar assumption of elevated risk may underlie rules that give higher weight to prior violent crimes, or reserve the highest criminal history categories for offenders with one of more violent priors (Hester 2015; see also chapter 10, *infra*). One of the purposes of such rules may be to identify for separate treatment "violent offenders" and "nonviolent offenders"—those who are thought to be more likely than the average offender to commit a violent crime in the future, and those who are less likely to do so.
- *Custody status*. In the majority of guidelines systems, one or more criminal history points is added for committing the current offense while in one of several designated criminal justice custody or supervision statuses (see chapter 10). Such individuals may pose a higher risk of recidivism than others not in one of these statuses, thus meriting extra punishment to deter or incapacitate them. Although empirical support is limited, it is plausible to assume that custody-status offenders pose a higher risk of further crime, or at least a higher risk of supervision failure, since they were unwilling to obey the law even when under the direct control of officials. Moreover, the fact of custody status often means that the offender has one or more recent convictions, which, in turn, suggests that the offender's criminal career is still "active." Although recency of prior offending is rarely directly

recognized in criminal history scoring, custody status may function as a proxy for recency. But here too, there is very little actual research on the risk-predictive value of either recency or custody status.

- *Earlier violations of release conditions.* A similar rationale may underlie another element found in some criminal history scores: the offender's violation of previous release conditions, with or without revocation of release. Like custody status (which involves violation of current or very recent release conditions), such earlier violations suggest elevated risk of crime or supervision failure if the offender is again granted release. (On the other hand, such an inference seems much less plausible in cases where the release violation occurred many years earlier.)

C. Research on Criminal History as a Predictor of Re-offending

Studies exploring the link between past and future offending have been reported for decades now and the basic finding is uncontested: the more extensive the offender's prior record, the higher the likelihood of subsequent re-offending. This is true whether the measure of recidivism is subsequent arrest, conviction, or incarceration. For example, Grunhut (1948) reviewed European statistics collected in 1902 and concluded that "the probability of recidivism increases with the number of previous sentences" (389). More recently, a meta-analysis of 131 studies (Gendreau et al. 1996) found that various measures of criminal history were consistently among the strongest predictors or recidivism. In terms of guidelines, this suggests that the recidivism rate should rise as a function of the offender's criminal history score. But as was noted earlier, criminal history scores vary widely, and there is good reason to believe that some scoring formulas predict risk better than others.

Currently, the two principal sources of information about criminal history and re-offending are recidivism studies conducted by sentencing commissions and academic research. Some U.S. commissions publish recidivism statistics for different categories of offending, although this research is generally only bivariate in nature, recording the simple association between two variables (prior and future crimes). Academic research is more likely to include multivariate analyses that establish the magnitude of the relationship after controlling for a range of other variables correlated with the risk of re-offending.[4] In addition, a number of aggregate analyses exist. The challenge to "meta-analyses" of previous research is the variability in methodology.

Studies use different combinations of predictor (independent) variables, and varying definitions of outcome (dependent variables).

Recent research in three guidelines jurisdictions has found a clear relationship between an offender's guidelines criminal history score and the likelihood of subsequent recidivism. In the federal system, offenders with zero criminal history (CH) points have a rearrest rate of 30 percent, which is significantly lower than the 47 percent rearrest rate for offenders with 1 point (USSC 2017b, figure 1). The rearrest rate then rises for offenders with higher criminal history scores—offenders with 10 CH points have a 77 percent reoffending rate, and with 15 or more points the rate is 86 percent. Similarly, research on offenders sentenced under the Pennsylvania and Minnesota guidelines found that, in each system, recidivism rates rose steadily with increases in prior record score (Hester forthcoming; Laskorunsky 2018). Reoffending statistics from England and Wales and other jurisdictions reveal the same progressive relationship (Andrews and Bonta 2010; Ministry of Justice 2016; Helmus and Forrester 2017).

Many other studies have addressed the question of the strength of prior record and non-record factors as predictors of re-offending. The diversity of this research, in terms of the conceptual definition and variables included, defies any straightforward aggregation that might yield a single conclusion. The best that we can say is that criminal history appears at or near the top of all hierarchies of risk factors. This outcome is unsurprising in light of the bivariate finding that recidivism rates are strongly correlated with the seriousness of the prior record. Some examples are illustrative:

- The Florida Department of Corrections found that criminal history (as reflected in the number of prior prison commitments) was the single most powerful predictor of recidivism (2014b, table 2). This was true for male but not for female offenders, a finding that highlights the need for more gender-specific research in this area.
- The Risk Assessment Project of the Pennsylvania Commission on Sentencing (2015) found that the number of prior convictions was the best predictor of recidivism for all levels of offense gravity (table 3).
- Analyses of re-offending by a large sample of Australian offenders revealed that criminal history was the strongest predictor of re-offending (Hsu et al. 2009).

The fact that criminal history appears high in rankings of recidivism predictors does not alone justify record-based sentencing enhancements; it remains one factor among many that predict re-offending, and criminal history is not always the best predictor of recidivism. The literature is replete with examples of research where other factors, usually demographic variables, are more important. We will return to research on non-prior-record factors in chapter 3. And in chapter 10 we discuss the risk-predictive value of several problematic components of many guidelines criminal history scores: juvenile adjudications, adult misdemeanor priors, patterning rules, heavy weighting of higher-severity prior crimes, and custody status.

D. Fit between Increments in Recidivism Risk and Increments in Guidelines Prison Terms

Even if a more extensive prior record indicates a higher risk of future offending, we need to address questions relating to the architecture of enhancement structures. How well do existing guideline enhancements correspond to empirical trends in risk? For example, is it appropriate to increase recommended prison terms in a linear fashion, with each increase in prior record? Does the risk of re-offending rise in a linear fashion?

Prior record enhancements are imposed to reflect the heightened risk posed by repeat offenders. The Criminal History axis of a sentencing grid therefore represents a proxy for the dimension of risk, with offenders assigned to different points along the axis. Comparing the re-offending rates with increments in sentence severity reveals that the two dimensions (severity, in terms of time in prison; risk of re-offending as reflected in empirical recidivism rates) are actually poorly matched. Later we will attempt to explain this mismatch; first however we document the phenomenon.

Our review suggests that severity increments fail to track re-offending rates in the following ways:

- Although first offenders represent a much lower risk of re-offending than repeat offenders, grids do not make a correspondingly greater distinction between these two groups of offenders;
- Among recidivists, distinct categories of criminal history, carrying very different presumptive sentences, are often associated with comparable re-offending rates;
- Although severity increases in a linear fashion across the CH axis, re-offending rates tend to level out at higher CH levels.
- Increases in severity often substantially outstrip increases in re-offending rates.

These problems are due in part to the decision to assign offenders to one of a limited number of criminal history categories. This arrangement is analogous to assigning all offenses to a small number of offense seriousness levels—where that is done, crimes of variable seriousness may be assigned to the same level, and at category boundaries crimes of roughly similar seriousness end up in categories with different severity rankings. Similar problems can arise with respect to the criminal history dimension: some offenders with variable risks of re-offending may be assigned to the same prior record category, while other offenders (especially at higher criminal history levels), who do not represent distinct levels of risk, may be assigned to different prior record categories.

1. *First Offenders Insufficiently Distinguished from Recidivists*

Another significant group of findings from the federal, Pennsylvania, and Minnesota research casts doubt on the common guidelines policy of enhancing sentences, across criminal history categories, according to a linear or other constant formula. In all three of these jurisdictions, the greatest increase in recidivism was between the lowest and next-lowest criminal history categories. In the federal system, offenders in CH Category I (0 or 1 CH point) have a re-arrest rate of 34 percent, while the rate for CH Category II (2 or 3 points) is 54 percent; this 59 percent increase (54/34) is much greater than the average category to category increase of 10 percent across the remaining categories, II through VI (USSC 2017b, figure 2). Similarly, Hester (forthcoming) and Laskorunsky (2018) found that the greatest difference in terms of recidivism risk was between the lowest CH category (0 points) and the next category (1 point).

These findings lend further support to our model, under which there is a greater difference in recommended sentence severity between first offenders and modest recidivists than between each of the higher criminal history categories. The lesson is clear: if the primary rationale for prior record enhancements is preventive, guidelines should make a greater distinction between first offenders and all recidivists. Since retributivist theory also makes a greater distinction between first offenders and recidivists with differing criminal histories, both rationales would appear to point to the same policy (see discussion in Roberts 2010; Bagaric and Alexander 2014). The convergence of retributive and preventive positions was noted by the U.S. Sentencing Commission when it described offenders with minimal prior criminal history: "Not only do they have substantially lower recidivism rates, but they are considered less culpable" (USSC 2004b, 15).

2. Levelling Out of Re-offending Rates

Comparison of recidivism rates by criminal history category or score reveals that these rates level out—a finding inconsistent with a linear severity premium that assigns more imprisonment to reflect each additional prior conviction or criminal history point. This problem was noted by Rappaport a generation ago as justifying a limited number of criminal history categories. He cited unpublished analyses by the U.S. Sentencing Commission, which found that after a certain point additional convictions "do not significantly increase predictive accuracy" (1997, 185). This flattening of recidivism probability also emerges from the academic literature on re-offending. For example, Piquero et al. (2007) report a stabilizing of recidivism probabilities after the fourth conviction (see also Zara and Farrington 2016, table 2.18). Yet on most guidelines grids the increments in sentence severity as offenders move to higher criminal history categories are uniform and independent of the re-offending rates associated with each prior record category. As noted previously, research suggests that the difference in recidivism risk between offenders in the two lowest categories is much more significant than the differences between higher categories, yet the increment in recommended sentence severity is usually about the same. One explanation for this anomaly is that the record-based enhancements are purposively regularized to promote consistency of application. An alternate hypothesis is that the enhancement structure reflects a desire to simply punish repeat offenders more harshly, which is therefore independent of the empirically derived risk values.

Because recidivism rates increase by declining amounts as the criminal history score rises, there are often only small differences between categories even where the latter carry quite divergent sentence length recommendations. For example, the federal recidivism study, cited previously, found that the rearrest rate for offenders with 6 CH points (CH category III) was only 4 percentage points (6 percent) lower than the rate for offenders with 7 points (category IV) (USSC 2016b, figure 6).[5] These results confirm published findings from an earlier Commission recidivism study (USSC 2004a, exhibit 2), and raise questions about the justification for substantial penalty differences between groups of offenders in different criminal history categories who do not have substantially different probabilities of re-offending. Similarly, the Pennsylvania and Minnesota studies found that the small differences in recidivism rates between some adjacent criminal history categories were not statistically significant (Hester forthcoming; Laskorunsky 2018). Recidivism studies in other guidelines states have likewise found comparable recidivism rates for offenders with quite different criminal history profiles. The

Massachusetts Sentencing Commission's comprehensive recidivism study provides a good illustration. The recidivism rate of offenders in the "serious record" group was only 3 percent higher than the group with a "moderate" criminal record (2002, table 16).

3. *Minor Differences in Recidivism Trigger Significant Sentence Severity Increments*

We can illustrate this problem by again drawing upon recent federal recidivism data.[6] The overall recidivism rate for offenders with 2 CH points (CH category II) is 56 percent, and the rate is only moderately higher (71 percent) for those with 7 points (CH category IV) (USSC 2016b, figure 6). The difference in risk of re-offending may be modest but the resulting increase in recommended severity is substantial. Consider offenders at severity level (row) 36 of the federal grid. The recommended (cell midpoint) sentence for a row 36 offender with 7 CH points is 295 months, which is approximately five years longer than the recommended 236-months term for an offender with two CH points (USSC 2016a). The same patterns can be seen by comparing Criminal History Categories and, for the highest categories, the mismatch between increased risk and increased sentence severity is just as dramatic. CH category VI offenders have an overall rearrest rate (80 percent) that is 7 percent higher than the rate for category IV offenders (75 percent) (USSC 2017b). But on row 36, CH category VI offenders are recommended for prison terms 24 percent higher than for category IV offenders (365 versus 295 months, USSC 2016a).

Can these dramatic increase in sentence severity be justified by the relatively modest increase in recidivism rates? Assigning the same increment in sentence severity all the way along the criminal history dimension assumes that increases in recidivism rates across the early (less serious) CH categories replicate all the way across the grid, yet they clearly do not.[7] Nor can it be assumed that "recidivism" means the same thing at lower and higher levels of criminal history. Although it might be assumed that offenders with a higher criminal history score will be more likely to recidivate with a violent or other serious crime, Laskorunsky (2018) found that the opposite was true in Minnesota: the proportion of offenders convicted of a property crime rises with each increase in criminal history category, making up almost half of all offenders in the highest category (6 or more points). And offenders in that category are almost three times more likely to recidivate with a property offense than with a person offense.[8]

The federal, Pennsylvania, and Minnesota findings described in the preceding paragraphs all demonstrate the poor fit between criminal history categories, recommended sentence severity, and re-offending rates. But such efforts to validate criminal history enhancements are rare; most prior record schemes lack any empirical basis. Guidelines systems simply assign criminal history points to offenders based on the number and nature of their prior crimes, and use the point total to assign the offender to one of a limited number of criminal history categories (for example, the federal guidelines use six categories, Minnesota uses seven, and Pennsylvania uses eight). When each category carries a distinct increase in recommended punishment severity, the assumption must be made that offenders in different categories represent an equally distinct difference in their risk of re-offending. But the research previously cited calls that assumption into question. In all three guidelines systems that have studied these issues, first offenders have much lower recidivism rates than the lowest category of repeat offenders, after which recidivism rates rise at a much slower pace; indeed, several adjacent higher categories are indistinguishable in terms of their re-offending rates. Yet in each system, recommended sentence severity rises steadily across all criminal history categories.

Risk of re-offending is not smoothly and continuously distributed in a way that reflects the number of prior convictions, and this reality has consequences for the grouping of offenders into distinct categories. Guidelines adopt a points-based scheme merely because unlike other sentencing factors (such as premeditation or remorse), criminal history can be counted, and scored; an offender's criminal past can be unitized. But this unitization is meretricious; it implies a degree of continuity that is unsupported by the recidivism research. The consequence is that categorizing offenders according to their criminal history score maps poorly onto the smoothly accelerating increments of sentence severity mandated by the guidelines. A trivial increase in risk of re-offending should not trigger a substantial jump in sentence length.

There is no clear or obvious relationship between the increase in severity that is appropriate to a given increase in risk of re-offending. We cannot, for example require a 10 percent increase in risk of recidivism to trigger a 10 percent increase in sentence length; matters are far more complex than that. However, as a general rule, minor increases in ascribed risk should attract equally modest increments in severity. Yet under current guidelines, a dramatic increase in severity is often imposed to achieve what appears to be a modest increase in prevention. It may be argued that this arrangement is the penal equivalent of imposing a drastic increase in motor vehicle insurance premiums in response to a modest increase in the aggregate risk of an accident. In short, before the State imposes a significant increment in sentence severity, it needs to satisfy a proportionality requirement, between the degree of additional recommended punishment and a demonstrated higher risk of re-offending.

Treating criminal history as a dimension and dividing the distribution into categories creates an inherent inflationary pressure. For example, if an extra year's imprisonment is added to the first category of criminal history (above the sentence imposed for first offenders), this is apparently assumed to require equivalent increments all along the range of categories. If each category is ascribed a separate sentencing range, and there are multiple categories, one of two outcomes arise. Either the distance between category ranges is minimal, in which case the maximum enhancement remains modest, or by the time the most serious category is reached the enhancement will be very significant. Grid-based guidelines favor the latter approach, creating a number of problems that we identify in this volume.

4. Explaining the Divergence between Re-offending Rates and Severity Increments

Why are prior record enhancements not calibrated more closely to reflect risk—which they are designed to reduce? One response is that the two-dimensional grid was created with another purpose in mind. In fact, documentation relating to the origins of the Minnesota guidelines supports such an interpretation. The Commission's analyses of pre-guidelines data revealed a powerful association between several criminal history variables and sentence outcomes. The variable with the strongest association was the number of prior felony convictions (Minnesota Sentencing Guidelines Commission 1979, 3). The Commission found that in making dispositional (prison/no-prison) decisions judges relied on two factors of roughly equal importance: the severity of the conviction offense, and the criminal history of the offender; it also found that the parole board considered the same two factors in making prison release decisions. The Commission therefore set about constructing a two-dimensional grid, based on these two factors, to structure judicial discretion in deciding prison disposition and prison duration in a determinate (no parole board) sentencing system.

In other words, criminal history was incorporated as a grid dimension and structured accordingly to reflect prior judicial and parole board practice rather than track empirical re-offending patterns. The Commission's report to the state legislature in 1980 notes that in developing the criminal history dimension the Commission was guided by four objectives, none of which invoke any link with preventing further crime.[9] Perhaps the Commission should have been less concerned with consistency and ease of application, and more with ensuring that prior record enhancements tracked empirical recidivism patterns. But the Commission was strongly influenced by proponents of retributive, "just deserts" sentencing (Roberts 2019; Parent 1988); and even if it had wanted to base prior record enhancements on recidivism risk, it lacked the time, data, and research resources to construct and validate such a model (Parent 1988).

Since 1989, the primary goal of Minnesota sentencing has been to ensure public safety (MSGC 2017b, 1), and this is certainly a major goal of all guidelines systems. Forty years after the initial drafting of the Minnesota guidelines we know a great deal more about the effectiveness of prior record enhancements as well as their costs and adverse consequences. Guidelines commissions in Minnesota and other jurisdictions also have much more data with which to assess and improve the crime control effectiveness and efficiency of criminal history enhancements. The architects of the original Minnesota grid would have had little reason to doubt the preventive effectiveness of prior record enhancements, or to be troubled by normative concerns about prior crimes as an aggravator at sentencing. But their faith in prior record enhancements appears, in retrospect, unjustified. Clearly, the Commission should revisit these issues.

Summary

The findings in this Part raise concerns about the current architecture of most sentencing grids. The punishment increments associated with criminal history categories do not closely correspond to risk-based distinctions between offenders (as reflected in categorical re-offending rates). The increments in severity assume progressive and regular increases in risk of re-offending, yet the statistics demonstrate that this is in fact not the case. The current approach (using discrete categories each carrying an additional, fixed quantum of punishment) promotes consistency of application. But consistency should follow, and not precede, a determination of the appropriate level of enhancement for this offender convicted of this offence with this particular criminal history. We will return to these issues and further discuss the architecture of record-based enhancements in our concluding chapter.

E. The Importance of Giving Judges Power to Individualize Prior Record Enhancements

The absence, in most guidelines systems, of individualization in the application of prior record enhancements is inconsistent with the treatment of other sentencing factors. For example, in determining how much enhancement is appropriate to reflect premeditation, or how much mitigation is justified for remorse, courts consider the individual offender and the circumstances of the offense. How extensive was the planning? How genuine is the remorse? Yet the current use of criminal history scores denies courts the discretion to consider individual offenders' levels of risk arising from their prior crimes. For this reason, our model regime outlined at the end of the volume incorporates a degree of individualization. It is not necessary to have to choose between a unitized, aggregate regime and one that is wholly individualized. Intermediate options are possible.

Individuals could be assigned, on the basis of their prior record score, to just three broad categories of risk—low, medium, and high. Each category would carry an associated sentence range and these ranges might overlap. Courts would have some discretion to individualize the record-based enhancement within the given risk range. The consequence would be that some offenders classified initially as high risk (on the basis of their criminal history score) might attract a modest enhancement if the court recognized that particular circumstances suggested that the offender was not a high risk. For example, the offender may have completed treatment for a problem relating to his offending, or may have addressed the causes of his earlier offending in some other way. Such a scheme would promote a generally consistent approach to prior record enhancements while at the same time acknowledging that the determination of risk, like blameworthiness, is a matter for individualization.

1. *Criminal History as a Static or Dynamic Factor?*

The research that links prior to future crimes answers the primary question of whether previous offending is a risk factor for future criminality, but the matter is more complicated. The link implies a static risk level. Indeed, sentencing guidelines and risk scale manuals usually place prior offending into the category of static rather than dynamic factors, on the simplistic assumption that an offender cannot change the fact that she acquired a felony conviction, say eight years previously.[10] In several respects, however, prior convictions are actually a dynamic risk factor. First, the predictive power of a prior conviction will in most cases decline over time, as the offender ages out of offending; the consequence is that risk is dynamic not static. Practitioners and scholars have recognized the declining significance of prior convictions over time (e.g., Hillier 1997). More recently, research by Kurlycheck et al. (2006, 2007) and Amirault and Lussier (2011) questions the static conceptualization of prior record. If previous offending is a stable risk factor it should exercise a constant influence. Yet these researchers demonstrated that risk declines over time and the result is that if a person remains crime-free for a period of several years, his or her risk of a new offense is similar to that of a person without a record (Kurlycheck et al. 2006, 485; see also Blumstein and Nakamura 2009; Ezell 2007).

Of course, the individual has not remained crime-free—the current conviction is evidence of that—but the point is that the predictive significance of prior convictions declines over time. Kazemian (2010) notes that a recent criminal record is a much more reliable predictor of re-offending than an older record. An offender with two priors committed 10 years earlier is a lower risk than one with the same two previous convictions recorded a year ago. Yet as we demonstrate in this volume, U.S. guidelines do not generally discount priors as they become older. They should, and we recommend such true decay provisions in our model. Young adults soon leave the high crime years, and older offenders enter low crime periods. These age-related changes mean that prior record enhancement schemes should incorporate temporal limits and decay factors (this topic is further discussed in chapter 10).

2. Considering the Individual's Efforts at Desistance

The second reason priors should be considered dynamic rather than static is that the predictive significance of a prior crime will diminish if the ex-offender takes steps to address the causes of that prior offending, or if there are changes to his living circumstances. If the offender lowers his risk of re-offending, he is effectively diminishing the predictive power of the prior crimes; previous offending is therefore not invariant but dynamic, with its significance changing in response to actions by the offender. Two obvious examples are substance abuse and marital status. If alcohol abuse has contributed to an offender's previous crimes and he is now abstinent, the predictive power of the previous conviction is obviously not the same as if he had not addressed the problem. Similarly, starting a family and committing to a stable relationship will also mean that the probative value of the previous offense is changing. Kazemian (2010) and others have noted that while criminal history information indicates higher risk of re-offending, there is a tendency to assume that the risk is stable. Ezell (2007) and Kazemian and Farrington (2006) both report that lifestyle changes were better predictors of re-offending than criminal history scores.[11] One of the key lessons of the research upon criminal careers and desistance is that these offending patterns are volatile; prior record enhancements assume a degree of stability, which is belied by the research (see Kazemian 2010).

Conceptualizing criminal history in dynamic rather than static terms carries significant implications for the architecture of the guidelines. The principal lesson is that prior offending should not be regarded as carrying an unchanging risk-based punitive weight. Prior convictions should be regarded as changing markers of re-offending, and for this reason we advocate greater use of decay provisions that down-weight and eventually disregard older priors. Simply put, if a prior crime's predictive value has declined, it should be accorded less weight in aggravation.[12] If the prior crime has lost most or all of its predictive power, it should be disregarded. No existing guidelines incorporate adequate decay rules and look-back limits. Our proposals recognize the research-based reality that the predictive significance of a prior conviction changes over time, and in response to events in the offender's life.

F. The Critical Need for Further Research

As we have stressed throughout this book, the first step in sentencing policy analysis is to clarify the punishment goals that criminal history enhancements are intended to serve. If these goals include prediction and management of offender recidivism risk, sentencing commissions and outside researchers should examine the extent to which the current criminal history score and each score component accurately predicts offender risk, and should also consider whether risk-predictive accuracy would be improved if factors other than criminal history were taken into account (such factors will be further discussed in chapter 3). Even if a particular prior record or other factor has risk-predictive value, a further question is whether it is fair to base sentencing on such a factor, and even if it is, whether that factor's predictive and crime control benefits are outweighed by added correctional costs, racially disparate impact, or other negative consequences such as interfering with an offender's partially successful efforts at desistance (see further discussion in chapter 4)—sentencing should reward such efforts, not undercut them.

Validation of the risk-predictive value of criminal history score components can be based on guidelines monitoring data over a period of several years, identifying which sentenced offenders reappear in the sentencing data for later years, and examining how the likelihood, frequency, and/or seriousness of re-offense varies with overall criminal history scores, the presence of particular score components, and other predictors. Anyone interested in conducting such research can find useful templates in the work done by the federal, Pennsylvania, and Minnesota sentencing commissions.[13]

This validation research will allow sentencing commissions and researchers to identify criminal history score components that provide little additional predictive value, or for which the added predictive value is outweighed by negative consequences such as racial disparate impact or substantial added correctional costs. Such components should then be dropped or at least given less weight. An example of this kind of evidence-based policy change was the decision of the U.S. Sentencing Commission to drop the "recency" point from the federal criminal history score because that component was found to have a substantial prison bed impact, but only slight added risk predictive value (USSC 2010, 18–21).[14]

Conclusion

This chapter has reviewed the research relating to the question of whether prior offending is a reliable predictor of future offending. A recent recidivism report published by the U.S. Sentencing Commission (2017b) is entitled "The Past Predicts the Future." This may be true, but only up to a point. Our review of the research relating prior to future crimes suggests that previous convictions do enhance the risk of re-offending, but in complex ways, and not always reliably. Moreover, we have shown how the categorical enhancements imposed by grid-based guidelines fail to closely track re-offending rates of offenders assigned to criminal history categories.

We have further argued that, although the existence of a previous conviction is an unchanging fact of the offender's profile, the prior crime's predictive significance—on which the preventive justification is founded—changes over time. For this and other reasons, judges must be given power to adjust recommended guidelines sentences, to account for case-specific variations in recidivism risk that are not captured by generally applicable prior record scores and formulas. In particular, and as further discussed in chapters 3 and 4, guidelines systems should also consider allowing judges to consider non-prior-record risk factors that indicate lower or higher recidivism risk than would be expected given the offender's prior conviction record.

Finally, we propose that the risk-predictive accuracy of each guidelines system's criminal history score, and of all score components, should be validated using recidivism data. Criminal history scoring formulas vary widely across guidelines systems, and it is unlikely that all existing criminal history scores are equally accurate and efficient in their risk-predictive power. The risk-predictive value of each score component should also be measured against the added costs, racial disparate impact, and other negative consequences of the sentence enhancements associated with that component.

3 WHAT OTHER FACTORS INDICATE HIGH OR LOW RECIDIVISM RISK?

In the previous chapter we examined the extent to which guidelines criminal history scores and score components accurately and efficiently predict an offender's higher and lower risk of re-offending. However, criminological research has identified a number of additional offender characteristics (e.g., age) and offense factors (e.g., the current offense is a property crime) that predict higher or lower risk of recidivism. Yet guidelines systems rarely incorporate any of these other risk factors into the criminal history or offender score, and only a few systems expressly allow such factors to be considered as an adjustment to the criminal history score or a basis for departure. This seems unwise. If prior record enhancements are primarily or even substantially justified as a way to manage offender risk, policymakers need to consider other, non-record risk factors that may improve risk-prediction accuracy and efficiency. As will be discussed in the next chapter, non-criminal-history risk factors (and even some based on criminal history) raise additional ethical and legal issues, but these issues are manageable in many cases.

Part A of this chapter examines the limited extent to which guidelines systems have directly or indirectly incorporated non-criminal-history-related risk factors into their guidelines (usually as a ground for departure after the recommended sentence has been determined based solely on current offense and prior conviction record). Part B examines offense- and (non-criminal-history) offender-based factors such as the offender's current age, that criminological research has found to be good predictors of the risk of re-offending, but that have not generally been given any formal role in guidelines sentencing. Part C summarizes the risk factors found in several widely used risk assessment instruments. Part D presents our recommendations for further jurisdiction-specific research and policy change, to improve the accuracy and cost-effectiveness of risk predictions at sentencing.

A preliminary caveat stated at the start of the previous chapter, examining prior record as a risk-prediction tool, is worth repeating here. This chapter assumes that sentencing courts and policymakers wish to identify offenders who pose especially high or especially low risk of further crime, and that, to do so, they are willing to consider additional, non-prior-record risk factors. But as we discuss in the next chapter, it should not simply be assumed that giving more severe criminal penalties to higher risk offenders will, on balance, prevent future crimes, or that it will do so in a cost-effective way; indeed, the available research on incapacitation and deterrence effects of more severe punishment casts serious doubt on the crime-control benefits of penalty increases for higher-risk offenders.

A. Non-criminal-history Risk Factors and Assessments Found in Existing Guidelines Systems

A few jurisdictions expressly or implicitly recognize, as a basis for departure from the recommended guidelines sentence, the limitations of criminal history as a risk prediction tool. The federal guidelines' "inadequacy of criminal history" provision permits departure up or down if the offender's criminal history score "substantially" understates or overstates "the seriousness of the defendant's criminal history *or the likelihood that the defendant will commit other crimes*" (USSC 2016a secs. 4A1.3(a)(1) and 4A1.3(b)(1) (emphasis added).

Three states authorize criminal history score adjustments, albeit in one direction only, and although these adjustments are not expressly linked to risk prediction, that may be at least part of their rationale. Washington State permits upward departure if the omission of certain prior crimes from the offender's criminal history score yields a recommended sentence that is "clearly too lenient" (Wash. Rev. Code secs. 9.94A.535(2)(b)–(d) (2013)). A similar Pennsylvania provision entitled "Adequacy of the Prior Record Score" permits the sentencing court to consider prior convictions and juvenile adjudications or dispositions that were not counted in the calculation of the score (204 Pennsylvania Code sec. 303.5(d) (2015)). Minnesota permits downward departure based on a showing that the offender's multiple prior convictions were all entered in one or two prior court appearances (a single appearance, if the current offense is of medium severity; no more than two appearances, if the current offense is low severity) (MSGC 2017a, sec. 2.D.3.a (4)). Under these circumstances the offender's criminal history score will usually overstate the number of prior interventions he has received, and to which he has failed to respond. The underlying assumption may be that offenders with fewer prior interventions are generally less dangerous and/or more "amenable" to a community-based sentence than their criminal history score would suggest.

Several jurisdictions (Minnesota, North Carolina, Ohio, and Utah) expressly recognize the probable-low-risk concept of "amenability to probation" (or similar, differently worded concepts) as a basis to depart and grant probation in lieu of the recommended prison term. Most of these jurisdictions also recognize a corresponding, high-risk concept of "unamenability to probation" as a basis for upward departure from a recommended non-prison sentence. Some systems recognize these factors in case law, while other systems include them, or similar factors, in lists of permitted grounds for departure.[1]

A few guidelines systems have used or are planning to use validated risk assessment tools at sentencing. Under the Virginia guidelines a finding of low risk permits imposition of a non-prison sentence on a nonviolent offender for whom ordinary guidelines rules recommend a prison sentence; for certain sex offenders, a finding of high risk authorizes a longer prison term than would otherwise apply (Virginia Criminal Sentencing Commission 2014, 41–51; 2017, 28–34). Factors currently employed to identify low-risk larceny or fraud offenders include the offender's relatively older age at the time of the current offense, female gender, and limited number of prior adult felony convictions and adult incarcerations, and that the offender was not legally restrained at the time of the offense (*Id.* 2018b, Sec. D; *id.* 2018c, Sec. D).[2] Factors used to identify high-risk sex offenders include the offender's relatively younger age, limited education and/or employment history, relationship to the victim, the location of the crime (e.g., in the offender's but not also victim's residence), and the number of prior adult person-crime arrests, prior incarcerations, prior participation in treatment programs, and (for aggravated sexual battery) that the offense involved actual or attempted penetration (*Id.* 2018d, Sec. A (Part 1); *Id.* 2018e, Sec. C).

In practice, high-risk sentencing enhancements are used sparingly, and far less frequently than low-risk sentencing mitigations: for example, in fiscal year 2017 the number of offenders receiving a low-risk mitigation was about 40 times greater than the number subject to a high-risk enhancement.[3] Nevertheless, the magnitude of the allowed high-risk enhancement (up to 300 percent above the otherwise-applicable guidelines term) raises a serious risk that these offenders are receiving disproportionately severe sentences. Low-risk mitigation raises the opposite problem, although disproportionate leniency is arguably less problematic, at least under a limiting or negative retributive theory (see Frase 2013a for further discussion of limiting retributive theories; see also chapter 1, *supra*, discussing retributive and utilitarian arguments in favor of asymmetric proportionality principles). Some writers reject this distinction and argue that, as a matter of principle, sentence severity should never be enhanced or mitigated on the basis of demographic or socioeconomic characteristics such as age, education, or employment (these issues will be examined further in chapter 4).

In 2015 Utah made substantial changes in its guidelines, designed to emphasize risk management and risk reduction based on validated risk/needs assessments.[4] Kansas has used the LSI-R risk assessment tool to divert nonviolent higher-risk drug offenders from prison to community-based drug treatment programs (Monahan and Skeem 2016; LSI-R components are summarized in Part C.3). And under the advisory sentencing guidelines formerly used in Missouri, judges were provided with a validated risk assessment tool for use at sentencing, which included the following factors: prior convictions, prior prison incarcerations, a recent five-year gap in offending, prior probation and parole revocations, prior escapes, and several offender characteristics—current age, substance abuse, education, and employment (Missouri Sentencing Advisory Commission 2013, 127–30; see also Wolff 2008).

Pursuant to a 2010 legislative directive, the Pennsylvania guidelines commission is developing a system of risk assessments to be used as a screening tool at sentencing—not as grounds to impose a more or less severe sentence, but only to identify offenders who are recommended to receive further, offender-specific risk and needs assessments (Pennsylvania Commission on Sentencing 2018a, b). Two sets of risk assessment tools are proposed. One set includes nine risk scales that predict rearrest for any offense, depending on the offender's conviction offense severity level on the guidelines grids; the other tool is limited to predicting rearrest for violent ("person") offenses, and applies regardless of offense severity level (*Id.*, 2018a, 2).[5] The any-offense scale will identify about one-third of all offenders, including equal numbers judged to pose the highest and the lowest risks of future crime, using the risk factors found to be most predictive of high or low risk for offenders at each offense level (*Id.*, 2018c, 4). By contrast, the violent-offense scale will only be used to identify offenders at low risk of committing such crimes; this policy decision was made because violent crimes are rare, and error rates in prediction of high-risk offenders are much greater than for low-risk predictions (*Id.*, 2018c, 11; 2018e, 2).

Commission research determined that offender age and the number of prior convictions added significant any-offense predictive accuracy to all nine scales, whereas five other risk factors only added predictive value for some scales (i.e., at some offense severity levels); those other risk factors, and the number of risk scales including that factor, are gender (8 of the 9 scales), current conviction offense type (7), multiple current convictions (2), prior conviction offense type (8), and whether there had been a prior juvenile adjudication (8) (*Id.*, 2018d, 1–2). Except for multiple current convictions, the same risk factors were found to be significantly predictive of recidivism for violent crimes (*Id.*) The Commission controlled for, but chose to exclude from all of the risk scales, two predictive but normatively objectionable demographic factors: race and county of residence.[6] For this reason, the risk scales "are moderately biased in favor of black offenders in that they under-predict the recidivism rates of black offenders" (*Id.*, 2018f, 1).

B. Risk Factors Recognized in Criminological Research but Not in Most Guidelines

Research on recidivism and criminal careers has found that the following non-criminal-history factors consistently predict a higher risk of re-offending:[7]

> [Y]oung age, male gender, substance abuse, employment problems, antisocial associates, criminal thinking patterns (e.g., feeling entitled, rationalizing misconduct, poor empathy), and antisocial personality features (e.g., impulsive, hostile, pleasure seeking).

Other factors identified in the extensive criminal careers literature that help to predict a longer remaining ("residual") criminal career are early onset of delinquency (age at first arrest), and whether the current or prior convictions were for property or drug crimes (see generally Monahan and Skeem 2014, 163, 164 n.16; see also Monahan et al. 2017). A factor that consistently predicts a shorter residual career length is *older* current age; other factors that predict residual career length include the offender's levels of education, social support and quality of family or other relationships, residential stability, and the degree of urbanization of his or her home community.

No guidelines system has incorporated any of these validated risk factors into the computation of its criminal history score, and only the five systems noted (Kansas, Missouri, Pennsylvania, Utah, and Virginia) have expressly recognized some of them as relevant criteria within guidelines ranges or as grounds for departure. However, factors such as current employment and social support are sometimes considered in applying the risk-related concepts of amenability and unamenability to probation that were discussed previously.

C. Factors Included in Risk Assessment Instruments

Many of the validated risk factors summarized in Part B have been incorporated into risk assessment tools designed for use by parole boards and other correctional officials. Three of the best known and most widely used risk assessment instruments are described below. One important thing to note is that two of these three instruments focus almost entirely on aspects of the offender's criminal history or current offense type and severity; except for age, these two instruments do not consider the offender's demographic, personality, or socioeconomic characteristics.

1. The U.S. Parole Commission's Salient Factor Score (SFS)

Almost all of the factors in the current (1998 version) of the Salient Factor Score relate to the offender's prior criminal record—prior adult convictions and juvenile adjudications, prior adult and juvenile commitments to custody, whether there was a commitment-free period of three or more years preceding commission of the current offense (or if not, whether no prior commitment exceeded 30 days), and whether the current offense was committed while on probation, parole, confinement, or escape status.

However, the offender's current age may be considered in two ways: (1) as part of a bivariate factor combining age with number of prior commitments (the lowest risk is predicted for offenders 26 years or older who have no more than three prior commitments; the highest risk ratings are for offenders aged 22 to 25 with five or more commitments, aged 20 or 21 with four or more commitments, or aged 19 or less regardless of their number of commitments); and (2) as a conditional factor to be considered only if the offender does not already have the maximum of 10 points (lowest risk)—in that case, an additional point is added for offenders 41 years or older at the time of the current offense (Hoffman and Beck 2004).

The United States Sentencing Commission has done validation research comparing the recidivism-prediction accuracy of the Salient Factor Score (SFS) and the offender's guidelines criminal history category (CHC). The commission found that the SFS was a better predictor, but that the difference was due to the SFS's inclusion of offender age; when age was combined with CHC, that measure and the SFS were equally good risk predictors. And when a "true" first-offender component (distinguishing offenders who had never even been arrested before the current offense) was also added to the age-plus-criminal history measure, that measure was a better predictor of risk than the SFS (USSC 2005, 12–15, 26).

2. The California Static Risk Assessment (CSRA)

This risk assessment tool contains 20 factors with a maximum possible score of 52 points (highest risk), arranged in the five groups listed below; four of these groups relate to the offender's record of prior conviction or misconduct while serving a sentence (Turner et al. 2009).[8]

- Demographic factors—current age (seven categories—age 60 or over scores 0 points; age 13–17 scores 6 points), and gender (male scores one point).
- Total number of felony convictions (maximum score is 5 points, for 5 or more convictions on separate dates, including the current conviction).
- Prior and current felony sentences, grouped in seven offense categories (maximum point scores for each category are shown in parentheses): homicide (1); sex crime (2); two or more violent property crimes (3); two or more weapons crimes (2); five or more other property crimes (5); three or more drug crimes (3); and escape (1).
- Prior and current misdemeanor sentences, grouped in nine offense categories (maximum point scores for each category are shown in parentheses): five or more non-domestic violence assaults (5); two or more domestic violence assaults or protective order violations (2); sex crime (2); other misdemeanors, including non-assault domestic violence (1); weapons offense (1); three or more property crimes (3); drug crime (2); escape (1); alcohol offense (1).
- Total number of sentence or supervision condition violations (up to 5 points, for 5 or more violations).

The CSRA developers explained that factors related to education, substance abuse, and juvenile record were not included in the instrument because reliable information on those matters was not available (Turner et al. 2009, 5). This point may have broader implications: unless it is known that a given risk factor was studied and found to have no significant added value, its exclusion from a particular risk assessment tool might simply mean that data were not available, or were deemed too unreliable and/or too often unavailable in practice, to permit the factor to be considered.

3. *The Level of Service Inventory-Revised (LSI-R)*

The current version of this widely used risk-needs assessment tool has 43 scored factors grouped into eight categories (called subcomponents); each factor can add one point toward a conclusion of high risk-needs; some facts about the offender and/or his criminal behavior can be counted under more than one factor (for example, the same crime can contribute or help to contribute a point under several of the criminal history factors) (Andrews et al. 2004).[9]

- Criminal history—this group has eight factors; one point is scored for each of the following: there are any prior juvenile dispositions or adult convictions; there are two or more of the above entered at different times; there are three or more of the above entered at different times; there were three or more charges in the most recent disposition or conviction; the offender was arrested or charged when less than 16 years old; any disposition or conviction led to incarceration; the offender was ever punished for institutional misconduct; the offender was ever charged with breaching probation, or had a revocation of community release (including pretrial).
- Education/employment—nine factors, scoring one point each for: the offender is currently unemployed or working less than 75 percent of the time; is frequently unemployed (worked less than 50 percent of the last 12 months he was in the community); has never been employed for a full year; has completed less than 12th grade or equivalent; has completed less than the 10th grade or equivalent; was ever suspended or expelled from school; has a low degree of school participation and performance; has no contact with, or has problems getting along with, fellow students or workers; has conflicts or other problems with teachers or work supervisors.
- Family/marital—four factors (one point for each): the offender has conflicts or other problems in his marital or equivalent relationship, or is not currently in such a relationship and is dissatisfied with his single status; the offender has a poor relationship with his parents or both are deceased; the offender has a poor relationship with other family members; a parent, sibling, other close relative, or spouse has a criminal record.
- Leisure/recreation—two factors: the offender has not within the previous 12 months participated in an organized activity (e.g., labor union, service

club, sports team or club, church); the offender has not been involved in a highly rewarding or satisfying activity such as stamp collecting or martial arts, and thus has a lot of idle time and may often be bored.

- Companions—four factors: some of the offender's acquaintances are involved in criminal activities or have criminal records; the offender has friends who are involved in criminal activities or have criminal records; the offender has fewer than three anti-criminal acquaintances (people who are not involved in criminal activities and don't have criminal records); the offender has fewer than three anti-criminal friends.
- Alcohol/drug problems—eight factors: the offender has ever had a drinking problem, the offender has ever had a drug problem, the offender currently has a drinking problem, the offender currently has a drug problem, the offender's drinking or drug problem has or could contribute to commission of a crime, the offender's drinking or drug problem has or could contribute to marital or family problems, the offender's drinking or drug problem has or could contribute to school or work problems, the offender's drinking or drug problem has or could contribute to his or her medical problems.
- Pro-criminal attitude or orientation—four factors: the offender places more emphasis on the positive than the negative consequences of his criminal acts, the offender has a low regard for conventional alternatives to crime and a criminal lifestyle, the offender shows little acceptance of responsibility for or appreciation of the harms caused by his crimes, offender shows little cooperation with assigned programming and little motivation to address criminogenic factors.
- Antisocial pattern—four factors: actual or likely diagnosis of Antisocial Personality Disorder; offender had severe adjustment problems as a child, and has a record of violence, escape, or violation of release conditions; offender has a criminal attitude (supportive of crime and/or poor attitude toward convention or supervision/treatment); offender has a pattern of generalized trouble, as manifested by at least four of the following: financial problems, three or more address changes in the last year, never employed a full year, less than grade 10 or equivalent completed, suspended or expelled at least once, poor relationship with parents, not involved in a highly rewarding or satisfying activity, few anti-criminal friends.

The LSI-R scale contains many factors in addition to prior convictions, and there is some evidence that those additional factors improve recidivism predictions, when compared to a guidelines criminal history score.

The Minnesota Commission examined reconviction rates of drug offenders released on probation or after serving a prison term, and found that the LSI-R risk levels of offenders correlated more strongly with their odds of subsequent reconviction than did the offenders' guidelines criminal history scores; the difference was particularly strong for probationers (MSGC 2015b, slides 31 and 32).

D. Recommendations for Further Research and Sentencing Policy Change

If the punishment goals of a guidelines system include management of offender recidivism risk, sentencing commissions and outside researchers should conduct research to determine whether additions to or adjustments of that system's criminal history formula will improve the score's accuracy and efficiency as a predictor of risk. This research should focus on risk factors, such as those discussed in Parts A, B, and C, that are not already included in the criminal history score but that have been recognized in the criminological literature, in risk assessment instruments, and/or in other guidelines systems. Researchers should also examine whether some of these additional risk factors are already being considered, even without formal recognition in the guidelines, when judges exercise their departure powers (which, as noted in Part A, are sometimes explicitly justified by criminal history scoring problems). To the extent that such factors are not usually recorded in existing court and sentencing data, they can be identified by conducting surveys of judges. If a factor is already being considered in many cases, formal recognition is less likely to be resisted by judges and practitioners and is more likely to improve the consistency of practices from case to case. Research should also address the ethical issues discussed in chapter 4, and decide how those issues should be resolved.

Non-prior-record factors that improve risk prediction accuracy and that are deemed acceptable in principle could then be added to that system's criminal history or offender score; alternatively, such factors could be taken into account through rules permitting judges to adjust the criminal history or offender score, or by adding such factors to the list of recognized grounds for departure. Such added factors must, of course, also be deemed consistent with offense proportionality, racial neutrality, and other guidelines' goals and principles in that jurisdiction. Although most added risk factors are likely to relate to the offender, some may relate to the offense, or to the interaction between offense and offender factors. To the extent that a risk prediction factor relates entirely to a proven aspect of the current conviction offense(s), treating that factor as aggravating or mitigating for risk-management purposes would be unlikely to interfere with offense proportionality goals, although it might raise concerns about racial disparate impact.

In our view, a particularly strong case can be made, from the perspective of accurate and cost-effective risk prediction, for mitigating sentences given to older offenders. One of the best-documented phenomena found in criminal-careers research is the "age-crime curve"—the odds of further crime steadily diminish with age, and this is generally true even for offenders who have accumulated a substantial number of convictions.[10] One early study of recidivist burglars for example found that the single best predictor of re-offending was age (Bartell and Winfree 1977). In fact, age is often a more powerful predictor of re-offending than criminal history. Notwithstanding the fact that older offenders have longer criminal records, they represent a much lower risk of re-offending.

Data from the U.S. Sentencing Commission illustrate the point. Offenders aged 21 to 25 at the time of sentencing had a 66 percent rearrest rate, compared to 22 percent for offenders between 51 and 60 years of age; comparing more extreme age groups reveals an even greater gap in rearrest rates (U.S. Sentencing Commission 2016a, Figure 11); see also BJS 2018, table 3).[11] In addition, as offenders grow older, if re-offending occurs it usually does so on a far more intermittent basis (see Baker et al. 2015), and at a lower level of offense seriousness (USSC 2017a, table 1). These findings have important consequences for our model; we recommend down-weighting prior record enhancements for older offenders. Other life course events are also as or more important than prior convictions in terms of predicting re-offending (see Ezell 2007; Kazemian and Farrington 2006).

A serious limitation of criminal history enhancements in guidelines systems is that they take no account of the offender's current age, and thus result in the confinement of large numbers of aging prisoners whose risk of re-offending is declining while the cost of holding them, especially medical costs, is rising. It is thus imperative to give particularly careful consideration to the possibilities of reducing the contribution of criminal history enhancements to the problem of aging prison inmate populations. This could be done, for example, by shortening the decay (washout or look-back) period for older offenders, or by downward adjustments to the total criminal history score based on a formula tied to advancing age.

Conclusion

Most guidelines systems use an offender's record of prior convictions as a proxy for risk of recidivism. To improve the accuracy and efficiency of predicted risk, judges should be allowed to take account of at least some of the well-documented risk factors beyond criminal history. This can be done as an addition or adjustment to the criminal history score, or as a permitted ground for departure, variance, or other alternative sanctioning. Some risk factors, both within existing criminal history scores and external to prior record, raise fairness and/or legal problems, but as further discussed in the chapter 4, these problems do not require exclusion of all such factors.

4 ARE RECORD-BASED ENHANCEMENTS A COST-EFFECTIVE AND FAIR WAY TO REDUCE CRIME?

Do prior record enhancements actually prevent crime? Even if criminal history, other risk factors, or some combination of history and non-history factors can predict higher and lower recidivism risk with some degree of accuracy, how should such assessments be used at sentencing? The design of sentencing grids appears to assume that most higher-risk offenders should be sent to prison, or be sent for longer, but is this a cost-effective way to reduce future crime? And even if it is, are such sentence enhancements fair, or even legal? This chapter will explore these further problems with risk-based sentencing enhancements.

Prior record enhancements have been a feature of American guidelines since their inception, yet no commission has ever attempted to validate the cost-effectiveness of this sentencing policy; indeed, to our knowledge no commission has even advised legislators of the need for such validation.[1] In light of the human and fiscal costs of this policy, the oversight is shocking. Many questions need answering: How many and what kinds of crimes are prevented by such enhancements? Are the preventive benefits, if any, outweighed by public and private costs and undesired consequences such as racial disproportionality in prison populations? In this chapter we are concerned only with the questions of whether severity enhancements based on prior offending or other risk factors reduce subsequent levels of crime (Part A), and whether such enhancements are fair to offenders and consistent with constitutional proof requirements (Part B). Later chapters will explore the magnitude, fiscal costs, and adverse consequences of record-based enhancements at sentencing.

A. Crime-Preventive Benefits of Increased Sentence Severity

Determining the crime control effectiveness of sentence enhancements based on prior record and/or assessed risk (or any other factor) is challenging; there are no direct tests of the hypothesis that imposing progressively harsher sentences reduces the number or seriousness of future crimes. Any preventive benefits of prior record or other enhancements will arise from one or more of the following mechanisms: incapacitation (that is, physically restraining offenders by sending them to prison instead of punishing them in the community, or by imposing longer prison terms), general deterrence of other would-be offenders who fear receiving similarly enhanced punishment for repeat offending, and special (or individual) deterrence of this offender through the experience of enhanced punishment on the current occasion and fear of receiving still greater punishment for future crimes.[2]

To assess the crime control benefits of prior record and other sentence enhancements, we thus need to answer the following questions:

- Is incapacitation through incarceration, based on the offender's prior record and/or other risk factors, an effective means of preventing re-offending?
- How effective is deterrence as a sentencing strategy to prevent offending by other offenders (general deterrence) and by this offender (special deterrence)?
- Prior record enhancements often take the form of imposing imprisonment instead of a community penalty. Does prison deter re-offending more effectively than less severe sanctions such as community penalties?
- Do longer terms of custody deter more effectively than shorter periods? This question is critical since sentencing guidelines impose progressively longer prison terms in response to the number of prior convictions.

1. *Incapacitation*

Incapacitation works by removing the offender from society and thereby restricting his ability to re-offend. The research literature on incapacitation as a general sentencing strategy is now vast (for recent reviews, see Kazemian 2010; Travis et al. 2014, and Hester et al. 2018), and it casts considerable doubt on the benefits of recidivist sentencing premiums as a crime control measure. The modest incapacitation benefits of increased sentence severity are attributable to a number of factors: (1) for some crimes, especially those involving drugs and other prohibited goods or services, incarcerated offenders are promptly replaced by other willing sellers and providers; (2) many crimes involve multiple offenders, so removing one or even several of them may not prevent the group from continuing to offend, recruiting new group offenders if necessary; (3) the benefits of incapacitation quickly reach the point of diminishing returns once a jurisdiction has achieved a high incarceration rate (as most U.S. states have, at least by historical and international standards)—as rates rise, more and more sentence enhancements are applied to relatively low-risk offenders; (4) the added years of incarceration produced by substantial sentence enhancements result in many aging offenders being held long after their criminal careers would have tapered off or ended; (5) any formulaic prior-record or other risk-based sentence-enhancement scheme is likely to overstate current risk by ignoring case-specific factors such as a recent gap or decline in offending (for an example of the new wave of "redemption" research, showing the importance of crime-free gaps, see Blumstein and Nakamura 2009);[3] 6) some offenders sent to prison or sent for longer are actually made more crime-prone by the experience of imprisonment (prisonization effects), and/or by the social stigma and adverse consequences of having a prison record; and (7) due to the combined effects of all of the above factors, the magnitude of criminal history enhancements in many jurisdictions (explored more fully in the next chapter) seems very unlikely to provide cost-effective incapacitation benefits.

2. *General Deterrence*

Empirical research on general deterrence usually examines the extent to which variations in the certainty, severity, and celerity of punishments affect the aggregate crime rate. A number of reviews have concluded that changes in the severity of punishments have little impact on aggregate crime rates (see for example, von Hirsch et al. 1999; Doob and Webster 2003; Durlauf and Nagin 2009; Nagin 2013; Travis et al. 2014; Hester et al. 2018)—sentencing policies that emphasize the severity of future sanctions carry little preventive benefit. Most of the general deterrence literature examines penalty differences or increases that were not directly related to criminal history or risk assessment; this literature has rarely addressed the kinds of graded, progressive sentence enhancements produced by guidelines criminal history scores or other formulas. However, empirical research has examined the deterrent effects of even more severe recidivist penalties—"Three Strikes" recidivist sentencing laws—and the results of that research offer little encouragement for the prior record enhancement approach to crime prevention (see Kovandzic et al. 2004; Chen 2008).

3. *Specific Deterrence*

Specific deterrence predicts that the experience of being punished will increase offenders' awareness of legal punishments, as well as their anticipation of future punishment, and that this will ultimately deter them from re-offending. Research on the causes of re-offending offers reason for skepticism regarding this prediction. Jurisdictions that operate grid-based guidelines clarify exactly how much additional punishment will be imposed in the event of reconviction, yet offenders seldom make such cost-benefit decisions. Nor do courts explicitly warn offenders that subsequent convictions will result in additional punishment as a result of their prior crimes.[4] Deterrence is a psychological phenomenon. Potential offenders must first be aware of the impending additional punishment; indeed, they must be continuously aware of the legal threat in order for it to influence their subsequent behavior. As discussed later on in the chapter, both the assumptions of deterrence theory, and the available research on specific deterrent effects, suggest little if any cost-effective crime-preventive benefits.

A deterrence-based justification for the recidivist sentencing premium makes a number of dubious assumptions about the impact of such a premium on offenders' behavior. First, it assumes that offenders are rational calculators who carefully weigh the expected gain and expected penalty arising from future offending. Second, a recidivist sentencing premium assumes that offenders consider the *additional* punishment that will be visited upon them for subsequent offenses, and that such increased punishment provides an extra deterrent. In reality, the imposition of greater punishment each time the offender reappears for sentencing is unlikely to have any significant impact on either aggregate crime rates or individual re-offending rates.

Ex-offenders, particularly ex-prisoners, often face barriers to reintegration, including restricted employment and housing opportunities as well as social isolation. Desistance is often hard, particularly when criminal opportunities represent a more expeditious means to economic resources. Many factors will influence whether an ex-offender returns to crime or "goes straight," and the anticipation of more time in prison as a result of his previous offending is unlikely to play an important role in the offender's decision-making. Research has confirmed this conclusion, using different methodologies, subject populations, and categories of offending. For example, one study of the decision-making of burglars found no evidence that the prospect of custody influenced their decision to offend or desist (Hearnden and Magill 2004).[5] Similar findings emerge from research has involved simulation studies with students (e.g., Piquero and Pogarsky 2002). Research has also shown no relationship between actual or perceived risks of punishment (e.g., Kleck et al. 2005; Kleck and Barnes 2008).

Bouffard, Niebuhr, and Exum (2016) provide one of the few tests of deterrence involving legal penalties. These researchers explored the effects of actual sentences for drunk driving upon offenders' intentions to re-offend. Results indicated limited deterrence with respect to the certainty of future punishment, and there was no deterrent effect with regard to severity. In fact, previous punishment was marginally related to "*higher* likelihoods of drunk driving" (1937, emphasis in original).

Sentence enhancements based on a specific deterrence rationale also implicitly assume that a given increment in penalty severity will have a predictable crime-preventive effect on the offender's future conduct. But it is unlikely that any penal intervention will exercise a consistent or uniform effect across all offenders and all offenses. Research confirms the hypothesis that the effects are variable; prison affects different people in different ways, and this is true for the deterrent effect. For example, Smith and Gendreau (2010) found that the criminogenic effect of incarceration was enhanced for low-risk offenders—another reason to oppose a prior record enhancement regime that imprisons first (or near first-time) offenders on the basis of their prior conduct alone. Cid (2009) and Weatherburn (2010) also found that the deterrent effect of imprisonment was mediated by the type of offense committed or the risk level of the offender. Prior record enhancements that apply consistently across different offense and offender categories fail to reflect this variation.[6] Ultimately, as Durlauf and Nagin (2009) suggest, imprisonment will enhance the likelihood of recidivism for some offenders, deter others, and have no impact on a third group of prisoners. If this is the case, a generic deterrence-based enhancement that increases the length of imprisonment and/or the likelihood of custody for all offenders in a defined offense and criminal history category makes no more sense than prescribing a drug that has very different effects upon patients with different profiles.

a. Three Key Predictions Arising from Deterrence Theory

As noted earlier, in U.S. guidelines systems prior convictions can have two clear impacts upon recommended sentence outcomes. In some cases, the form of the sentence will change because the offender is recommended to custody ("pushed-in") as a consequence of her prior record whereas, with fewer priors, she would have a recommended community-based sentence. And for all offenders with recommended custody terms (even those for whom, due to high offense severity, custody is the presumptive disposition for all offenders), the criminal history score increases the presumptive sentence length. This dual impact means that two areas of research are relevant to validating criminal history enhancements: the impact of custody versus community sanctions, and the effect of longer versus shorter prison terms, on subsequent recidivism rates.

Below we examine research relevant to three key hypotheses relating to the specific deterrent effects of prior record enhancements affecting the form of the sentence or the duration of custody:

- *Hypothesis a: Stronger recidivist enhancements deter more effectively than weaker premiums.*
- *Hypothesis b: Imprisonment deters more effectively than noncustodial sanctions.*
- *Hypothesis c: Longer prison terms deter more effectively than shorter terms.*

b. Do Stronger Prior Record Enhancements Generate Lower Recidivism Rates?

One way to answer this question would be to compare re-offending rates in low- and high-enhancement jurisdictions. Ideally one would compare recidivism rates in comparable jurisdictions, some of which exclude a criminal record from sentencing, and some of which pursue a rigid cumulative model of sentencing; if the recidivist sentencing premium is effective, recidivism rates should be systematically lower in the cumulative model jurisdictions. Unfortunately, the ubiquity of recidivist sentencing premiums precludes any broad comparative analysis of this kind; nevertheless, the available evidence strongly contradicts the first hypothesis.

Western Australia is perhaps the only modern jurisdiction in which courts are prohibited from taking prior record into account at sentencing. Section 7(2) of the Sentencing Act 1995 states that: "An offence is not aggravated by the fact that . . . (b) the offender has a criminal record or (c) a previous sentence has not achieved the purpose for which it was imposed." If prior record enhancements prevent re-offending (and/or have general deterrent effects) recidivism rates should be higher in that jurisdiction, yet they are in fact lower than in other Australian states where prior record is a legitimate aggravating factor at sentencing (Department of Corrective Services 2014, table 2). Moreover, comparing recidivism rates to international trends suggests that they are lower in Western Australia—in 2013–2014, one third of all sentenced adults in Western Australia were reconvicted within two years whereas, as noted later in this chapter, reconviction rates tend to be higher in other countries.

Deterrent effects can also be assessed by comparing jurisdictions with relatively weaker or stronger enhancements, at least those that also routinely publish recidivism statistics (Zara and Farrington 2016, 14).[7] Prior convictions play a more powerful role in the United States than in England and Wales (Roberts and Pina-Sanchez 2014), yet recidivism rates in the two countries are comparable. Comparisons between the two countries are complicated by differences in data definition and collection. Nevertheless, they offer little reason to believe that the more powerful prior record enhancements across the United States are associated with lower re-offending rates. For example, a multistate study of state prisoners released in 2005 reported a within-one-year rearrest rate of 43 percent (BJS 2015a, table 4). This may be compared to a 40 percent one-year re-offending rate of releases in 2008 in the United Kingdom (Ministry of Justice 2010, 12). Previous convictions also play a relatively modest role at sentencing in Germany (see Roberts and Harrendorf 2019). Jehle (2014) provided comparative reconviction statistics for Germany and other European nations and similarly concluded that, despite their differing sentencing practices, reconviction statistics were comparable. Similarly, in a systematic review of recidivism rates worldwide, Fazel and Wolf (2015, table 1) reported a 48 percent recidivism rate for prisoners in Germany and a 45 percent rate for the same three-year follow-up period in the United States.

Finally, one recent study tested the intensity of enhancement hypothesis across U,S, jurisdictions. Using county-level data for 39 of the most populous urban counties in the United States, D'Alessio and Stolzenberg (2017) compared the weight assigned to prior convictions at sentencing in each county to the likelihood of repeat offending (as measured by the length of prior records of offenders sentenced in that county). The researchers found little relationship between the two variables and concluded that "the likelihood of repeat offending is not substantially lower in counties that punish repeat offenders more severely than first time offenders" (12).

These simple comparisons lack the controls of matched sample research (discussed later on in the chapter), but we can at least say that they are inconsistent with the hypothesis that a more robust prior record enhancement generates lower rates of re-offending.

c. Does Imprisonment Result in Lower Recidivism Rates than Noncustodial Sanctions?

In recent years, researchers in many countries have compared recidivism rates associated with offenders receiving different sentences.[8] Most of this research involves comparisons between prison and noncustodial alternatives. The research question is simple: Does prison (a harsher sanction) deter more effectively than a community penalty (a more lenient sanction)? The latest research employs sophisticated statistical matching procedures that control for a priori differences in the risk of re-offending (higher risk offenders are more likely to be sentenced to prison; lower-risk offenders are more likely to receive a community penalty).

Two recent studies using matching procedures found weak and sometimes negative deterrent effects of imprisonment. Aarten et al. (2015) compared re-offending rates for two carefully matched samples of Dutch offenders, some of whom had received a custodial sentence, others a suspended sentence. These researchers found that offenders sentenced to prison were *more* likely to re-offend. Mears and Cochran (2018) used propensity score and other matching techniques to assess the relative deterrent effects of four sentence types on Florida offenders: prison, jail, intensive probation, and regular probation. Their study addressed two questions: (1) Among offenders convicted of a felony for the first time, are subsequent recidivism rates lower for offenders receiving a more severe sentence type, and vice versa? (2) Among offenders convicted of a second felony, are subsequent recidivism rates lower for offenders who received a more severe sentence type at their second sentencing than at their first, and vice versa? For each question there were six comparisons between prison and one of the non-prison sentence types. As to each question, only two of the six comparisons suggested a deterrent effect. In one second-felony comparison of offenders initially receiving probation there was no significant recidivism difference between offenders who again received probation and matched offenders sentenced to prison; in the remaining seven comparisons, prison was associated with significantly *higher* recidivism rates.[9]

The finding of negative deterrent effects—*higher* re-offending rates for offenders sentenced to prison, compared to those receiving community-based sanctions—has emerged repeatedly over the past 40 years (e.g., Bartell and Winfree 1977). As noted, the most recent tests of the "prison deters more effectively" hypothesis employed sophisticated statistical controls that greatly reduce the likelihood that variables other than the nature of the sentence may have caused the outcome. For example, researchers in the United

Kingdom examined the recidivism rates of a large sample of offenders some of whom had been incarcerated, others who had received a community order. Individuals in the incarcerated sample were significantly more likely to subsequently commit another offense (Jolliffe and Hedderman 2015).

The Ministry of Justice in the U.K. has conducted a series of studies comparing re-offending rates of offenders sentenced to custody with a control group sentenced to community-based sentences. After controlling for the background variables of offenders this study found higher rates of re-offending in the group sent to prison than for offenders who received a community order (Ministry of Justice 2015, table B9). Similarly, offenders sentenced to a community order re-offended at a slightly higher rate than similar, (matched) offenders who received a less severe sanction such as a fine (Ministry of Justice 2016, figure 7). This finding, that a more severe sanction had a worse recidivism outcome than a less severe sanction, is also inconsistent with specific deterrence theory.

Many systematic reviews of this literature have now been published, summarizing research from many countries.[10] The general conclusion of this research, which has used diverse sources of data and definitions of re-offending, is that prison is not associated with lower recidivism rates than less severe penalties, principally community-based orders.[11] For example, Villettaz et al. (2006) reported that across the five most stringent studies, imprisonment was associated with a 5 percent *higher* rate of re-offending (compared to noncustodial sanctions). These same authors more recently updated their review and confirmed that re-offending rates were lower for offenders assigned to a community sanction rather than a custodial order (Villettaz et al. 2015). Cullen et al. (2011) also note that: "With some confidence, we can conclude that, across all offenders, prisons do not have a specific deterrent effect. Custodial sentences do not reduce recidivism more than noncustodial sanctions" (2011, 60S).

The research summarized in this Part, finding the same or higher recidivism rates for custody than for community sanctions, is consistent with research documenting the criminogenic effects of custody due to various forms of inmate worsening (prisonization) combined with the adverse social and economic consequences of having a prison record (see further discussion in Section A.4).[12] These findings thus undermine one of the foundational assumptions of prior record enhancements—that switching to a harsher form of sentencing reduces re-offending. More specifically, it calls into question the structure of many grids whereby repeat offenders, convicted of medium- or low-severity crimes, are "pushed into" prison on the basis of their prior convictions alone; at lower criminal history, they would have been recommended for a community sanction. The comparative work on sanctions of variable severity supports a critical element in our prior record enhancement model, namely that prior offending alone should justify incarceration only under exceptional circumstances.

d. Do Longer Terms of Custody Generate Lower Re-offending Rates?

Even if a more severe form of sanctioning (prison) fails to deter re-offending more effectively than less severe sanctioning options (community-based punishments and suspended sentences), it remains possible that, among offenders sentenced to prison, the threat and imposition of more prison time for higher-record offenders might provide additional specific-deterrent effects. This appears to be the assumption supporting the architecture of criminal history enhancements, namely, that the preventive benefit of incarceration is additive—longer prison terms deter more, and proportionately more, than shorter terms. As a Pew Center review of the issue noted: if increasing the length of sentence is beneficial in terms of crime prevention, then "offenders serving more time in prison should have lower recidivism rates than those serving less time" (2012, 33).[13] Once again, however, research findings offer little support for the prior record enhancement prediction. Studies over the past 30 years have compared recidivism rates for offenders released after serving different periods of imprisonment. The deterrence hypothesis would predict a negative relationship between the length of imprisonment and subsequent re-offending rates, yet recidivism rates were generally unrelated to the amount of time the offenders had spent in prison.

Early studies failed to demonstrate a link between length of time served and subsequent re-offending. A study of offenders released in the mid-1970s concluded that "no evidence was found to suggest that time served has any influence on subsequent offense severity, or to support hypotheses of specific deterrence." (BJS 1984, 4). A decade later, Champion reviewed the literature and concluded that "no research has ever demonstrated conclusively that longer prison sentences make ex-offenders less likely to commit new crimes" (1994, 97). Nothing published since then has contradicted these opinions. Andrews and Bonta (2003) in Canada, and Fink and Ducommun-Vaucher (2014) in Switzerland, reported similar findings: recidivism rates were actually slightly higher for offenders released after longer prison terms than after shorter terms. This finding is consistent with research (discussed in Section A.4) showing that, at least for some offenders, a longer prison term steadily worsens the offender's ability to reintegrate and live a law-abiding life.

The U.S. Sentencing Commission recidivism data provide a good example of the simple comparison between offenders who have spent short rather than longer periods in custody. Offenders who had served shorter periods of imprisonment generally had lower recidivism rates. Thus offenders who had received prison terms of up to six months had a rearrest rate of 37.5 percent, compared to 55.5 percent of offenders sentenced to terms between five and nine years (USSC 2016b, figure 10). State recidivism statistics reveal the same trend. For example, the recidivism rate of determinate sentence offenders serving one-year sentences was significantly lower than the rate for offenders sentenced to three-year terms (48 percent versus 65 percent; California Department of Corrections 2011, figure 9; see also Pennsylvania Commission on Sentencing 2011, figure 5). Academic studies echo this finding, which undermines the deterrent claim.[14]

Studies that focus on specific categories of offending have reached the same conclusion. Baay et al. (2012) report that longer terms of imprisonment were associated with higher recidivism rates in their sample of homicide offenders. A major study of sex offenders examined the relationship between time served and re-offending and concluded that "the data do not warrant any general conclusion about an association between the level of recidivism and the amount of time served" (BJS 2003, 19).

As with most of the research that has accumulated in recent decades, the most recent studies are also the most rigorous, incorporating a wider range of variables and more sophisticated statistical techniques to overcome the absence of random assignment of offenders to different durations of imprisonment. Wermink et al. (2017) evaluated the relationship between time served in prison and subsequent recidivism, using a longitudinal and nationwide sample of Dutch offenders. Their findings illustrate the perils of simple comparisons among groups of offenders. Comparing the uncorrected recidivism rates of different groups revealed that re-offending rates declined as the length of time served increased—consistent with the underlying assumption of prior record enhancements. For example, the reconviction rate for the offenders who had served the longest time in prison was approximately half that of the group who had spent the shortest time in custody (see Wermink et al., 2017, table 3). Yet when the researchers introduced the appropriate statistical controls, these differences evaporated, and they concluded that there was "no clear effect of length of imprisonment on recidivism" (23).[15] This conclusion is supported by a number of reviews of the literature (see, e.g., Pew Center 2012). United States' and Canadian scholars have reached similar conclusions (e.g., Smith et al. 2002; Nagin and Snodgrass 2013; Cochran et al. 2014).[16]

4. Adverse, Criminogenic Consequences of Imprisonment

Finally, we add a word about research documenting the negative effects of imprisonment on offenders, and of longer prison terms. Determining the causal effects of imprisonment is challenging, to say the least. Advocates of a strong prior record enhancement may point to the association between prior imprisonment (as a result of prior offending) and subsequent re-offending as evidence of a criminal propensity. The prior crimes reflect an underlying disposition toward offending, which produces further offending. Yet it is equally plausible to argue that the prior incarceration was not just a consequence of prior offending but a cause of further offending. Paradoxically, the sanction imposed may be a partial cause of the behavior it is designed to prevent.

The negative effects of prison on an ex-offender's life and employment prospects are now well-documented. There is also a growing body of "dose-response" research on prison time. As noted previously, increasing the "dose" of prison time imposed and served has no apparent overall deterrent benefit in terms of future offending. That is probably because, even if some offenders are deterred by prison, and deterred more by a longer term, for other offenders imprisonment or a longer term in prison will have adverse, criminogenic effects, reducing their opportunities for employment, housing, government benefits, and marriage. For example, Ramakers et al. (2017) found that longer terms of custody had more dramatic effects on employment prospects than shorter terms of imprisonment. Since unemployment is itself a well-known risk factor for offending and re-offending, this undesirable effect of imprisonment may in the longer term contribute to re-offending.

B. Ethical Objections and Legal Barriers to Risk-Based Sentence Enhancements

Even if aspects of an offender's prior record and/or other offense or offender factors accurately predict higher or lower recidivism risk, and even if sentence enhancements (or some of them) based on higher risk serve to prevent future crimes in a cost-effective manner, important normative and legal issues must be resolved—risk-based sentence enhancements may not be acceptable due to principled objections and/or legal barriers. As discussed later in the chapter, some of the problems raised in these objections are valid, while others are overstated or can be minimized.

1. Ethical Objections

Some prior-record factors, and most non-record risk-related factors, raise serious issues of fairness even if they are cost-effective.[17] As will be discussed more fully in chapter 10, almost every guidelines jurisdiction includes at least some juvenile adjudications in the adult criminal history score, despite the diminished culpability of juveniles and the reduced procedural safeguards in juvenile court. Objections can also be raised to inclusion of the offender's custody status (incarcerated or on conditional release at the time of the current offense), especially when pretrial release and/or detention are treated as qualifying statuses—these people are legally presumed innocent, and detained suspects do not freely choose that status; moreover, the latter are even more disproportionately poor and nonwhite than the typical criminal defendant or convict. For these and other reasons discussed more fully in chapter 10, we argue that juvenile adjudications and all forms of custody status should not be included in criminal history scoring, even if they can be shown to improve the accuracy of recidivism risk predictions, and even if resulting sentence enhancements are shown to be cost-effective.

The use of non-prior-record, risk-related factors to enhance punishment raises even greater fairness concerns. For example, it would strike many people as unfair to enhance the sentence of a 20-year-old offender simply because he or she belongs to an age group with an elevated risk of recidivism—people cannot change their age. Moreover, there is mounting evidence that the culpability of young adults is diminished, albeit to a lesser degree, in the same way that juvenile culpability is diminished—many young adults are still emotionally and cognitively immature.[18]

Some have argued that because gender is likewise a characteristic an offender cannot control, it should have no bearing on the severity of punishment (Starr 2015).[19] It has also been argued that the use of employment history or status, educational attainment, and family or living arrangements as risk factors is invalid because these reflect legitimate lifestyle choices (or conversely, lack of real choice due to bias or disadvantage), and that such factors have a disparate impact on nonwhite offenders (Tonry 2014, 171–74; Starr 2015, 23). Many of these critical views find support in guidelines provisions that expressly prohibit departure based on factors such as gender and socioeconomic status (see, e.g., MSGC 2017a, sec. 2.D.2).

These are all valid concerns, but there are also arguments on the other side. If females are given reduced penalties reflecting their lower risk, this policy is not necessarily unfair to male offenders provided that the penalties given to the latter are proportionate to their current offenses and prior convictions (for more discussion see Frase 2014, 147–51). Similarly, the rejection of young age as an aggravating factor does not necessarily mean that old age cannot be considered in mitigation. And as to both of these demographic factors, risk-based mitigation of sentences (for women and older offenders) results in more favorable treatment for groups that have traditionally been victims of discrimination. Thus, unlike race-based distinctions, there is little reason to fear that differential treatment is motivated by bias or would worsen inequality; nor is the premise for such treatment—lower risk—likely to reinforce negative stereotypes about these groups.[20]

As for the use of socioeconomic risk factors, the documented disparate impact of such factors on nonwhite offenders is a matter of great concern, especially since racial neutrality is often an important goal of guidelines reforms. However, these factors (for example: current full-time employment) occasionally benefit nonwhite offenders, suggesting lower risk than would otherwise be predicted by their current offense(s) and criminal history; at least in those cases it should be permissible to take such factors into account.[21] It also seems appropriate to recognize the lower predicted risk of an offender, based on his or her educational attainment and/or employment record, in cases where the offender achieved these characteristics despite substantial personal, family, or neighborhood disadvantage (Tonry 1995, 45). This ground for mitigation should be available to offenders of all races, but it is likely to be more often applicable to nonwhite offenders, given the strong correlations between race and disadvantage.

Sentence *enhancements* based on socioeconomic risk factors are more problematic, especially when these factors relate to circumstances over which the offender has little control. For many offenders (especially nonwhite offenders), limited education, poor employment history, and residential instability are not matters of choice or cause for blame; nor is the fact that one's parent, sibling, spouse, or close relative has a criminal record. But offenders usually have more control over things such as marital status, whether they live with and support their children and spouse or partner, and who their friends and companions are. And although choices about these matters are usually not illegal (although nonsupport may be), are such "lifestyle" decisions really beyond the law's power to consider when assessing risk of further criminal behavior? Some legal "choices" (for instance: heavy use of alcohol, choice of criminal friends and associates) clearly cause or at least correlate with higher risk. It can be argued that sentencing courts should be permitted to take account of legal but risky behavior, at least as long as the enhanced penalties given to higher-risk offenders do not exceed the punishment they deserve for their crimes (see generally Frase 2013a, 2014). Conversely, since some offender choices result in lower risk, it seems appropriate for sentencing courts to recognize and reward such choices (for example, when an offender addresses his substance abuse problem by undergoing treatment, goes back to school, or seeks job-related training).

With respect to factors such as the defendant's support of and by her family, it should be noted that even jurisdictions such as Minnesota that forbid such a factor as a ground for departure, allow it to be considered along with other factors in deciding whether the offender is particularly amenable to probation and thus eligible for downward departure from the recommended prison sentence (see, e.g., *State v. Soto* (2014)).

The treatment of an offender's alcohol and drug abuse may also raise ethical concerns. On the one hand, such abuse is correlated with higher risk of repeat offending; for this reason, some guidelines systems expressly forbid mitigation on this ground (see, e.g., USSC 2014, sec. 5H1.4), and several of the risk assessment tools discussed in chapter 3 essentially treat it as an aggravating factor. On the other hand, addicted offenders are arguably less culpable due to their reduced power of self-control. To reconcile these conflicting considerations, several compromise positions are available. For example, mitigation might be permitted if treatment has never been offered to the offender.[22] Conversely, sentence enhancement based on heightened risk might be allowable if the offender has previously been offered treatment but has failed to accept it or otherwise take steps to try to address his substance abuse.

2. *Legal Barriers to Risk-Based Sentence Enhancements*

One further consideration, when adding or expanding offense or offender-based risk prediction factors, is that their use as aggravating factors may trigger jury-trial and proof-beyond-reasonable doubt requirements under *Blakely v. Washington* (2004).[23] This would not be a problem for any offense-related factor that corresponds to an element of the conviction offense (since those are already subject to heightened proof requirements); nor would there be any problem adding a risk factor inherent in the elements of a prior conviction, or otherwise sufficiently related to conviction and court records that it falls within the prior-convictions exception to *Blakely*. (And of course, mitigating factors are not subject to *Blakely* requirements, so that case puts no limits on the use of factors that predict low risk of recidivism.)

But almost all non-criminal-history risk factors will neither correspond to a proven current-offense element nor fall within *Blakely*'s prior-convictions exception; in these cases, contested facts needed to establish that risk factors will have to be found by the jury beyond a reasonable doubt. This will also be the case for contested facts related to some components of American guidelines criminal history scores. Examples of such elements and contested facts include the following:

- "Patterning" enhancements (see further discussion in chapter 10)—are the past and current offenses the "same," or at least "similar" (enough)?
- Custody status enhancements (also discussed in chapter 10)—was the offender in fact (still) subject to the alleged qualifying incarceration or release status at the time of the current offense?[24]
- Recency points—was the current offense committed within the applicable time period following commission of the relevant prior offense, or where applicable, discharge from sentence for that offense?
- Rules giving higher weight to prior "person" offenses (unless these offenses are fully defined by law)—was the prior crime in question committed in a violent or other qualifying manner?

Conclusion

This chapter has examined two further problems with sentence enhancements based on prior record and/or other risk factors: (1) Even if the prior record score or other risk factors are shown to accurately predict recidivism risk (the questions explored in chapters 2 and 3), are the resulting sentence enhancements a cost-effective way to reduce future offending by this or other offenders? (2) Even if such enhancements reflect demonstrated higher risk, and efficiently prevent crime, are they fair to offenders, or even legal?

As to the first problem, we reviewed the research testing the extent to which a policy of imposing harsher punishments to reflect the offender's criminal history, or other indications of higher risk, actually works to prevent crime by means of incapacitation, general deterrence, or specific deterrence. We conclude that the net crime-preventive benefits of such enhancements are very limited, and unlikely to be cost-effective, at least at the substantial magnitudes of enhancement imposed in many guidelines systems (see further discussion of enhancement magnitudes in chapter 5). Indeed, many studies suggest the opposite of a specific deterrent effect: there is actually a mild but detectable criminogenic short-term effect of imprisonment—compared to community-based sanctions, prison is associated with slightly *higher* re-offending rates. Similarly, increments in sentence length appear to have little or no demonstrable increased deterrent effects on subsequent re-offending; for some offenders, longer prison terms increase the odds of further crime.

These findings, considered alongside the criminal history category re-offending rates discussed in chapter 2, create a powerful two-fold objection to the robust and steadily rising prior record enhancements imposed in most existing guidelines systems. First, offenders in a higher criminal history category do not always represent a greater threat in terms of re-offending, and even when they do, the sentence enhancements imposed at these higher-record levels are disproportionate to risk. Second, the additional time in prison imposed to reflect a higher criminal history score, and the substantially elevated costs of these sentence enhancements, appear to be unjustified by the likely crime-control benefits of these sentence enhancements. The same will often be true for added prison time based on non-criminal-history risk factors.

With respect to normative and legal problems, we noted that some criminal history components, and many non-criminal history risk factors, raise serious ethical and legal issues when these components and factors are used to impose more severe penalties. However, we have argued that mitigation based on low history or low assessed risk poses fewer problems.

Given the normative and legal problems of risk-based enhancements, and the substantial body of research suggesting modest crime-control benefits (or even counterproductive effects), we conclude that the robust and formulaic, steadily escalating prior record enhancements found in many guidelines are unwarranted, wasteful, and counterproductive, causing more crime rather than preventing crime.

5 THE EFFECTS OF PRIOR CONVICTIONS ON SENTENCE SEVERITY

Co-author: Rhys Hester

All U.S. guidelines recommend harsher sentences for repeat offenders, but how much do prior convictions enhance severity, and in what specific ways? This chapter explores the degree to which a higher criminal history score increases the severity of recommended and imposed sentences. Establishing the magnitude of the criminal history enhancement in a jurisdiction is another way of answering the question: *How much more are repeat offenders punished in this particular system because of their prior convictions?* More powerful enhancements have both positive and negative effects. As discussed more fully in chapters 2 to 4, strong criminal history enhancements may better serve rationales that depend on offender risk (provided that criminal history scores reflect risk of re-offending, and that more punishment severity reduces risk or prevents crime in a cost-effective manner). But significant enhancements also have a number of negative consequences that will be explored in this and the next three chapters.

The impact of criminal history on sentence severity can be measured in a variety of ways. Some measures assess the extent to which high criminal history scores translate into increased sentencing severity. Other measures relate to the criminal history formula itself—the components of the score and the ways in which each component is weighted; these rules determine how quickly offenders can acquire a high score, triggering the most severe impacts, and they also determine which offenders are most likely to receive high criminal history scores. This chapter focuses on the effects of criminal history scores and different criminal history formulas on sentence severity. Throughout, the chapter illustrates the great variation across the United States in terms of the magnitude of prior record enhancements as well as the specific ways that different guidelines count and weight prior convictions. The next chapters examine the negative consequences of powerful prior record enhancements, namely: impacts on the proportionality of sentences relative to conviction-offense seriousness and on the offense and risk-level mix of inmates (chapter 6); the disparate impacts of these enhancements on racial and ethnic minorities (chapter 7); and the impacts on prison bed needs and costs (chapter 8).

Part A of this chapter examines the impacts of criminal history scores on two key measures of sentence severity: whether the offender will be sent to prison, and the duration of any custodial sentence. Part B explores the various components and other features of a system's criminal history formula that cause larger numbers of offenders to receive high scores (thereby triggering more severe punishment). Part C presents our proposals for regulating the magnitude of prior record enhancements.

A. Measuring the Impact of Criminal History Scores on Sentence Severity

Sentence severity depends on both the form and the quantum of punishment, and it is useful to apply separate measures to each of these severity dimensions. In the U.S. context the most important question regarding the form of punishment is whether the offender will receive an executed prison sentence or a community-based sentence—a choice that is sometimes referred to as the "disposition" (or "in/out") decision. Imprisonment is a particularly severe penalty because prison terms usually have a maximum duration longer than one year, are served in a state-run facility that is often geographically remote from the offender's home community, and impose the substantial social stigma of a "prison record."[1] As for the amount of punishment, the key variable is the length of the executed custodial (prison or jail) term—the "duration" decision. The impact of criminal history enhancements on dispositional severity will be examined in Section 1 of this Part; Section 2 examines the impact on durational severity. In both sections, guidelines systems are examined both in theory and in practice. The systems are first compared "on paper," based on recommended sentence dispositions and durations in each system. The practical impact of criminal history enhancements on dispositional and durational severity is then compared in selected guidelines systems for which sufficient sentencing data are available ("in-practice" measures). We have limited our multi-jurisdictional comparisons to the 12 grid-based guidelines systems that have either a single grid or a main grid. The five non-grid systems, and the two systems that have only specialized grids for different offense types, are not easily compared to each other or to systems that operate a main grid.[2]

1. *The Impact of Criminal History on Dispositions*

A high criminal history score will often make an offender eligible for a recommended prison sentence when she would otherwise have a recommended community-based sentence.

a. On-Paper Measures

Our on-paper impact measure is the proportion of grid cells in which prison is the recommended disposition due to the offender's elevated criminal history score. On most grids, offenders convicted of medium- or low-severity offenses are recommended for community-based sentences if their criminal history score is below a certain level, and for prison if their score is above that level. Offenders above the threshold are thereby "pushed into" prison as a result of their prior crimes. Our measure of dispositional enhancement (or "push-in") is the number of prior-record-driven, recommended-for-prison cells as a percentage of all cells in the grid.

Figure 5.1 illustrates this calculation, using Minnesota's main grid as an example. As with most grids, it can be divided into three zones. Zone 1, at the top of the grid, includes high offense severity offenders who are all recommended for prison, regardless of their criminal history. For offenders in this group, prior convictions simply increase the amount of recommended prison time. Zone 2 contains the cells central to the dispositional magnitude measure: were it not for their higher levels of criminal history, offenders in Zone 2 cells would have been in Zone 3 and be recommended for a non-prison sentence (unless a mandatory-prison statute or an exceptional guidelines rule applies).[3] These cells contain the offenders who are "pushed into prison" by reason of their prior crimes. There are 20 cells in Minnesota's Zone 2, and a total of 77 cells on the entire grid. Thus 26 percent of the cells on the grid recommend prison due to the offender's criminal history.

Disposition recommendations constitute an important policy decision, and one on which criminal history can have a major impact. Jurisdictions with grids that have a relatively high proportion of "push-in" cells will have higher proportions of offenders recommended for prison because of criminal history. In turn, these jurisdictions will confront larger prison populations and face increased risk of the undesired criminal-history-related impacts

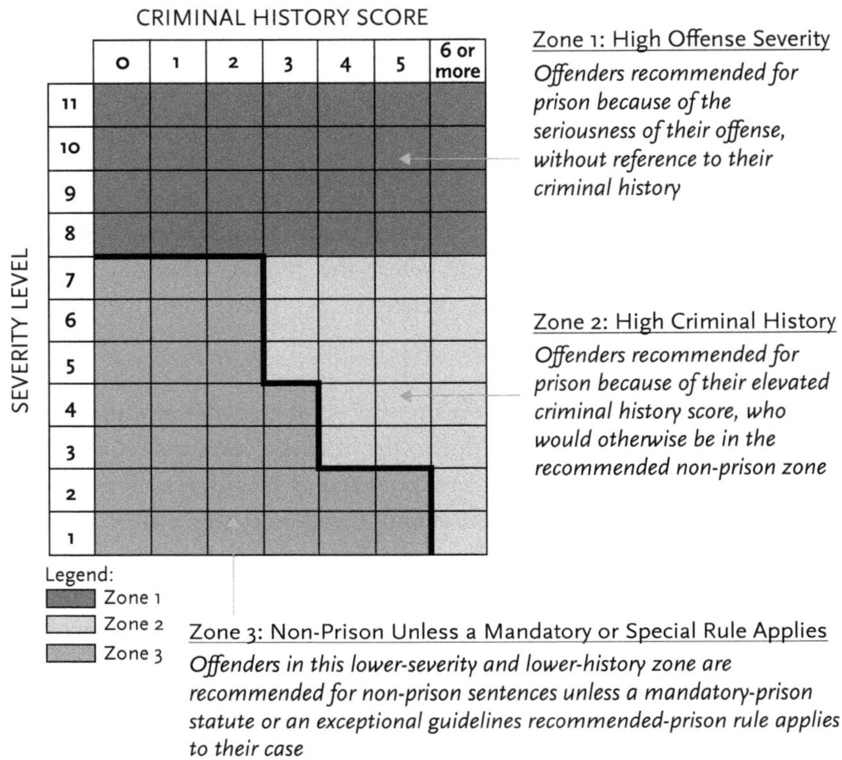

FIGURE 5.1: Calculating the on-paper dispositional magnitude measure using the Minnesota grid as an example

discussed in the next three chapters. Other significant adverse effects were noted in chapter 4: a "prison record" substantially reduces an offender's opportunities for employment, housing, government benefits, and marriage, thereby greatly increasing the odds of re-offending while also imposing major hardships on the offender and his or her family.

b. Great Variation in Dispositional Magnitude Measure

Table 5.1 ranks the jurisdictions using our disposition measure. The mean for these 12 grids is 18 percent, which means that across the guidelines included here, approximately one cell in five results in a committal to prison as a result of the offender's record. The table reveals considerable variation in the percentage of cells in which prison is recommended based solely on criminal history—ranging from a low of 9 percent under the federal guidelines to a high of 28 percent in Utah. Utah thus has over three times as many "push-in" cells as the federal guidelines. The Utah prison population is likely to differ

Table 5.1. Magnitude of criminal history dispositional enhancement—percent of cells in which offender is imprisoned for prior convictions

Federal	9%
Oregon	11%
Arkansas	13%
Tennessee	16%
Kansas	17%
Massachusetts	17%
Pennsylvania	19%
North Carolina	19%
Washington, D.C.	22%
Washington	22%
Minnesota	26%
Utah	28%
Mean:	18%

Note: Percentages reported refer to the "on-paper" dispositional magnitude measure (i.e., the percent of grid cells recommending prison due to an elevated criminal history score [grid Zone 2]). The comparisons are presented by rank order and are based on the primary grids from the indicated jurisdiction as of the end of 2015. Grid rows that include offenses that do not meet the traditional definition of a felony (i.e., do not carry a statutory maximum penalty of more than a year of incarceration) are excluded from the calculations. Rows in which life imprisonment is recommended or authorized are also excluded.

in composition from states with fewer "push-in" cells. It will contain a higher proportion of recidivists convicted of less serious offenses. This helps to explain why nonviolent offenders comprised almost two-thirds of defendants sentenced to prison in that state in 2013 (Pew Charitable Trusts 2015, 3). In addition, to the extent that a powerful prior record enhancement creates unanticipated consequences (see later chapters) a state such as Utah will be disproportionately affected.

On-paper measures are useful since recommendations are the only way to compare a large number of guidelines systems, including those without sufficiently complete sentencing statistics to construct in-practice measures. In addition, guideline recommendations reflected in on-paper measures are the public-facing enhancements, and clearly affect any plea discussions involving the parties. However, when data are available it is also useful to examine empirical patterns of enhancement—what we refer to as "in practice" measures of the impact of previous convictions.

b. In-Practice Measures

On-paper measures represent theoretical increments in severity, and presuppose that offenders are distributed evenly across all criminal history and offense severity categories. In reality, of course, there are fewer offenders in certain criminal history and severity categories. In order to measure the systemic impact of enhancements we need to incorporate the pattern of actual cases into the analysis. An analogy illustrates the point. Imagine that a company's annual salary increments for productivity range from 5 percent to 50 percent. The magnitude of enhancement is therefore a ratio of 10:1; the most industrious employee may receive an increase up to 10 times higher than the most indolent (who must receive 5 percent). However, if in practice only 1 employee in 10 receives an increase above 20 percent, and none above 30 percent, the in-practice salary enhancement is far more modest than the on-paper or theoretical range. We apply this logic to the context of criminal history enhancements; but as we shall see, unlike this workplace example, in the world of sentencing the divergence between theory and practice sometimes operates in the opposite direction, producing variations that are greater in practice than on paper.

Our in-practice magnitude measures are based on the actual number of offenders found in each grid cell, and the number who actually received an executed prison sentence. Such data-based measures yield different dispositional magnitude estimates for any given grid, and potentially different rank orders of grids, in comparison to the on-paper (recommended-sentence) measures reported previously.[4] Because the magnitude measures presented later on in the chapter are based on actual cases, these measures provide a more accurate estimate of the impact that policy choices about criminal history enhancements have on actual sentencing decisions and prison populations. These comparisons are therefore of particular interest to commissions and correctional authorities.

We selected two jurisdictions, Minnesota and Washington, to illustrate how measures based on sentencing data complement the on-paper analysis.[5] These two states have relatively similar guidelines systems: they both have legally binding rules with a robust appellate review and almost no parole-release discretion, well-maintained sentencing data, and similar recommendations regarding the effect of criminal history on dispositions. Despite their similarities, however, these states show contrasting patterns on our dispositional magnitude measures. As shown in table 5.2, the impact of criminal history on disposition decisions is lessened in Minnesota when based on actual cases sentenced than when measured on paper, while in Washington the impact is greater using in-practice measures.

Table 5.2 contains two in-practice measures. The first examines the proportion of all sentenced offenders who were convicted in "push-in" (Zone 2) cells; thus, unlike our on-paper dispositional magnitude measure, which is based on the proportion of Zone 2 cells to total grid cells, this first in-practice measure takes account of the uneven distribution of cases across cells of the grid. Our second in-practice measure (third row of figures in the table) is based on actual sentencing practices, and computes the number of prison sentences imposed on offenders in Zone 2 cells, as a percent of all sentenced offenders. In both states, the second in-practice measure (based on actual prison sentences) yields lower magnitude estimates than the first in-practice measure (based on number of offenders convicted in push-in cells), because sentences reflect decisions by judges to depart from the prison-commitment recommendation that apply to all Zone 2 cases.

Thus, the biggest difference between these two states is revealed by the first in-practice measure (second row of figures in the table—percent of convicted

Table 5.2. Comparison of dispositional magnitude measures, on paper and incorporating sentencing data, for two states

	Minnesota	Washington
On Paper: % of cells in Zone 2	26%	22%
In-Practice-1: % of defendants	18%	40%
In Practice-2: prison commits	13%	32%

Note: The comparisons are based on primary grids only and are operationalized as follows:

On Paper indicates the percentage of grid cells that fall into Zone 2 (these figures are also shown in table 5.1).

In-Practice-1 indicates the percentage of all convicted defendants who are found in those Zone 2 cells.

In-Practice-2 indicates the percentage of all convicted defendants who are found in Zone 2 cells and sentenced to prison (some Zone 2 defendants receive a non-prison sentence via downward dispositional departure).

The two *In-Practice* measures use 2014 sentencing data from each state.

offenders): when compared to the on-paper, percent-of-cells measure (first row of figures), criminal history's dispositional impact drops in Minnesota under the first in-practice measure, but rises substantially in Washington. These differing patterns reflect, in turn, both the structure of these states' grids and the distribution of cases across the grids. In both states, the majority of defendants fall into lower offense severity levels; but in Washington a much higher fraction of those lower-severity offenders end up in Zone 2 because that zone has twice as many cells as Zone 3 (low severity and criminal history). In Minnesota, Zone 2 only has about two-thirds as many cells as Zone 3, so there are relatively fewer Zone 2 defendants. In other words, Washington's substantially higher criminal history dispositional impact reflects that state's decision to include many additional lower-severity, medium-history grid cells in Zone 2, the recommended-prison zone.

The contrasting patterns in these two states are worthy of further research. Table 5.1 suggested that criminal history carries comparable weight in these two jurisdictions, yet table 5.2 reveals this to be an oversimplification. In Washington, a much higher proportion of offenders are committed to prison on the basis of their prior convictions. This finding underscores the need to examine both on-paper and in-practice measures of impact. Only the Washington Commission would know why they decided to create so many Zone 2 "pushed-in" placements. More importantly, only that Commission can state whether they were aware of the consequences for offenders when they constructed their guidelines.

c. The Problematic Practice of Imprisoning for Prior Crimes

In our proposals we advocate minimizing the practice of imprisoning the offender when a comparable defendant with a lower criminal history score would be sentenced to a community sanction. We have several justifications. Of the two principal ways in which previous convictions enhance sentence, the impact on dispositions is potentially more troubling. Increasing an offender's sentence by a few months to reflect relevant prior convictions is easier to justify than sending him to prison as a result of those prior crimes (for which he has previously been punished). Changing the disposition from community to prison represents a more radical transformation of the sentence than simply increasing sentence length when the offender was going to prison anyway (to reflect the seriousness of his current crime). Principally, the difference between community and prison is so stark, and the consequences of imprisonment so profound for the offender that this sets a dispositional change apart from a durational enhancement.

In effect, dispositional enhancement based on the offender's prior convictions triggers a regime change—from punishment in the community to confinement in a state-run institution (or in a federal prison, often located in another state). And, as we noted in chapter 4, the research on the effectiveness of prison versus probation refutes rather than supports a preventive justification for changing the disposition imposed on the basis of prior crimes. Simply put, compared to community-based penalties, imprisonment is often associated with equal or higher rates of re-offending. This reality undermines the preventive justification for imprisoning on the basis of the offender's prior record score. Despite this, as can be seen in table 5.1, in many systems significant numbers of guideline cells recommend prison for offenders who, if convicted of the same crime but with a lower criminal history score, would not be recommended for prison.

Finally, offenders are likely to regard dispositional enhancement as being more unfair than durational enhancement. This in turn will undermine perceptions of the legitimacy of sentencing. After all, it is one thing to have some months added to your prison sentence, but quite another to find yourself in a state or federal prison solely on the basis of your prior crimes. The defendant's appeal against prior record enhancements on grounds of double punishment is also more powerful when the additional (record-based) punishment results in imprisonment. In our view, a guideline system should limit the power of prior crimes to effect such a significant transformation in sentencing. Our proposals summarized at the conclusion of this chapter explain how this should be accomplished.

2. *The Impact of Criminal History on Prison and Other Custody Durations*

We now turn from disposition to duration and document how much longer recommended and imposed custodial terms are for those in the highest criminal history category compared to those in the lowest category. As with dispositional magnitude, we first compare systems using guideline recommendations, then look at selected systems using in-practice measures.

a. On-Paper Measures

Our on-paper measure compares the custody (prison or jail) terms recommended for offenders in the highest criminal history category with the custodial sentence recommended for offenders in the lowest category.[6] Where a range of durations is provided for one or both groups of offenders, we use the midpoint; where a single recommended duration or a specific number within a range is provided, we use that number.[7] For each offense severity level on a system's grid, we compute the enhancement ratio of the recommended custody term for highest-history offenders divided by the recommended term for lowest-history offenders; those ratios are then averaged to yield an overall durational magnitude measure for the entire grid.

Figure 5.2 illustrates the calculation of the enhancement ratio for an offense severity level, again using the main Minnesota grid as an example. At severity level 8 on the grid, offenders with a criminal history score of 6 or more have a recommended prison term of 108 months, whereas for offenders with a criminal history score of 0 the recommended term is 48 months. Thus, the recommended sentence for offenders with the highest criminal history is 2.25 times greater than the recommended sentence for offenders with the lowest criminal history.[8]

We can express the degree of durational enhancement in another way. For severity level 8 offenders in Minnesota's highest criminal history category who receive the midpoint sentence (108 months), over half their prison sentence reflects prior rather than current offending. If the offender receives the sentence at the top of the Category VI range (129 months), almost two-thirds of the sentence is explained by her previous crime, for which of course she has already been punished. As further discussed in chapter 6, we take the view that offense-based proportionality is excessively undermined when the prior crime carries more weight than the

CRIMINAL HISTORY SCORE

	0	1	2	3	4	5	6 or more
11	306 261–367	326 278–391	346 295–415	366 312–439	386 329–463	406 346–480[2]	426 363–480[2]
10	150 128–180	165 141–198	180 153–216	195 166–234	210 179–252	225 192–270	240 204–288
9	86 74–103	98 84–117	110 94–132	122 104–146	134 114–160	146 125–175	158 135–189
8	48 41–57	58 50–69	68 58–81	78 67–93	88 75–105	98 84–117	108 92–129

108 ÷ 48 = 2.25

FIGURE 5.2: Formula for calculating the on-paper durational magnitude measure using the Minnesota guidelines main grid as an example

current offense. There is also a case to answer regarding perceptions of the legitimacy of repeat offender premiums when they assume this degree of enhancement. Our proposed model sets limits on the magnitude of the durational enhancements.

b. Enhancement Ratios Decline as the Offense Severity Level Increases

Figure 5.2 also illustrates another important aspect of criminal history's impact on recommended custody duration: the highest-history/lowest-history ratios vary across offense severity levels. Although there are many idiosyncratic variations, enhancement ratios generally tend to be lowest at the highest (most serious) offense severity levels. For example, at Minnesota severity level 11 the ratio is only 1.39 (426 divided by 306) while, as noted previously, the ratio is 2.25 for severity level 8; at severity levels 1 to 7 (not shown in figure 5.2) the ratio varies from a low of 3.17 to a high of 12.0. Some state guidelines grids have even greater variation in their high/low ratios across severity levels (in Washington the ratios run from 1.71 to 33.33). To capture these variations within grids, we average the separate ratios computed for each level to provide a single overall durational magnitude measure for that grid; for example, and as further discussed later in the chapter, Minnesota's main-grid average ratio is 4.7. Nevertheless, it should be kept in mind that the grid-average measures reported below conceal the far greater and lesser magnitudes of criminal history enhancement that exist in some of these systems for certain offense severity levels on the grid.

Why should criminal history premiums decline in magnitude as the level of seriousness increases? Although studies of sentencing practices have found that higher levels of offense seriousness attract a lower ratio of enhancement than that applied to less serious crimes (see Vigorita 2001; Cassidy and Rydberg 2017), this seems paradoxical. If one adopts a retributive justification for enhancing sentence severity based on prior record, such justification would appear to be more compelling when the instant offense is more serious. The same would be true under a preventive rationale, at least to the extent that the current offense predicts the offense of reconviction (although it generally does not; see chapter 10 for further discussion).

One explanation for this paradoxical pattern of enhancements is that commissions believe offenders convicted at the highest offense levels are less likely to be deterred by the prospect of additional punishment in the event of reconviction. But this explanation seems unlikely, both historically (the paradoxical pattern first appeared in the late 1970s, when research into offense or offender-specific deterrence was in its infancy) and empirically (as discussed in chapter 4, research consistently shows little if any added deterrent effect of heightened sanction severity). Alternatively, perhaps commissions assume that low-severity offenders pose higher risks of re-offending, and that this justifies longer periods of incarceration and/or supervision. Research lends support to the first assumption (see, e.g., Hester Forthcoming, Laskorunky 2018) but, as discussed in chapter 4, casts doubt on the crime control benefits of giving longer prison terms to higher risk, low-offense-severity offenders.

In the end, perhaps the paradox is simply a necessary consequence of the long sentences of imprisonment imposed in contemporary U.S. sentencing regimes, for serious offenses. If prior record enhancements rose at the same rate, in percentage terms, regardless of offense severity, then either the enhancements for low-severity crimes would have to be far smaller (even though these offenders generally pose a higher risk or repeat offending), or the absolute magnitudes of enhancement given to high-severity offenders would have to be enormous. If we return to the Minnesota example, we see that if the main-grid average ratio of 4.7 were applied at offense severity level 11, offenders in the highest criminal history category would have recommended sentences of 1,438 months (306 times 4.7)—120 years! On the actual grid, each added criminal history point at level 11 increases the recommended sentence by 20 months, which is already a very burdensome penalty increase based on a single prior conviction; applying the grid-average high-low ratio of 4.7, each additional point would add 189 months—almost 16 years!

c. Average Ratios of Enhancement Vary Greatly across Jurisdictions

As can be seen in table 5.3, the magnitude of durational enhancement in Minnesota is dwarfed by several other systems. Table 5.3 provides grid averages, in rank order, for the main grids in 12 guidelines systems. In several jurisdictions at the top of the table (Washington DC, North Carolina, federal, and Massachusetts) the recommended custody sentence for highest-history offenders is roughly double the recommended term for lowest-history offenders; at the other extreme, Washington and Arkansas have average ratios of about 10, and in Kansas the ratio is over 14. Across all guidelines included here, the recommended custody sentence for the most serious recidivist is more than six times longer than the sentence recommended for the first offender convicted of the same offense.[9]

In later discussions we will occasionally focus on some or all of the following four jurisdictions included in table 5.3: North Carolina (low durational

Table 5.3. Magnitude of criminal history enhancements—on-paper durational measure (length of prison or jail term)

Washington, DC	1.7
North Carolina	2.2
Federal	2.5
Massachusetts	2.5
Minnesota	4.7
Tennessee	5.5
Utah	6.8
Oregon	7.2
Pennsylvania	7.7
Washington	9.8
Arkansas	10.5
Kansas	14.4
Mean	6.3

Note: These durational magnitude measures represent grid averages of the ratios, for each offense severity level in that system, of recommended custody (prison or jail) durations for highest- versus lowest-history offenders. The grid-average ratios are listed in rank order. Only the primary grid in each jurisdiction (as of 2015), is examined (several systems have specialized grids for certain crimes). Grid rows that mostly include offenses that do not meet the traditional definition of a felony (i.e., do not carry a statutory maximum penalty of more than a year of incarceration) are excluded from the calculations. Rows in which life imprisonment is recommended or authorized are also excluded.

magnitude); Minnesota (low-medium magnitude); Washington (medium-high magnitude); and Kansas (high magnitude). These four jurisdictions were chosen not only to represent a wide range of durational magnitudes but also because they are similar in other respects and thus readily comparable: they are all states, they have the high quality sentencing data needed for the comparisons in question, they retain a permanent sentencing commission, they have abolished most parole release discretion, and they have legally binding rather than advisory guidelines (see generally Frase 2013a, chap. 3, noting the many similarities between these four systems).

d. What Specific Policy Choices Produce High-Magnitude Durational Enhancements?

Magnitudes of durational enhancement due to criminal history depend on both the low end and the high end of the range for each offense severity level. Reducing the recommended sentence for offenders in the lowest criminal history category will increase the high-low ratio for that offense level, and so will raising the recommended sentence for offenders in the highest criminal history category. The separate effects of reducing low-history sentences and raising high-history sentences can be illustrated by comparing the recommended sentences for highest-history and lowest-history offenders in three guidelines systems noted previously that have very different average high-low ratios: Minnesota (4.7), Washington (9.8), and Kansas (14.4). These comparisons reveal that the much higher Washington and Kansas high-low ratios are primarily due to those states choosing recommended sentences for highest-history offenders that are on average about 60 percent longer than the corresponding recommendations in Minnesota. Indeed, Washington's much higher ratio is *entirely* a product of its longer recommended sentences for highest-history offenders (since average recommended terms for lowest-history offenders are longer than in Minnesota). But shorter recommended sentences for lowest-history offenders are an additional contributing factor to Kansas's higher ratio: the average recommended custody sentence for lowest-history offenders is 29 percent shorter in Kansas than in Minnesota.

As we discuss further in chapter 6, there are strong retributive and crime control justifications for sharply reducing penalties given to first offenders. Therefore, the numerous problems caused by high-magnitude durational prior record enhancements must be attacked at the high end—by reducing recommended custody durations for high-history offenders.

e. In-Practice Durational Magnitude Measures

As with measures of dispositional magnitude, it is useful to also examine durational magnitude in practice, based on cases actually sentenced. As discussed later on in the chapter, our first In-Practice measure is based on the recommended prison terms for offenders convicted at each offense severity level, and is designed to adjust for the uneven distribution of case volume across severity levels. Our second In-Practice measure is based on the average sentences imposed on highest-history and lowest-history offenders; this measure adjusts not only for variations in case volume but also for judges' decisions to depart from custody-duration recommendations. We selected the same two jurisdictions with extensive and well-maintained sentencing data (Minnesota and Washington), to illustrate how measures based on sentencing data complement on-paper analysis.

As shown in the third row of table 5.4, the estimates of durational magnitudes based on actual sentences imposed are much higher in both states, roughly doubling the on-paper estimates. But this effect is produced in very different ways in the two states. In Minnesota, almost all of this increase in estimated durational magnitude occurs at the stage of sentencing (third row in the table), and results from the ways in which judges exercise their remaining discretion as to the choice and duration of custody, in particular their decisions to show substantial leniency to low-history offenders, executing very few prison terms and imposing jail terms much shorter than the midpoint of the allowed range (zero to 12 months). The distribution of cases on the Minnesota grid is not a major factor—the unweighted and weighted grid average recommended-duration ratios (first and second rows in the table) are almost identical.

Table 5.4. Comparison of durational magnitude measures, on paper and incorporating sentencing data, for two states

	Minnesota	Washington
On Paper: unweighted grid average, recommended durations	4.7	9.8
In-Practice-1: weighted grid average, recommended durations	5.0	22.6
In-Practice-2: weighted grid average, actual sentence durations	9.3	19.0

Note: The comparisons are of primary grids only and are operationalized as follows:

On Paper indicates the unweighted grid average of the ratios, for each offense severity level in that state, of recommended custody durations for highest- versus lowest-history offenders (also shown in table 5.3).

In-Practice-1 recomputes each state's grid average of highest- versus lowest-history custody recommendations, weighting the ratios for each offense severity level according to the number of offenders convicted at that level.

In-Practice-2 computes highest- versus lowest-history ratios for each severity level based on the average duration of the custody sentences (prison or jail) imposed on highest- and lowest-history offenders, and again weights these severity-level ratios by the number of offenders convicted at that level.

The two *In-Practice* measures use 2014 sentencing data from each state. For Washington, both calculations exclude severity level 13 due to the very low number of offenders at that level.

In contrast, all of the increase in estimated durational magnitude for Washington is found in the second row of the table, and arises from the distribution of cases on the Washington grid—the bulk of defendants are convicted at the lowest offense severity levels, and those are also the levels that have by far the highest ratios of recommended custody for highest-versus-lowest-history offenders. Switching to sentence-based estimates (third row in the table) does not further increase estimated durational magnitude, probably because Washington's sentencing ranges are quite narrow for offenders at the lowest offense severity levels with zero criminal history (thus limiting the degree of durational mitigation available without departure).

f. Dispositional and Durational Measures of Magnitude Are Unrelated

Comparison of the figures in tables 5.1 and 5.3 reveals a counterintuitive finding: the two measures of impact—dispositional and durational—are not correlated with each other across guidelines systems. Intuitively one would expect a state that operates a robust recidivist premium to rank high on both measures of impact, and vice versa, but this is not the case. Kansas is a good illustration. This state operates the most powerful durational enhancement ratio—a whopping 14.4 (table 5.3)—yet it is much more modest in terms of the dispositional measure: only 17 percent of "push-in" cells compared to 28 percent in Utah and 26 percent in Minnesota (table 5.1). It is unclear why the Kansas grid-based guidelines adopt a different approach to that found in Utah and Minnesota. As with so many aspects of prior record enhancements, the guidelines documentation in these states is inscrutable; no explicit justification or explanation is offered for the differing approaches to prior record enhancements (see Roberts 2015b, 15–16.

The absence of a correlation between the two measures of impact may suggest that jurisdictions subscribe to different models of application regarding criminal history enhancements. A comprehensive analysis of the issue is beyond the scope of this chapter. However, two possible categories of explanation are the following. One relates to the underlying rationale of enhancements: a given jurisdiction may have followed the logic we advocate here, namely that it is more appropriate for prior convictions to influence the duration of custody if, and only if, the offender has committed a crime for which immediate imprisonment is justified (as reflected in the current crime's offense level). In such a state, "push-in" cells would be rare or absent from a grid, but prior convictions would enhance the recommended sentence lengths for offense where custody is recommended. Other jurisdictions may regard previous crimes as sufficiently important to both change the recommended disposition and enhance the duration of any custodial sentence recommended in the guidelines. The alternative (and more likely) explanation is that sentencing commissions constructed their record-based enhancement schemes without considering the likely impacts on a variety of issues, including those explored in this volume.

Finally, we relate the findings from this chapter to an issue explored in chapter 4, namely the effects of prior record enhancements on re-offending rates. The key lesson from that chapter was that research over the years and across jurisdictions has generated little support for the preventive justification for record-based sentencing enhancements. Neither the use of prison versus probation, nor the imposition of longer prison sentences, appears to reduce re-offending rates. Much of that research, particularly the more recent studies, used sophisticated research designs to disentangle causal effects; those findings substantially undercut crime-control arguments for "push in"—sending offenders to prison solely because of their prior convictions.

B. Aspects of Criminal History Formulas That Generate High Criminal History Scores

The impacts of criminal history enhancements on sentence severity, prison populations, and other policy concerns to be discussed in later chapters, depend not only on the ways in which high history scores translate into more severe disposition and duration decisions (as discussed in Part A), but also on criminal history scoring rules that determine how many and which kinds of offenders end up with higher scores.[10] In particular, such scoring rules involve: the kinds of prior crimes and other components that are included in the score (discussed in Section B.1); the weight each component receives, and whether some crimes trigger more than one component and thus are effectively counted two or more times (Section B.2); and the rules governing the timing of prior convictions (Section B.3)—How far back in time are they counted? And are all recent convictions counted, even collateral counts that are being sentenced at the same time?

1. Components That Are Most Often Included in Criminal History Scores

Criminal history score components vary substantially across American guidelines systems (the formulas are extensively discussed in Frase et al. 2015). Subject to the timing rules discussed in Section B.3 all guidelines systems include prior adult convictions for felonies. All but one guidelines system includes at least some juvenile adjudications, but with major variations: in some jurisdictions only crimes that would be felonies are counted, whereas other jurisdictions also count misdemeanors; a few states stop counting qualifying juvenile adjudications after the adult offender has reached a certain age, but most states do not. As for prior adult misdemeanor convictions, three guidelines jurisdictions include all of them, four include all but minor traffic, seven include only the most serious misdemeanors, two include an even more select group of offenses, and two do not include any misdemeanors.

A majority of guidelines systems include as a component of criminal history scoring some aspect of what is usually referred to as custody status—the offender was incarcerated in a criminal justice institution or on probation, parole, or another form of conditional release at the time he or she committed the current offense being sentenced.[11] In about half of these jurisdictions, custody status includes being on bail or another form of pre-conviction release or in pretrial detention; the other half count only post-conviction statuses. Some jurisdictions count only release statuses, not any form of incarceration. A few guidelines have criminal history scoring systems that include a component similar to on-release custody status—one or more points are added if, prior to commission of the current offense, the offender has ever violated conditions of release (with or without revocation of release).[12] For certain offenses in some guidelines systems, another component of criminal history relates to whether a prior offense was the same or similar to the current offense (such "patterning" rules will be further examined in chapter 10).

2. *Weighting of Criminal History Score Components*

Most guidelines systems assign differing weights to prior adult felony convictions, usually based either on the guidelines severity level ranking for that felony, the severity of the sentence imposed for the prior offense, or whether the prior offense was violent or nonviolent (Hester 2015). The most serious prior felony convictions usually carry between 3 and 10 times the weight of the least serious felonies. In terms of the impact on the total criminal history score, a single very serious prior felony conviction will, on average, push the offender about halfway across the guidelines grid, and in some systems almost three-quarters of the way across.

Not surprisingly, prior misdemeanor convictions receive less weight, and they are usually (but not always) subject to a cap—such convictions, no matter how numerous, add at most one or two points to the criminal history score. Juvenile adjudications are also usually each given less weight, and their total contribution is often capped, but in a few systems qualifying juvenile priors are not capped, and also receive the same weight as adult convictions for those crimes. The custody status component of criminal history is also generally limited to one or two points, but in some guidelines systems that still means that this component carries as much or more weight as some prior felony convictions (for further discussion see chapter 10). Premiums for similarity between current and prior crimes likewise generally only add one or two points to the criminal history score (or a larger but roughly equivalent proportion of points, in systems where criminal history scores run to much larger numbers[13]).

Another form of weighting relates to whether a single prior offense can add points under more than one component of the criminal history score. Such double-counting could arise if points are added not only for the prior conviction itself, but also for one or more of the following score components: custody status (e.g., current crime committed while on probation arising from a conviction that is also scored), earlier violations of release conditions (imposed in connection with a conviction that is also scored), similarity between current and prior crimes where the latter are also included in the score, and/or whether the latest prior conviction was very recent.

Some kinds of prior convictions carry extra weight in the sense that they are required in order for the offender to be eligible for inclusion in the highest criminal history category or categories (or conversely: some crimes carry less weight in that they can only move an offender from a low-level to a mid-level criminal history category, Hester 2015).

3. *Prior Conviction Timing Rules*

Another variation in criminal history formulas that affects the magnitude of resulting enhancements, by limiting which convictions may be included in the criminal history score, relates to when those convictions were entered. There are two kinds of timing rules. The first rule, variously referred to as a decay, look-back, lapse, or washout rule, excludes prior convictions because they are too old—after the passage of a certain number of years that conviction is no longer counted in the criminal history score (for further discussion, see chapter 9). A variation on this kind of rule requires the offender to have remained crime-free during a specified period immediately before the current offense (or during a specified period following completion of sentence for the prior offense). However, about half of the guidelines systems have no look-back limits for certain categories of prior convictions (usually those for the most serious crimes), or have no such limits for any crimes—they are all counted for the entire lifetime of the offender. And even where a look-back limit is specified for some or all crime types, the period can be as long as 15 years, and may not begin to run until final discharge from the prior sentence (thus continuing to count prior convictions that were entered much further back in time than the 15-year or other specified look-back period).

A second kind of timing limit works in the opposite way, in that it tends to exclude convictions because they are *too recent* (for further discussion, see Frase 2015b, 2015c). The strictest rules (excluding the largest number of convictions) specify that a "prior" conviction must have been entered before the offender committed the current offense(s) being sentenced. But most guidelines systems also count convictions entered after the current offense commission date, provided they were entered before the date of sentencing on the current offense. And a few systems treat some or all multiple current convictions, that is, collateral counts being sentenced on the same day, as "prior" convictions when sentencing some current offenses.

4. A Comparative Illustration

To demonstrate some of the many ways that policy choices about criminal history affect sentence severity, we offer this brief comparison showing how the recommended sentence for an armed robbery would be derived in three jurisdictions: Kansas, Minnesota, and Pennsylvania. For this illustration, we constructed a series of hypothetical cases around a base offense of aggravated robbery, described as follows: the offender approached an individual on a public sidewalk, brandished a handgun, took the victim's cash and jewelry but did not inflict any physical injury. We consider how this offender's recommended sentence changes in each jurisdiction, with changes in the following elements of prior record:

Hypothetical A	No priors, or only minor ones (lowest criminal history category)
Hypothetical B	One prior armed robbery conviction
Hypothetical C	Same as B but add 1 serious and 3 less serious misdemeanors
Hypothetical D	Same as C but add 2 juvenile offenses
Hypothetical E	Same as D but add custody status

Each of these three jurisdictions has a different recommended sentence for the first-time offender. For the purposes of this illustration we are not interested in comparing first-time offender robbery sentences across jurisdictions; instead, we wish to focus on how various elements of criminal history enhance an offender's punishment relative to the first-time offender. Thus, we use the first-offender sentence as a baseline, and measure the sentence enhancements under each hypothetical as a percentage increase over the first-offender sentence. The results are presented graphically in figure 5.3.[14]

As the figure illustrates, the three jurisdictions vary considerably in whether and how they incorporate these criminal history enhancements, and the total effect on the offender's sentence can be quite substantial in relation to what a first-time offender might expect to receive. In Minnesota the enhancements are comparatively modest when considered individually, but each of the four hypotheticals adds to the premium, giving the individual in Hypothetical E a sentence 80 percent longer than what would have been recommended for a criminal history score of 0. In Kansas, the impact of the one prior armed robbery (Hypothetical B) is three times that in Minnesota, quickly taking the offender over halfway across the Kansas grid to a premium of 60 percent. However, two of the remaining enhancements would not be considered in Kansas, and the one that would be—the juvenile offenses—adds only a

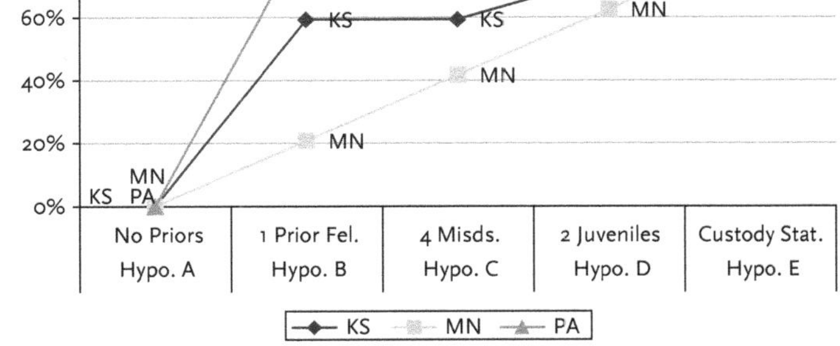

FIGURE 5.3: Comparison of criminal history enhancements in three jurisdictions, using armed robbery hypotheticals

Sources: Kansas Sentencing Commission 2014; MSGC 2017a; Pennsylvania Commission on Sentencing 2012a.

modest premium. Thus, while the Kansas premium rose more quickly than in Minnesota with a single prior felony conviction (Hypothetical A), the end result (Hypothetical E) is a smaller percentage enhancement increase in Kansas due to that state's more limited inclusion of other criminal history score components. Finally, the initial enhancement is greatest in Pennsylvania, nearly doubling the recommended minimum sentence of the offender on the basis of the one prior alone. The additional point for misdemeanors also adds substantially to the premium, as would the juvenile points, were it not for the special eligibility rules in place that reserve the highest prior record categories for offenders who have committed multiple very serious offenses.

The results of this comparison are highly dependent upon the current conviction offense as well as the assumed prior record facts.[15] For instance, in this example, ultimately the Kansas offender experiences the lowest multiplier, but as reported in table 5.3, Kansas actually has the highest average on-paper durational magnitude, which is attributable to the large row multipliers at lower offense severity levels for that state. The example provided in figure 5.3 uses armed robbery, a serious crime that is found in the upper rows of each grid where less variation in multipliers exists. Figure 5.3 illustrates that the policy choices of what to include in criminal history, together with the magnitude of enhancement added by each additional point, has a significant impact on the sentences imposed.

Summary

Naïve assumptions about the uniform treatment of previous convictions across the United States have been dispelled by this review. It might have been expected that as with some other sentencing factors that constitute a dimension, prior convictions would operate in the same way, and exercise approximately the same aggravating effect across systems.[16] Not so. Despite sharing common rationales, guidelines enhance sentences in different ways, and with divergent degrees of enhancement. Our review of the counting and weighting rules, look-back limits, and other determinants of the criminal history score reveals an equally diverse pattern. Accordingly, the ways in which previous crimes affect sentence severity across the U.S. guidelines systems cannot be easily summarized, or explained. The same criminal history profile carries very different consequences for the offender, depending on the jurisdiction in which he or she is sentenced. In addition, radically different models appear to be applied. The systems in which prior crimes have a powerful effect on the decision to imprison are not the same systems that apply a strong enhancement in terms of sentence length.

Finally, variations in the operationalization of criminal history enhancements do not appear to reflect different core underlying rationales, evidence-based analysis, or any other systematic influence. Rather, it suggests that criminal history enhancements have been conceived haphazardly over time, without sufficient regard to the consequences for offenders, crime prevention, or prison populations and costs. Prior record enhancements have reflected intuitive reactions on the part of the commission members more than any principled or evidence-based analysis. Hence the necessity for a root-and-branch review of current practices.

C. Our Reform Proposals

The varying criminal history scoring rules summarized previously, especially in combination with each other, can cause many offenders to receive very striking sentence enhancements based on criminal history, greatly increasing the severity of sentences they receive, contributing to substantial growth in prison populations, and causing other undesired consequences. Here are our proposals to limit the magnitude of such enhancements.

- *Dispositional Magnitude*

Imprisoning an offender when a first offender or one with a more modest criminal history score would receive a community sentence is a radical transformation of the sentence. As such it undermines offense-based proportionality and raises questions about perceptions of legitimacy. For these reasons the practice should be strictly limited. "Push-in" prison-commitment recommendations should be restricted to offenders with the most serious criminal histories, and even then only when the current offense is very serious, or is of medium seriousness and the offender has one or more prior violent-crime convictions.[17]

- *Durational Magnitude*

With respect to enhancing the length of sentence for cases in which the crime alone justifies incarceration, we propose a simple rule of thumb: namely that the prior offending should never carry more weight than the current crime. This rule converts into a cap upon the degree of enhancement: the sentence for the highest criminal history category should be no more than twice as long as the length of sentence for the lowest criminal history category.[18] The worst recidivist should not receive a sentence that is more than twice as long as the sentence imposed on a first-time offender convicted of the same offense.

- *Durational Magnitude Increments across Criminal History Categories*

As we noted in chapter 1 (and will further discuss in chapters 6 and 11), there is a principled basis for applying a non-linear enhancement formula that provides sharply reduced recommended sentences for first offenders, with a much "flatter" slope of enhancement across all of the higher history categories (the enhancement curve would be roughly in the shape of an ice hockey stick held with the blade pointing down; a sample grid incorporating such nonlinear enhancements is shown in chapter 6, figure 6.2). The basic assumption of this approach is that first offenders are qualitatively different, and merit much lower punishment severity on both risk and retributive grounds.

- *Other Reforms Designed to Reduce PRE Magnitudes*

As noted previously and discussed more fully in later chapters, there are many questionable counting rules in guidelines criminal history formulas that increase the numbers of offenders with high history scores, thereby unjustifiably increasing dispositional and durational PRE magnitudes. We will recommend dropping or greatly limiting these score components, including: rules that count very old prior convictions (chapter 9), and rules that add criminal history points for juvenile adjudications, adult misdemeanor convictions, custody status, similarity between current and prior offenses, and upweighting of higher-severity priors (chapter 10).

- *Prior Conviction Timing Rules: How Recent, Relative to the Current Offense Date?*

If a jurisdiction justifies its criminal history enhancements solely or primarily on a retributive rationale (that recidivists are more blameworthy for their latest crime), then "prior" convictions should only be counted if they were entered before the date on which the current offense was committed—an offender's deserved punishment for the current offense is not affected by events occurring after commission of that crime. As noted previously, however, existing rules in many guidelines systems count any conviction entered before the date of the current sentencing, even if it was for a crime committed after the current offense. Rules that count convictions entered after the current offense date can only be justified on the basis of assumed greater offender risk, not retribution. Accordingly, post-current-offense convictions should only be counted in the criminal history score to the extent that validation research shows that their addition significantly improves the accuracy of the score as a predictor of recidivism risk.[19]

• *Judicial Power to Depart Based on Atypical Criminal History Circumstances*

Jurisdictions should give judges express authority to mitigate the sentence when the offender's criminal history score overstates his or her recidivism risk and/or culpability. This element of the model recognizes the importance of a degree of individualization in the determination of the appropriate degree of prior record enhancement. In very exceptional cases, judges may also be given power to enhance the sentence based on a case-specific finding that the criminal history score understates the offender's risk and culpability (*both* are required; enhanced punishment must be both useful and deserved).

Conclusion

Prior record enhancements in U.S. guidelines jurisdictions have very substantial effects on the form and severity of recommended and imposed sentences. Many offenders convicted of low- or medium-severity crimes are sent to prison solely because of their prior record, which causes them to be "pushed in" to guidelines grid cells recommending prison. An offender's prior record also greatly enhances the duration of his prison term. In this chapter we have suggested several measures to quantify these enhancement effects and compare them across jurisdictions, both in theory ("on-paper" measures) and, where data is available, as applied ("in-practice" measures). We also show how the magnitude of prior record enhancements depends on decisions to include and/or give greater weight to various criminal history score components. In light of the negative consequences of prior record enhancements (discussed in the next three chapters), and the questionable justifications for these enhancements (discussed in chapters 1 to 4), we make several recommendations to limit the degree to which higher criminal history scores translate into imprisonment and longer prison terms. Later, in chapters 9 and 10, we make further recommendations to cut back or eliminate questionable criminal history score components and counting rules that unjustifiably raise scores and thus contribute to higher PRE magnitudes.

6 ADVERSE IMPACTS ON OFFENSE-BASED PROPORTIONALITY AND PRISON-USE PRIORITIES

Co-author: Rhys Hester

The previous chapter explored the impact of powerful criminal history enhancements on sentence severity generally, focusing on prison-commitment and custody-duration decisions. But such enhancements also have several other problematic effects. Their disparate impacts on nonwhite offenders, and resulting contribution to racial disproportionality in prison populations, will be discussed in chapter 7. Chapter 8 will examine bed and budget impacts. This chapter examines three further impacts of criminal history enhancements, each of which has the potential to undermine important goals of many sentencing guidelines systems.

Part A shows how criminal history enhancements tend to undermine the nearly universal guidelines goal of making punishment severity proportional to the seriousness of the offense for which the offender is being sentenced. Part B addresses the adverse impacts of criminal history enhancements on another frequent goal of guidelines reforms: reserving scarce and expensive prison beds for offenders convicted of violent crimes. Powerful criminal history enhancements can undermine that goal by shifting the balance of prison admissions and inmate stocks toward property, drug, and other nonviolent crimes. Part C examines the impact of criminal history enhancements on the composition of prison populations by risk level. Since older offenders tend to have more prior convictions but steadily declining recidivism risks, criminal history enhancements increase the number of aging, low-risk prison inmates; the formulaic nature of such enhancements is also likely to over-predict the risk level of some younger offenders. In each of the contexts discussed in Parts A to C, data is presented from several jurisdictions to illustrate these adverse effects of criminal history enhancements. Part D presents our proposals for limiting these adverse effects.

A. Decreasing the Proportionality of Sentence Severity Relative to Offense Severity

Sentencing proportionality is an important goal of almost all guidelines reforms—more serious crimes should attract correspondingly more severe sanctions. Offense-based proportionality is deemed particularly important under a retributive theory of punishment, but it also has value as a means of effective crime control—penalties that increase in proportion to crime seriousness tend to match punishment costs with expected deterrence, incapacitation, and other crime-control benefits, while also sending valuable norm-reinforcing messages about the relative seriousness of different crimes (Frase 2008, 2012, 2013a).

Offense-based proportionality thus requires the severity of sentence to be primarily determined by the seriousness of the crime. If severity is greatly affected by offender factors—for example, because the individual represents a high risk or has a long criminal record, proportionality is undermined. There is a zero-sum relationship between offense and offender variables: as one becomes more important in determining sentence outcomes, the other must become less important. And this is exactly what happens when prior convictions carry great weight at sentencing: the importance of the current crime diminishes.

Under sentencing guidelines, recommended and imposed sentence severity depends primarily upon two factors: the severity of the conviction offense and the magnitude of the offender's criminal history score. Accordingly, the greater the magnitude of criminal history enhancements, the less the sentence depends on the severity of the offense being sentenced, thus lowering the proportionality of punishment for that offense. The sentencing policy issue is one of degree; from the perspective of proportionality, the policy question is this: To what extent should the punishment be driven primarily by the current offense with comparatively modest criminal history enhancements, versus having the punishment determined in substantial part by criminal history at the expense of the current offense?

One way to measure the extent to which criminal history enhancements undercut conviction offense proportionality is to examine the degree of overlap between recommended sentencing ranges for adjoining offense severity levels. Such overlaps cause high-history offenders to be recommended for sentences more severe than sentences for many lower-history offenders convicted of more serious crimes, even if none of these cases involves case-specific aggravating or mitigating facts.[1] These disproportionality effects can be seen on the main Minnesota guidelines grid, displayed in figure 6.1. For example: the highest-history offenders (those with 6 or more criminal history points) convicted at offense severity level 1 (e.g., fourth-degree assault or fleeing a police officer) have a recommended prison duration of 19 months, which is more severe than the recommended 18-month duration specified for lowest-history offenders convicted at severity level 5 (e.g., residential burglary or simple robbery).

With respect to dispositional recommendations, the highest-history level 1 offender's recommended executed-prison sentence is more severe than the recommended suspended-prison sentence for lowest-history offenders at level 7. Similar examples of offense disproportionality are found at offense severity levels 2 through 5 on the grid: offenders who fall in the highest criminal history category have recommended prison durations equal to or more severe than lowest-history (zero-points) offenders two to four severity levels higher up the grid; in terms of disposition, the recommended executed-prison sentences for level 2 through 5 highest-history offenders are more severe than the recommended suspended-prison sentences for lowest-history offenders two to five offense levels higher.

The extent of offense disproportionality in a given system can be captured in a single, on-paper measure by asking what percentage of cells on a guidelines grid are "fully proportionate" relative to crimes of greater and lesser severity, that is: the recommended, typical-case prison term in that cell is *shorter* than in all cells at higher levels of offense severity on the grid, and is also *longer* than in all cells at lower offense severity levels. The main Minnesota grid shown in figure 6.1 has 77 cells, of which only 18 cells (23.4 percent) are fully proportionate in the double sense defined previously (these cells are shown with dark shading, on figure 6.1). For example: all of the cells at severity level 10 are fully proportionate except the cell at zero criminal history, where the 150-month recommended prison sentence is shorter than the recommended 158-month term for level 9 offenders in the highest criminal history category.[2]

As discussed in chapter 5, on-paper measures should be supplemented whenever possible by measures based on actual cases sentenced, in order to take account of the uneven distribution of offenders across guidelines grids as well as judges' decisions to depart from guidelines recommendations. Applying this approach to the 77 cells on the main Minnesota grid reveals even greater

SEVERITY LEVEL OF CONVICTION OFFENSE (Common offenses listed in italics)		CRIMINAL HISTORY SCORE 0	1	2	3	4	5	6 or more
Murder, 2nd Degree (intentional murder; drive-by-shootings)	11	306 *261–367*	326 *278–391*	346 *295–415*	366 *312–439*	386 *329–463*	406 *346–480*[2]	426 *363–480*
Murder, 3rd Degree; Murder, 2nd Degree (unintentional murder)	10	150 *128–180*	165 *141–198*	180 *153–216*	195 *166–234*	210 *179–252*	225 *192–270*	240 *204–288*
Assault, 1st Degree	9	86 *74–103*	98 *84–117*	110 *94–132*	122 *104–146*	134 *114–160*	146 *125–175*	158 *135–189*
Aggravated Robbery, 1st Degree; Burglary, 1st Degree (w/Weapon or Assault)	8	48 *41–57*	58 *50–69*	68 *58–81*	78 *67–93*	88 *75–105*	98 *84–117*	108 *92–129*
Felony DWI; Financial Exploitation of a Vulnerable Adult	7	36	42	48	54 *46–64*	60 *51–72*	66 *57–79*	72 *62–84*[2]
Assault, 2nd Degree; Burglary, 1st Degree (Occupied Dwelling)	6	21	27	33	39 *34–46*	45 *39–54*	51 *44–61*	57 *49–68*
Residential Burglary; Simple Robbery	5	18	23	28	33 *29–39*	38 *33–45*	43 *37–51*	48 *41–57*
Nonresidential Burglary	4	12	15	18	21	24 *21–28*	27 *23–32*	30 *26–36*
Theft Crimes (Over $5,000)	3	12	13	15	17	19 *17–22*	21 *18–25*	23 *20–27*
Theft Crimes ($5,000 or less); Check Forgery ($251–$2,500)	2	12	12	13	15	17	19	21 *18–25*
Assault, 4th Degree; Fleeing a Police Officer	1	12	12	12	13	15	17	19 *17–22*

FIGURE 6.1: Minnesota main grid, 2016 (sex and drug crimes have separate grids)

Presumptive sentence lengths in months

Italicized numbers within the grid denote the range within which a judge may sentence without the sentence being deemed a departure. Sentences of 12 months are actually for one year and one day.

- Cells above the black disposition line indicate presumptive (recommended) commitment to state prison (executed prison sentence). First Degree Murder is excluded from the guidelines by law and continues to have a mandatory life sentence.
- Light-shaded cells below the disposition line indicate a presumptive stayed (suspended) prison sentence; at the discretion of the judge, up to a year in jail and/or non-jail sanctions can be imposed as conditions of probation. However, certain offenses in this section of the grid always carry a presumptive commitment to state prison, pursuant to Guidelines policy or applicable mandatory-sentence statutes.
- Dark-shaded cells at the top [added by the authors] have fully offense-proportionate recommended prison durations (see text for further discussion).

disproportionality than the on-paper measure presented previously: in 2014, only 2 percent of offenders sentenced on that grid were convicted in a cell with a fully proportionate prison duration as defined previously.

The extent to which a jurisdiction's criminal history enhancements undermine offense proportionality is related to the overall durational magnitude of enhancement in that jurisdiction (one of the magnitude measures discussed in chapter 5). As shown in table 6.1, guidelines systems ranking low on that magnitude measure tend to have higher proportions of fully proportionate grid cells, and vice versa (excluding offense severity levels allowing life imprisonment, or where most offenses are misdemeanors). For example, in the District of Columbia (lowest durational magnitude) over half of the grid cells are fully proportionate; in Kansas (highest durational magnitude), only 2.2 percent of grid cells are fully proportionate.

The federal system is a notable outlier, having both low overall durational magnitude and an extremely low percentage of fully proportionate cells—*none* of the cells on the federal grid is fully proportionate! That anomaly may be due at least in part to the fact that, as shown in the right-hand column of table 6.1, the federal grid has more cells than any other grid. With a very high number of grid cells the overall range of recommended custody terms in a system (from 3 to 365 months on the federal grid, using cell midpoints) must be divided into more segments; in order to keep those segments from being too narrow, greater overlaps between cells and severity levels are required, which lowers offense proportionality.

This effect of PRE—undermining offense-based proportionality—is troubling not least because one of the goals of the guidelines movement was to promote this form of proportionality, moving to a more desert-oriented model of sentencing (Parent 1988).

B. Undercutting the Goal of Reserving Prison Beds for Offenders Committing Violent Crimes

Sentencing guidelines permit policymakers to set priorities in the use of limited and expensive prison resources. Many guidelines systems have chosen to give higher priority to the incarceration of offenders convicted of violent crimes, and to use community-based measures to sanction nonviolent crimes.[3] But since nonviolent offenders often have high recidivism rates (see, e.g., Langan and Levin 2002), they tend to accumulate higher criminal history scores. Powerful criminal history enhancements thus send many of these

Table 6.1. Effects of high-magnitude criminal history enhancements on the proportionality of recommended sentences relative to conviction offense severity (main grids only)

	Durational Magnitude (grid average)[a]	Fully Proportionate[b] Grid Cells (% of all cells)	Number of Grid Cells[c]
District of Columbia	1.7	55.6%	45
North Carolina	2.2	37.0%	54
Federal	2.5	0%	192
Massachusetts	2.5	12.5%	30
Minnesota	4.7	23.4%	77
Tennessee	5.5	20.0%	25
Utah[d]	6.8	11.1%	45
Oregon	7.2	15.2%	99
Pennsylvania	7.7	1.0%	89
Washington	9.8	4.0%	150
Arkansas	10.5	6.7%	60
Kansas	14.4	2.2%	90

Notes:

[a] These durational magnitude measures were previously reported in table 5.3.

[b] A fully-proportionate grid cell is one for which the recommended, typical-case prison or jail sentence (i.e., the single recommended duration, or the midpoint of the custodial range if no single presumptive sentence is provided) is both: (1) less severe than in all cells on the grid for offenses of greater severity (which are usually located higher on the grid), and (2) more severe than in all cells on the grid for offenses of lesser severity (usually located lower on the grid).

[c] The number of grid cells shown in the right-hand column excludes offense severity levels in which life imprisonment is recommended or authorized, or where all or most offenses are misdemeanors. Grids analyzed for each jurisdiction are as of the end of 2015.

[d] Utah figures exclude severity level C, where the guidelines only specify the statutory range (1 to 15 years) for all offenders, and severity level E, which has no consistent severity ranking. Depending on the criminal history category, prison durations in severity level E fall between levels F and G, are equal to severity level G, or fall between levels G and H (level H crimes are the least serious).

offenders to prison, and increase the length of their prison terms, thereby undermining the violent-crimes priority policy.

In order to quantify these impacts, it is again useful to focus on offenders who were convicted of low- or medium-severity crimes and who were only recommended for an executed prison sentence because their elevated criminal history score pushed them across the applicable grid into a recommended-prison grid cell—in chapter 5 we referred to these as "Zone 2" offenders. As table 6.2 shows, at least two-thirds of the Zone 2 offenders in each of the three jurisdictions we analyze (Minnesota, North Carolina, and Washington) were being sentenced for a non-person offense in 2014. In Minnesota, for example, 66 percent of Zone 2 offenders sentenced in 2014 had been convicted of a non-person crime. Even if we use a broader definition of potentially violent crimes and include felony DWI, 59 percent of Minnesota Zone 2 offenders were convicted of nonviolent crimes (that is: a property, drug, non-person sex crime such as failure to register, or some "other" crime). Moreover, all of the figures above *overestimate* the proportion of truly "violent" crimes represented in Zone 2—many "person" crimes are ranked at low severity and involve no serious injury or weapon use (only threats, minor injury, or potential injury). For example, 80 percent of Minnesota main-grid Zone 2 "person" offenders convicted in 2014 were ranked at severity level 4 or lower on that grid (shown in figure 6.1) and were not charged with using or carrying a dangerous weapon.

Of course, an offender whose most recent (current) offense was nonviolent could have had prior convictions for violent crimes, but this is often not

Table 6.2. Distribution of offense types in three states, 2014, for offenders convicted in Zone 2*

Offense Type	MN	NC	WA
Person	34%	29%	27%
Property	32%	32%	48%
Drug	15%	16%	14%
Other	19%	23%	11%
Total Non-Person	*66%*	*71%*	*73%*

* In each state, Zone 2 offenders are those convicted of medium- or low-severity offenses who are recommended for prison rather than probation because of their elevated criminal history scores. Figures are based on sentencing data from each state.

the case. In Minnesota, for example, about one-third of Zone 2 offenders sentenced in 2016 had a totally nonviolent record—none of their current *or prior* convictions was for a person or sex crime (and again, many "person" offenses do not involve actual or even potential serious injury).

In the three states examined previously, most offenders convicted in Zone 2 and recommended for prison do receive an executed prison term, and the odds of imprisonment do not vary by offense type—among Zone 2 offenders sentenced to prison, the offense type percentages are almost identical to the figures shown, for all convicted offenders, in table 6.2. As discussed more fully in chapter 8, these prison sentences, caused by the offenders' criminal history scores not by the seriousness of their current offenses, have very substantial prison-bed and budgetary impacts.

Once again, these findings raise questions about the choices made by commissions when creating their grids. Did the federal Commission realize, when it constructed a grid with such a large number of cells, that one effect would be to undercut a central purpose of its guidelines, namely to promote offense-based proportionality? Did the Minnesota Commission realize, when it created a PRE with a relatively high durational magnitude, that the result would be fewer fully proportionate grid cells? Did the Commission appreciate the role that its criminal history enhancement would play in undermining the objective of reserving prison places for violent offenders?

C. Sending More Aging and Other Low-Risk Offenders to Prison

Targeting high-risk offenders for imprisonment is another commonly endorsed sentencing priority.[4] Criminal history enhancements would seem to help achieve this goal since prior record is generally viewed as an indicator of an offender's recidivism risk. But many offenders with higher criminal history scores are already well past their peak offending years, or will reach that past-peak age well before they finish serving an enhanced prison term.

Arrest data and criminological research have repeatedly demonstrated a strong "age-crime curve"—the frequency of criminal behavior tends to peak in the teens and early twenties, and declines steadily thereafter (see, e.g., Piquero et al. 2007; Sampson and Laub 1995; Hirschi and Gottfredson 1983). By the time people have reached their forties and fifties their rates of offending have substantially declined, and most of them have desisted entirely, or soon will. Even the small subset of "chronic," "career," or "life course persistent" offenders display this pattern: most eventually desist, albeit more slowly.[5] Moreover, older offenders tend to have more extensive criminal records. Yet despite these well-documented patterns, criminal history enhancements and other sentencing rules generally apply without regard to the offender's current age.[6]

High-magnitude criminal history enhancements thus are likely to contribute to an aged, low-risk inmate population—and an expensive one: medical and other costs of incarcerating aging offenders can be quite high (Fellner and Vinck 2012). Given their declining risk level, the incarceration of aging offenders becomes increasingly less cost-effective as they grow older. These may not be major concerns for sentencing policymakers who support punishment for purely retributive reasons and believe repeat offenders are more culpable.[7] But for those motivated by public safety and related utilitarian concerns, prisoner age profiles are of great interest. Sending many older offenders to prison results in a mismatch between criminal history enhancement and efficient risk management. And although imprisonment of aging and other lower-risk offenders could potentially promote public safety through general deterrence if there were any general deterrent value of prison, the available evidence suggests that longer prison terms have little if any additional deterrent value (see further discussion in chapter 4).

Apart from the problem of aging offenders, criminal history enhancements can also result in over-prediction of risk for some younger offenders, further increasing the numbers of low-risk offenders sent to or retained in prison. This occurs because these enhancements are typically imposed according to a formula that disregards the actual risk level of particular offenders. Although the likelihood of such over-prediction is reduced at the individual case level, given the generally higher risk of younger offenders, the aggregate over-prediction effect could be as great as for aging offenders, given that younger offenders are far more numerous.

Of course, formulaic application of criminal history enhancements can also under-predict risk levels, and given the age-crime curve this seems particularly likely to occur for the youngest offenders—their risk level is already higher than average, whereas for older offenders the risk is lower than average. But we do not support sentence enhancements for young offenders based on an ascribed characteristic such as age over which the offender has no control. As discussed in chapter 4, a 20-year-old offender cannot help being in a higher-risk age category, and the culpability of such an offender is often reduced due to age. Sentence mitigation based on advancing age is different; although likewise based on an ascribed characteristic, such mitigation raises no issue of fairness to the offender, and it is arguably not unfair to younger offenders if their punishment does not exceed what they deserve for their offenses (for further discussion of these issues, see Frase 2014 and Tonry 2014).

D. Our Proposals

Three problematic consequences of powerful criminal history enhancements were discussed previously—(1) undermining the proportionality of sentence severity relative to conviction-offense severity, (2) undercutting the goal of using limited prison beds for offenders convicted of violent crimes, and (3) sending more aging and other low-risk offenders to prison. Most of these undesirable effects could be mitigated by lowering the overall dispositional and durational magnitudes of these enhancements; thus, all of our proposals in chapter 5, to reduce those magnitudes, will help to reduce the problematic impacts discussed in this chapter. In the next Sections we offer some additional proposals, each one designed to address a particular problematic impact of these enhancements.

1. Proportionality

To better serve the goal of maintaining proportionality between sentence severity and the seriousness of the conviction offense, we make two recommendations. First, guidelines systems should design their sentencing grids so that the recommended custody durations in adjacent offense severity levels overlap only for first offenders—as explained in chapter 1, we believe those offenders merit substantial mitigation, justifying recommended sentences less severe than the sentences for highest-history offenders committing the less serious offenses ranked one severity level lower on the grid. An example of such a mostly non-overlapping grid is provided in figure 6.2. This example is a revised version of the main Minnesota grid, which was shown in figure 6.1.[8] (For these illustrative purposes, figure 6.2 shows only the cell midpoints, and unlike figure 6.1, it includes some recommended custody terms of less than 12 months.) As was noted in Part A, less than one-quarter of the cells on the actual Minnesota grid are fully proportionate (more severe than all cells below that row on the grid; less severe than all cells above that row); on the sample grid shown in figure 6.2, over three-quarters of the cells are fully proportionate in terms of recommended custody duration (all but eight cells at zero history and eight cells in the highest-history category).

SEVERITY LEVEL OF CONVICTION OFFENSE (Common offenses listed in italics)		CRIMINAL HISTORY SCORE 0	1	2	3	4	5	6 or more
Murder, 2nd Degree (intentional murder; drive-by-shootings)	11	293	326	346	366	386	406	426
Murder, 3rd Degree; Murder, 2nd Degree (unintentional murder)	10	149	165	176	187	198	209	220
Assault, 1st Degree	9	65	98	104	110	116	123	130
Aggravated Robbery 1st Degree; Burglary, 1st Degree (w/Weapon or Assault)	8	39	58	62	66	70	74	78
Felony DWI; Financial Exploitation of a Vulnerable Adult	7	28	42	44	47	50	53	56
Assault, 2nd Degree; Burglary, 1st Degree (Occupied Dwelling)	6	18	27	28	30	32	34	36
Residential Burglary; Simple Robbery	5	15	23	23	24	24	25	26
Non-residential Burglary	4	10	16	16	17	18	19	20
Theft Crimes (Over $5,000)	3	9	13	13	14	14	15	15
Theft Crimes ($5,000 or less); Check Forgery ($251–$2,500)	2	7	10	10	11	11	12	12
Assault, 4th Degree Fleeing a Police Officer	1	5	8	8	8	9	9	9

FIGURE 6.2: Illustrative Minnesota main grid with mostly non-overlapped offense severity ranges (only cell midpoints are shown)

Presumptive sentence lengths in months

- White cells indicate presumptive (recommended) executed custody sentence (state prison or local jail).
- Shaded cells indicate presumptive stayed (suspended) prison or jail sentence.

Under the model illustrated in figure 6.2 there is still substantial offense-based disproportionality with respect to disposition, that is, whether the recommended custody term is executed or suspended—high-history offenders at Severity levels 1 to 6 have recommended dispositions more severe than lower-history offenders convicted of the more serious crimes at level 7. This remaining form of disproportionality can only be eliminated by making the dispositional line horizontal (so that all offenders at a certain severity level are recommended for suspended prison terms, while executed prison terms are recommended for all offenders convicted at the severity level immediately above). It can be argued, however, that offense disproportionality as to prison duration is a more serious injustice, or at least that disproportionality as to disposition is more tolerable because it serves important practical goals. If two offenders commit the exact same offense but one of them appears much more likely to succeed on probation, it is wasteful to insist that both offenders be immediately sent to prison. But if the probation sentence is later revoked, so that both offenders end up going to prison, they should serve the same prison term, to reflect the equal severity of their crimes. This distinction has been adopted in most guidelines systems; the grids in these systems, like the Minnesota grid shown in figure 6.1, prescribe offense-proportional prison durations but use disposition lines that are decidedly not horizontal.[9]

Our second proportionality-promoting recommendation is that recommended typical-case sentences for offenders in the highest criminal history category should be well below the statutory maximum penalties for those crimes, in order to leave room for further enhancement based solely on aggravating offense facts (this is in fact how the guidelines grids in Minnesota and many other U.S. guidelines systems are constructed). Commissions should not assume that each guidelines grid row must use up substantially all of the legislatively authorized punishment range; the statutory maximum is designed to accommodate the "worst" cases not only in terms of the offender's prior record but also in terms of the most serious ways of committing that offense. If highest-history offenders are recommended for prison terms at or close to the statutory maximum, there is no further room for enhancement based on aggravated offense factors.

2. *Prison-Use Priority for Violent Crimes*

To limit the number of nonviolent offenders recommended for prison commitment or for longer prison terms due to their prior convictions, we recommend that guidelines systems adopt an approach used in several guidelines states—offenders should not become eligible for inclusion in the highest criminal history category or categories unless they have at least one prior conviction for a violent crime (for further discussion of these rules, see Hester 2015). In our view a better, more restrictive version of this rule would specify that an offender cannot enter the highest-history categories unless both the current offense and one or more prior crimes were violent. Alternatively, eligibility for the highest criminal history categories could be limited to offenders whose current and at least one prior crime were ranked at high severity (even if not violent).

3. *Prison-Use Priority for High-Risk Offenders*

To limit the number of low-risk offenders sent to prison or held for longer terms based on their prior convictions, we make two recommendations. First, in light of the declining risk and increasing costs of incarcerating aging offenders, special rules should apply when older offenders are sentenced (or when the length of the sentence otherwise recommended would eventually cause the detention of an aging offender). This could be done, for example, by means of a formula that steadily reduces the criminal history score, or the recommended prison term, in proportion to the offender's current age (or expected age at release from the prison term that would otherwise apply). Since such a rule would be based on the statistical fact that offender risk generally declines with age, the rule would only affect the presumptive sentence applicable to typical or ordinary cases; judges would retain the power to not apply the rule, or apply it less strongly, where admitted or proven facts demonstrate that a particular offender poses a higher risk than his or her age would otherwise indicate.[10]

It is important to be clear about the rationale for this recommendation. PREs are imposed in large measure to reduce the risk of re-offending, using the prior record as a marker of risk. There is clear evidence that for older defendants, prior convictions are less probative of re-offending, in part because the base rate of re-offending in such individuals is lower, and in part because an older offender's priors are likely to be further back in time and therefore less probative of recidivism. For this reason, the severity increment imposed on an older offender results in a degree of over-punishment. There may also be retributive reasons for down-weighting prior crimes when the offender is older. Being further in time from their early offenses, these people can more plausibly claim to be a different person, even if they have now been reconvicted. At the very least, when a court is sentencing an older person with a relatively high criminal history score it should conduct a more thorough examination of whether in light of the offender's age, the prior crimes have the same significance for sentencing that they would have if the offender were younger.

Our second recommendation addresses the problem of offenders who, for reasons other than their advancing age, pose a lower risk than their criminal history score would suggest. To deal with this problem, judges should be given explicit authority to grant a downward departure when specific case facts demonstrate that the offender's criminal history score overstates his or her recidivism risk. If a jurisdiction did not want to have a special rule based on our first recommendation, this departure power could be stated broadly enough to also apply to aging offenders. In exceptional cases, and in compliance with the constitutional requirements of *Blakely v. Washington* (2004), judges could also be given authority to depart upward based on proof of unusually high risk. Several guidelines systems give judges the power to adjust the criminal history score or impose a departure sentence, based on atypical criminal history patterns (for further discussion of these rules, see Frase 2015a).

Conclusion

High-magnitude criminal history enhancements undermine the conviction-offense proportionality of sentences, increase the proportions of prison inmates convicted of nonviolent crimes, and increase the proportions of aging inmates whose risk level is declining while the costs of incarcerating them are rising. In each guidelines jurisdiction, commission and/or outside researchers should examine the extent to which that system's criminal history enhancements are causing these problematic impacts, and propose steps to reduce those impacts in the ways we have suggested above.

7 DISPROPORTIONATE IMPACTS ON MINORITY OFFENDERS

Co-author: Rhys Hester

Sentencing enhancements based on the offender's prior conviction record have the potential to substantially increase racial disproportionalities in prison populations, since racial minorities tend to have more extensive criminal histories. This chapter explores that problem, focusing on states that have well-maintained offender-level sentencing data. Part A briefly reviews the larger problem of disproportionate minority confinement in the United States, and the serious negative consequences of such disparities. Part B examines data on the extent to which racial differences in prior conviction records contribute to disproportionate minority confinement. Part C presents our proposals for reducing these contributions by identifying and revising criminal history enhancement rules that have the largest and least defensible disparate impacts.

In most of this chapter we will focus on black-to-white disparities, since blacks are the largest nonwhite group in most states and there is more detailed criminal justice data for blacks than for most other nonwhite groups. But major disparities also exist for several of these groups, particularly Hispanics and Native Americans. For example, in 2014 the all-states per capita prison rate for Hispanics was 1.4 times the non-Hispanic white rate, and in four states the Hispanic rate was over three times higher (Nellis 2016, table D). In addition, as will be shown in Part B.2, some states have prison disparities between Native Americans and whites that are as great as black-to-white disparities.

A. The Problem of Disproportionate Minority Confinement

1. Scope of the Problem

Studies comparing incarceration rates by race have found wide variations among American states. For example, in December 2014 the ratio of black-to-white per capita incarceration rates (prison inmates of each race with sentences of more than one year, per 100,000 state population of that race) ranged from a high of 12.2 in New Jersey to a low of 2.4 in Hawaii—New Jersey's black-to-white disparity ratio was over five times greater than Hawaii's. These variations are summarized in table 7.1 which (for the reasons explained later in this Section) also includes data on the overall (all-races) per capita incarceration rates for each state.[1]

As we have done throughout this book, this chapter focuses on prior record enhancements in sentencing guidelines systems. But it is important to recognize that racial disparities are probably just as big a problem—albeit one that is harder to quantify and address—in systems without guidelines, and that the contribution of criminal history to those disparities may also be very substantial in non-guidelines systems. The 17 states that currently have some form of sentencing guidelines (shown with bolded type in table 7.1) are widely distributed across these racial disparity rankings, with about equal numbers of guidelines states found in the first (higher-disparity) and second (lower-disparity) halves of the table. Thus, there does not appear to be any simple relationship between the use of sentencing guidelines and racially disproportionate prison populations. Perhaps the clearest pattern evident in table 7.1 is the tendency for states with low per capita prison rates (both guidelines and non-guidelines states) to have high black-to-white incarceration ratios, and vice versa, a pattern that appears to reflect differing state incarceration priorities interacting with racial differences in conviction offenses.[2]

Disparate inmate populations are, of course, part of a larger problem of racial and ethnic disparity throughout the criminal justice system (Tonry 1995; Sampson and Lauritsen 1997; Cole 1999; Walker et al. 2007; Tonry and Melewski 2008; Kutateladze et al. 2014; Rehavi and Starr 2014). Some studies suggest that disparity is cumulative, steadily increasing at each successive stage of criminal processing (see, e.g., Sentencing Project 2008). But this may not be equally true in all jurisdictions. And in any given jurisdiction, some stages of the process or some legal and extralegal decision criteria contribute much more heavily to disparity or certain forms of disparity. Research has only just

Table 7.1. Black-to-white incarceration-rate ratios and total per capita prison rates, 2014 (guidelines states are shown in bold type)

Rank order of B/W ratios	State	Black-to-white ratio	Per capita prison rate (all races)
1	New Jersey	12.2	241
2	Wisconsin	11.5	371
3	Iowa	11.1	282
4	**Minnesota**	**11.0**	**194**
5	Vermont	10.5	241
6	Connecticut	9.4	326
7	**Pennsylvania**	**8.9**	**394**
8	Illinois	8.8	375
9	California	8.8	349
10	Nebraska	8.4	283
11	Rhode Island	8.3	178
12	New York	8.0	265
13	**Massachusetts**	**7.5**	**188**
14	**Utah**	**7.3**	**237**
15	Colorado	7.3	383
16	**Kansas**	**7.0**	**322**
17	**Michigan**	**6.6**	**437**
18	New Mexico	6.4	329
19	Montana	6.3	360
20	Maine	6.0	153
21	**Washington**	**5.7**	**254**
22	**Oregon**	**5.6**	**378**
23	**Ohio**	**5.6**	**444**
24	North Dakota	5.2	214
25	New Hampshire	5.2	219
26	**Virginia**	**5.0**	**449**
27	South Dakota	4.8	421

Table 7.1. Continued

Rank order of B/W ratios	State	Black-to-white ratio	Per capita prison rate (all races)
28	Arizona	4.8	593
29	**Delaware**	**4.8**	**440**
30	Indiana	4.8	442
31	Idaho	4.7	489
32	**Maryland**	**4.7**	**346**
33	Oklahoma	4.5	700
34	South Carolina	4.3	429
35	**North Carolina**	**4.3**	**358**
36	Nevada	4.1	434
37	Missouri	4.1	526
38	Texas	4.0	584
39	Louisiana	4.0	816
40	Alaska	3.8	374
41	**Arkansas**	**3.8**	**599**
42	**Tennessee**	**3.7**	**437**
43	**Florida**	**3.6**	**513**
44	West Virginia	3.5	372
45	Wyoming	3.5	408
46	**Alabama**	**3.3**	**633**
47	Kentucky	3.3	474
48	Georgia	3.2	517
49	Mississippi	3.0	597
50	Hawaii	2.4	257
	All states	5.1	412

Sources: Black/white ratios: Nellis 2016, table C; all-races prison rates: BJS 2015, table 6. Ratios compare per capita prison rates for each race. Race-specific and total prison rates are per 100,000 residents, including juveniles.

begun to explore the contributions of each step in the criminal process to the bottom line of racially disproportionate prison populations.

2. Negative Consequences of Disproportionate Minority Confinement

Criminal history enhancements, and the higher incarceration rates they produce for offenders of all races, undoubtedly have some crime control value (although probably much less than is commonly assumed, given research showing the limited deterrence and incapacitation effects of increased punishment severity; see further discussion in chapter 4). Some people also believe that repeat offenders are more blameworthy, and thus deserve more severe sanctions to achieve retributive punishment goals (although, as noted in chapter 1, many retributive theorists reject all prior record enhancements). But criminal history enhancements also have many negative consequences, one of which is to increase racial disproportionality in prison populations. Even apart from racial disparate impact, some believe criminal history enhancements are unfair—that they punish the offender again and again for the same crime. And perceived unfairness is probably felt more deeply by nonwhites, many of whom generally view the criminal justice system and its processes with suspicion. Disproportionate minority confinement thus adds to and reinforces the perception, particularly in nonwhite communities, of systemic and societal unfairness, symbolizing our nation's failure to achieve its goals of racial fairness and equality. Perceived unfairness also undermines the effectiveness of punishment and crime control efforts generally; research shows that people are more willing to obey the law and cooperate with law enforcement if they believe they are being treated fairly (Tyler 2006).

Criminal history enhancements, and the increased penalties they impose on nonwhite offenders, also have a variety of more concrete undesirable consequences. Numerous studies (e.g., Mauer 1999; Western 2006; Clear 2008; Garland et al. 2008; Dolovich 2009; Tonry 2011) have revealed the many ways in which conviction and especially incarceration compounds individual, family, and community disadvantage. For many of these communities there comes a tipping point beyond which any further increase in incarceration rates causes more crime than it prevents (Mauer 1999; Clear 2007, 2008; Garland et al. 2008).

All of these negative effects compound each other and increase the odds of further criminal behavior by the offender, members of his or her family, and members of the community. Thus, if closer attention to the racially disparate impact of criminal history enhancements were to lead to proposals to reduce the magnitude of these enhancements in ways that send fewer nonwhite offenders to prison, or send them for shorter terms, the effect might very well be less crime, especially in the long run.

B. How Criminal History Enhancements Contribute to Prison Racial Disproportionality

This Part presents data from several guidelines states, showing how criminal history enhancements contribute to racially disproportionate prison populations. Section B.1 examines four guidelines systems that have sufficient data to generate cross-jurisdictional comparisons, and that have sufficiently similar guidelines systems to make such comparisons meaningful (all four systems have mostly abolished parole release discretion, and have legally binding guidelines). Section B.2 takes a closer look at one of these jurisdictions, Minnesota, to show how detailed sentencing data can provide a more complete understanding of the ways in which criminal history enhancements and other factors contribute to prison disproportionality.

1. Comparisons across Several Guidelines States

A number of researchers have noted the disparate racial impact of criminal history in sentencing guidelines systems generally (see, e.g., Tonry 1995, 168–69). In this Section we examine 2012–2014 sentencing data from four guidelines jurisdictions (Kansas, Minnesota, North Carolina, and Washington) to determine (1) whether and to what extent racial disproportionality increases across several key criminal justice stages, (2) whether black offenders have more extensive criminal histories than whites across multiple jurisdictions, and (3) the extent to which differences in criminal history contribute to overall racial disproportionality in sentencing. We find that disproportionality generally does increase across key stages, that blacks do have longer criminal histories than whites, and that, in three of the four jurisdictions, these racial differences in criminal history are the source of one-half or more of the black/white disproportionality in the frequency of recommended and executed prison sentences.

a. Racial Disproportionality across Key Stages of Case Processing

We begin by comparing the progression of black-to-white disproportionality across key processing stages: (1) felony convictions, (2) recommended prison sentences, and (3) executed prison sentences; these three stages lead to

(4) disproportionality in prison populations.[3] The comparisons of these four stages are shown in table 7.2, and the data is reported as ratios of per capita rates—the numbers in the table signify how much more likely blacks are to be represented at that stage in the process compared to whites, using per capita measures to control for the differences in state populations of each race.

Any disproportionality at the first stage, felony conviction, reflects actions that precede decisions about guidelines policy and case-level sentencing. The disproportionality here may be attributable to differences in offending, differences in police apprehension, differences in prosecutorial charging decisions, and so forth. Changes in guidelines policies would have no direct effect at this stage. Guidelines policies are, however, pertinent at the second, third, and fourth stages shown in the table. In all of these states there is a substantial increase in racial disproportionality from stage 1 (felony convictions) to stage 2 (guidelines prison recommendations). Such an increase is not necessarily unwarranted, or even related to offender criminal history—blacks could be more likely to receive a prison recommendation because, for example, they are convicted of more serious offenses. On the other hand, the increase in disproportionality might be unjustified if the additional

Table 7.2. Per capita black-to-white ratios at key stages in four states

	1. Felony Conviction	2. Recommended Prison	3. Executed Prison	4. Prison Population
Kansas	4.4	6.7	6.6	8.2
Minnesota	8.4	12.2	12.2	14.2
North Carolina	3.6	5.1	4.4	4.9
Washington	3.6	4.4	4.5	6.6
4-State Average	*5.0*	*7.1*	*6.9*	*8.5*

Notes: Ratios are based on per capita rates (per 100,000 in the adult population) derived from U.S. Census Bureau (2016) adult population, with Hispanic Origin excluded. Columns 1–3 use sentencing outcome data for 2012–2014 and base population estimates for July 1, 2012 (average time lag of one year). Column 4 uses year-end 2014 prison populations from BJS (2015b), and base population estimates for July 1, 2011 (3.5-year time lag). Frase (2009) discusses the use of population-base time lags so that race ratios at various criminal justice stages reflect base populations in the years when the crimes involved would have been committed.

disproportionality is not attributable to more serious violent offending or some other overriding public policy objective. Accordingly, we turn our attention to parsing out the sources of the increased disparity at the prison recommendations stage (which, as table 7.2 shows, largely carries over to stage 3, executed prison sentences, and to a lesser extent, also carries over to stage 4, prison populations).

b. Racial Differences in Average Criminal History and Offense Severity Scores

Figure 7.1 compares, for each state, the average criminal history scores and average offense severity scores for blacks versus whites. In all four states, blacks have both higher average severity scores and higher average criminal history scores compared to whites. In three states the racial difference in history scores is greater than the racial difference in severity scores. This can be confirmed both visually in figure 7.1 and by examining the ratios of black to white scores,

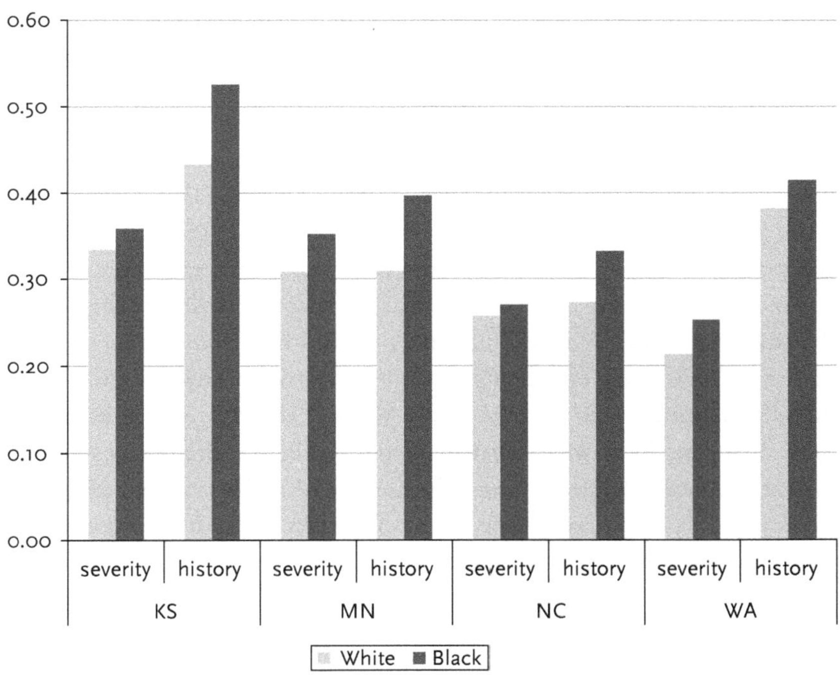

FIGURE 7.1: Average offense severity and criminal history scores by race in four states, 2012–2014 (main grids only)

Note: The bars represent, for each race group, that race's average offense severity level expressed as a percentage of the highest possible severity level in that jurisdiction, and that race's average criminal history score expressed as a percentage of the highest possible criminal history score.

Table 7.3. Average offense severity and criminal history score by race and by state, 2012–2014 (main grids only)

	Average Offense Severity	Average Criminal History
	Black: White Ratio	Black: White Ratio
Kansas	1.07	1.22
Minnesota	1.14	1.28
North Carolina	1.05	1.22
Washington	1.18	1.08

Note: The average severity levels and average criminal history scores for each race group are expressed as percentages, respectively, of the highest possible severity level and highest possible criminal history score, in that jurisdiction.

as shown in table 7.3. Thus, while some of the disparity in recommended and executed prison sentences is likely attributable to blacks being convicted of more serious offenses, for three of these jurisdictions an even greater race gap exists based on criminal history. Washington is the exception, having greater disparity in offense severity than criminal history.

These findings are consistent with other data and research from both guidelines and non-guidelines jurisdictions. Combined data for 1990 through 2006, from a sample of counties representing the 75 largest U.S. counties, shows that, by every measure, blacks had more substantial prior criminal history records (Frase 2009, 217–19, summarizing data compiled by the Bureau of Justice Statistics). Further, numerous studies have found that criminal history exerts a strong effect on sentencing severity (see, e.g., Weidner et al. 2005; Steffensmeier and Demuth 2006; Wang et al. 2009; Stolzenberg et al. 2013). Based on the existing research and our findings from the four states we analyze, it appears that the strong influence of criminal history on sentencing severity, and its disproportionate impact on blacks, are nearly universal phenomena among current U.S. sentencing jurisdictions.

c. Racial Disproportionality in Sentencing Attributable to Criminal History

Having found that racial disparity increases between the stage of felony conviction and the stages of recommended and executed prison sentences (table 7.2), and having confirmed that blacks have higher criminal history scores than whites (figure 7.1 and table 7.3), we conclude this multi-jurisdictional assessment by identifying the proportion of racial disparity in recommended and executed prison sentences that is attributable solely to criminal history enhancements.[4]

In most guidelines systems there are three paths by which offenders become eligible for a recommended prison sentence, one of which is by criminal history enhancements. Figure 7.2 uses the Minnesota main grid to illustrate these three paths to a recommended-prison sentence, which correspond to three groups of offenders and three zones on a guidelines grid: (1) high offense-severity areas of the grid, where all offenders are recommended for prison regardless of their criminal history scores (Zone 1); (2) high-criminal-history cells at lower levels of offense severity, where offenders are recommended for prison only because of their elevated criminal history scores (Zone 2); and (3) offenders in cells at medium or low offense severity, with relatively low criminal history scores, who are subject to a mandatory-minimum statute or other special rule that turns what would otherwise be a non-prison recommendation into a prison sentence (Zone 3). In Minnesota, blacks are overrepresented in all three of these grid zones, but because of the high volume of offenders of all races who fall into Zone 2 (high-history), that zone makes a particularly strong contribution to racial disproportionality

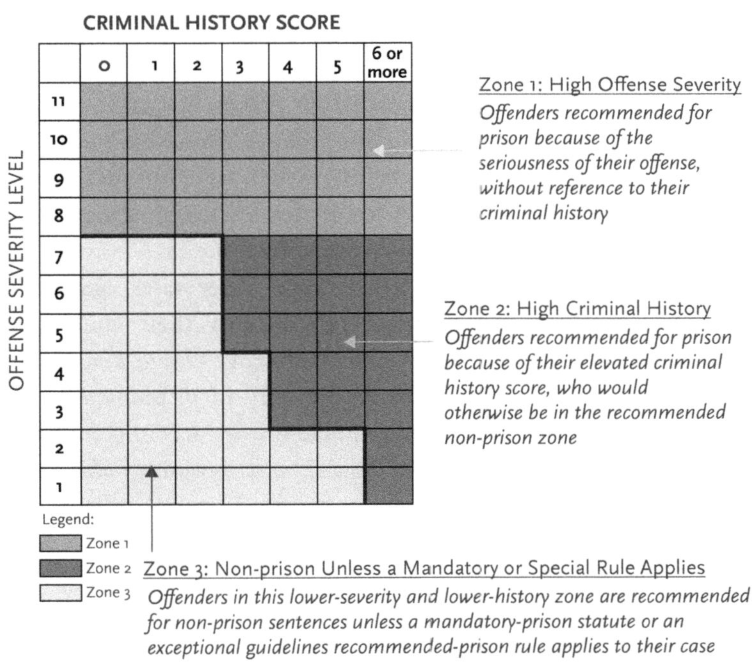

FIGURE 7.2: Minnesota standard grid: Grid zones contributing to prison commitment

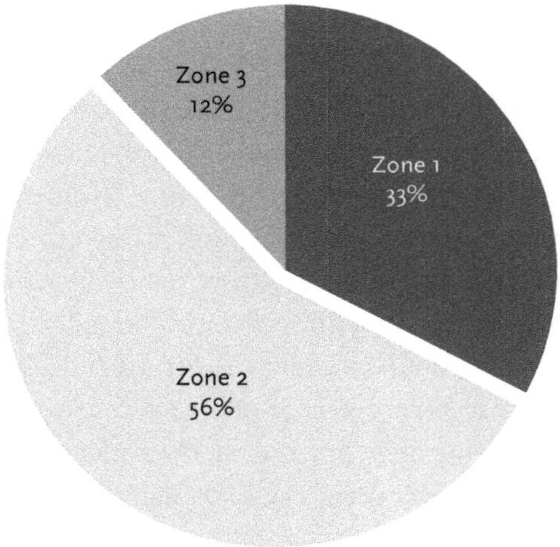

FIGURE 7.3: Proportions of black-to-white disparity in recommended prison sentences attributable to each grid zone, Minnesota standard grid, 2012–2014

in executed-prison recommendations, actual prison sentences, and prison populations.

For each of the recommended-prison paths and grid zones described previously, we compute the number of additional black offenders who were recommended for prison beyond the number that would be expected if blacks and whites were distributed across the grid in the same proportions.[5] We then express those "extra" blacks recommended for prison, in each zone, as a percentage of the total for all zones. The results for the Minnesota Standard Grid are presented in the pie chart in figure 7.3. As the chart illustrates, the largest source of black-to-white disparity in recommended prison sentences comes from racial differences in criminal history scores (Zone 2).

Table 7.4 expands the analysis above to three other states, again focusing on each state's primary sentencing grid (referred to as their main, standard, or felony grid).[6] In these four states criminal history (Zone 2) accounts for 30 percent to 60 percent of the racial disparity in recommended prison sentences; in Kansas and Minnesota criminal history accounts for well over half of the disparity. The much lower Zone-2 contribution in Washington is probably due to the fact that, as was shown in table 7.3, racial differences in average criminal history scores are much lower in Washington than in the other states, while differences in average offense severity are higher.

Table 7.5 repeats the three-zone analysis above for sentencing decisions—what proportion of racial disparity in executed prison sentences is attributable solely to criminal history enhancements? To permit direct comparisons

Table 7.4. Proportions of black-to-white disparity in recommended prison sentences attributable to each main-grid zone in four states, 2012–2014

	Zone 1 High Severity	*Zone 2* High Criminal History	*Zone 3* Mandatories & Other Special Rules
Kansas	41%	60%	–1%
Minnesota	33%	56%	12%
North Carolina	52%	48%	–1%
Washington	70%	30%	0%

Table 7.5. Proportions of black-to-white disparity in executed prison sentences attributable to each grid zone in four states, 2012–2014

	Zone 1 High Severity	*Zone 2* High Criminal History	*Zone 3* Mandatories & Other Special Rules
Kansas	44%	58%	−3%
Minnesota	35%	53%	11%
North Carolina	52%	48%	−1%
Washington	67%	33%	0%

to the data presented in table 7.4, we again examine only primary sentencing grids and focus on the population of defendants for whom prison was recommended. Changes between recommended and executed prison sentences reflect the degree to which court actors exercise discretion to depart from guidelines recommendations, and the extent to which such departures exacerbate or mitigate racial disproportionality. As table 7.5 shows, the allocation of disparity in executed prison sentences among those who had a prison recommendation closely tracks the allocation based on recommended prison sentences—the patterns of racial disparity found in recommended sentences are carried over with very little change into actual imposed sentences. In these four states criminal history accounts for 33 percent to 58 percent of the racial disparity in executed prison sentences and again accounts for over half of the disparity in Kansas and Minnesota, and almost half in North Carolina; the Zone-2 contribution in Washington remains much lower.

The three-zone analysis in table 7.5 shows the relative contributions of criminal history (Zone 2) and other factors (Zones 1 and 3) to racial disparity in imposed prison sentences, but the practical impact of such disparity depends on the number of offenders affected. On the Minnesota main grid for this three-year period, for example, there were a total of 1,270 additional blacks sentenced to prison, compared to the number that would be expected using the white executed-prison rate. Those 1,270 black offenders represented 38 percent of all imprisoned blacks sentenced on the standard grid for 2012–2014. Looking at this proportion the other way around, the actual number of imprisoned blacks (3,349) was 61 percent higher than the expected number (2,079).

To summarize: here are the most important findings of our examination of main-grid sentencing data from Kansas, Minnesota, North Carolina, and Washington, for the years 2012 to 2014:

- For each jurisdiction, a large degree of racial disproportionality exists prior to the sentencing phase, yet in each jurisdiction additional disproportionality is also introduced at sentencing (table 7.2).
- In each jurisdiction blacks have more extensive criminal histories than whites, and, except in Washington, racial differences are greater for criminal history than for offense severity (figure 7.1 and table 7.3).
- In all four jurisdictions criminal history accounts for a significant amount of the racial disproportionality in recommended and executed prison sentences (tables 7.4 and 7.5). We calculated the disproportionality attributable to higher proportions of blacks being convicted in three guidelines grid zones: Zone 1 (high offense severity), Zone 2 (medium or low offense severity but elevated criminal history), and Zone 3 (medium or low offense severity as well as low criminal history, but subject to a mandatory-prison law or other special rule). In three of the four states, about 50 to 60 percent of the disparity in recommended and imposed executed-prison sentences was attributable to criminal history enhancements (Zone 2); in Washington the Zone-2 contributions were only about 30 percent, due to the differing racial patterns of cases in that state (higher racial disparity in average offense severity and much lower disparity in average criminal history scores).

2. *In-Depth Analysis: Criminal History and Racial Disproportionality in Minnesota*

The most extensive research to date on the contribution of criminal history enhancements to racially disproportionate prison populations has been conducted in Minnesota (see, e.g., Frase 2009, 2013a). This is a state that is blessed with some of the most complete criminal justice data of any state but that, as was shown in table 7.1 and Section B.1, also has a high degree of racial disproportionality in its prison populations. This Section summarizes, updates, and expands the results of prior Minnesota research, and illustrates how commissions and other researchers can use sentencing data to identify the separate contributions of criminal history enhancements and other sources of racial disproportionality in punishment.

The earlier studies noted previously found that most of the black-white disproportionality in Minnesota prison populations was already evident at the point of arrest. Except for drug crimes, where racial disparities largely result from law enforcement decisions about where to enforce those laws, the large racial differences in arrest rates for serious crimes punishable with imprisonment appear to reflect racial differences in offending patterns. Those patterns, in turn, reflect very substantial differences in the socioeconomic status of blacks and whites in Minnesota.

Table 7.6 provides an updated summary of Minnesota's black-white disparities, along with comparable data for Native Americans and the more limited data available for Hispanics.[7] As was done in Section B.1, data on convictions and sentences is combined for the three-year period 2012 to 2014. As shown in the table, black and Native American families each have poverty rates about six times higher than the white rate; they have arrest rates five to eight times higher than the white rate, felony conviction rates eight times higher, recommended and imposed prison rates 9 to 11 times higher, and year-end imprisonment rates 12 times higher. Hispanic conviction rates, recommended and imposed prison rates, and year-end imprisonment rates are two to three times higher than the rates for non-Hispanic whites (there is no poverty-rate and arrest data for this group).[8]

The following discussion of the sources of racial disproportionalities in Minnesota prison populations will focus on sentencing policies and practices. But policymakers, attorneys, and judges should keep the "big picture" firmly in mind—many black and Native American offenders (and probably also many Hispanics) enter the criminal justice system and reach the sentencing stage in disproportionate numbers largely because of socioeconomic disparities; any

Table 7.6. Minnesota disparities in the community and at major stages of the criminal process (black, Native American, and Hispanic rate as a multiple of the white rate)

	Blacks	Native Americans	Hispanics
2010–2012 Poverty rates (% of families)	6.11	5.62	n.a.
2012 Adult arrest rates, per 100,000 adult population, for UCR Part 1 [serious violent + property] plus drugs	7.88	5.14	n.a.
2012–2014 Average annual felony conviction rates per 100,000 adult population	7.55	8.13	2.06
2012–2014 Average guidelines recommended-prison rates per 100,000 adult population	10.82	9.41	2.63
2012–2014 Average annual prison-sentence rates per 100,000 adult population	10.70	10.12	2.73
2015 Year-end prison population rates per 100,000 adult population	12.11	11.64	3.05

Notes

White, black, and Native American race categories include Hispanics, for consistency with arrest and Minnesota prison data that only report race data on that basis. The Census Bureau reports separate population estimates for each race "alone" (respondents who chose only that race) and for persons who chose a given race "alone or in combination." Because the latter estimates are higher for each race, especially for Native Americans, the per capita black/white and Native American/white ratios (2nd through 6th lines of data) are averages of the higher and lower figures produced by using these two population bases. Hispanic ratios equal the Hispanic rate as a multiple of the reported or estimated non-Hispanic white rate.

Per capita population bases are July 1, 2012 estimates. Conviction, recommended-prison, and prison-sentence rate bases are thus lagged an average of 1 year, while prison population rate bases are lagged 3.5 years. As further discussed in Frase 2009, time-lagging is done so that the population bases approximate the dates when the crimes being punished were committed; this is especially important for Minnesota, since the state's black population has grown much faster than its white population in recent years.

Sources: Minnesota Dept. of Corrections 2018b; Minnesota Bureau of Criminal Apprehension 2016; U.S. Census Bureau 2016; and the Minnesota Sentencing Guidelines Commission (2012, 2013, and 2014 sentencing data files obtained from the Commission).

criminal justice policy—including criminal history enhancements—that has a disparate impact on these offenders risks increasing their degree of socio-economic disadvantage, thus increasing the likelihood that they will return to crime, re-enter the criminal justice system, and further increase disparities within the system and in the community.

a. Racial Differences in Criminal History Scores

As was reported in Section B.1, black offenders in Minnesota have much higher criminal history scores than white offenders, and racial disparity on this measure is greater than for offense severity—in 2012–2014, average black criminal history scores were 28 percent higher than average white scores, whereas for offense severity the black average was only 14 percent higher for main-grid offenses (and on the sex crimes grid, average black offense severity is actually slightly lower).

Here is some additional detail on what is known about the nature of the differences between the white and black criminal history scores in Minnesota:

- The pattern of much higher average black criminal history scores is fairly consistent across offense groups—the same pattern occurs within 16 of the 19 offense severity levels on the two Minnesota grids used in 2012–2014 (all three exceptions are on the sex-crimes grid), and within all six major offense types (e.g., violent, property, etc.), although black-white criminal history disparities are highest for drug and felony DWI offenders.
- In terms of the components contributing to the total criminal history score, blacks are more likely than whites to receive points for custody status (e.g., in prison or on probation) at the time of the current offense; for juvenile record; and for prior felony convictions (in these years there were no consistent black-white differences in the presence of points for prior misdemeanor convictions).
- The prior-felonies component is the most significant, for several reasons: (1) about 40 percent of black offenders have a custody status point and less than 4 percent have a juvenile record point, but about 70 percent of black offenders have one or more felony points; (2) the contributions of custody status and juvenile record are almost always capped at a single criminal history point, whereas prior felony points are not capped; (3) prior felonies are weighted, up to 3 points each, according to their offense-severity ranking. As a combined result of these factors, the prior-felonies component accounts for over three-quarters of total criminal history points for both white and black offenders.

- Blacks also tend to have more highly ranked prior felonies, so that the black-white disparity on the weighted-felony component (1.31:1) is greater than it would be if prior felonies were weighted equally (1.17:1).
- There also appear to be racial differences in prior felony offense types, although this data is not routinely collected and as of this writing is only available for 2008 to 2010 and 2016. In all of those years black offenders were more likely to have prior convictions for actually or potentially violent ("person") crimes. In 2008–2010 black offenders were also more likely to have prior convictions for felony drug crimes.

b. Racial Differences in Recommended-Prison Rates

Prior Minnesota studies found that there is a major increase in racial disparity at the point where guidelines prison-commitment recommendations take effect. As was shown in Section B.1 (tables 7.2 and 7.3), black-white disproportionality in the rates at which Minnesota offenders were recommended for and received prison sentences in 2012–2014 was over 40 percent greater than black-white disproportionality in felony conviction rates (the procedural stage just before sentencing), and most of this increase appeared to be the result of the disparate racial impact of criminal history enhancements. Section B.1 further demonstrated that this sudden step-up in black-white disparity can also be observed in other guidelines systems, where it likewise appears to be largely driven by criminal history enhancements (tables 7.4 and 7.5).

Table 7.6 confirms the consistency and magnitude of the increase in black-white disparity between the stages of conviction and recommended sentence, and also shows that a smaller step-up in disparity at the recommended-sentence stage occurs for Native Americans and Hispanics—in these three years the increases in disparity at the recommended-sentence stage for blacks, Native Americans, and Hispanics were, respectively, 43, 16, and 28 percent. The remainder of this discussion (as well as the examination of fiscal impacts in chapter 8) will focus solely on black-white disparities, and the ways in which criminal history enhancements increase those disparities. That is because blacks are the nonwhite group with the highest recommended-prison rate in Minnesota, the highest average criminal history scores, and the largest number of offenders (hence, the largest absolute magnitudes of disparity).

c. Racial Differences in the Recommended Duration of Executed-Prison Sentences

Racial differences in the duration of recommended executed-prison sentences are smaller than the recommended-prison-commit differences discussed previously.[9] In 2012 to 2014 the average recommended black prison duration was 1.11 times the average for whites—53.7 months for blacks, versus 48.5 months for whites—and similar black-white differences are found in earlier years. Some of the higher black recommended prison length is due to blacks having higher average offense severity levels on the main grid. But an analysis of recommended prison durations within each severity level shows that higher black criminal history scores are also an important contributing factor—in 2012 to 2014, blacks had higher average recommended durations within most severity levels on the two grids Minnesota was using in those years.[10]

d. Guidelines Departure Decisions

There are two kinds of departures from recommended guidelines sentences: durational departures from the length of the recommended prison term and dispositional departures from the recommendation as to prison commitment (execution versus suspension [or "stay"] of the prison term). Only downward dispositional departures appear to reflect racial differences in criminal history that contribute to prison disproportionality. And, somewhat surprisingly, dispositional departures only do this indirectly—by magnifying racial differences in the durations of executed prison sentences.

In 2012 to 2014 blacks had higher rates than whites for both upward and downward durational departure on executed prison terms. For both races, downward durational departures are far more common than upward departures, so the overall effect is to reduce the length of executed-prison sentences, and this mitigating effect is slightly greater for blacks than for whites. Moreover, durational departure rates show no correlation with offender criminal history scores. Thus, it does not appear that racial differences in criminal history are worsening racial disparities when judges exercise their durational departure powers.

As for dispositional departures, upward departures are infrequent; only 5 to 6 percent of offenders with a recommended stay are given an executed prison term, and most of these departures are agreed to in plea bargaining (usually because the defendant is already in prison or heading to prison on other charges[11]). Some upward departures are based on judicial findings of unamenability to probation (Frase 2005a). Offenders who request upward dispositional departure or who are found unamenable tend to have higher criminal history scores (Frase 1993), so to that extent, criminal history increases sentence severity in a racially disparate manner. But the magnitude of the latter effect is quite small, not only because such upward departures are infrequent, but also because the black rate is often equal to or lower than the white rate, and is rarely more than modestly higher (in 2012 to 2014, the average upward dispositional departure rate for blacks was slightly *lower* than the white rate).

However, in most years rates of downward dispositional departure (stayed sentence instead of the recommended executed-prison term, as a percent of offenders with recommended prison terms) have been much lower for blacks than for whites. In 2012 to 2014 the downward departure rate for whites (36.6 percent) was 1.184 times the black rate (30.9 percent). Several studies have used multivariate models to examine the effects of race and other factors on downward dispositional departure decisions in years in which the apparent (bivariate) black versus white disparity was particularly great. In separate logistic regression models of recommended-executed-prison cases from 1987, 1989, 2000, 2001, and 2005, race was rarely a statistically significant predictor of a prison sentence after controlling for other legal and extralegal variables.[12] However, offender criminal history is consistently one of the strongest factors predicting downward dispositional departure. This finding underscores the important methodological point that treating criminal history as a control variable tends to conceal the "race effect" of that variable (Frase 2009, 2013b; Baumer 2013).

The combined effects of upward and downward dispositional departures in recent years have tended to cancel each other out so that, as discussed in the next subsection, black-white disparity in the frequency of actual executed-prison sentences is almost identical to the disparity in executed-prison recommendations.[13] However, dispositional departures do have an important racial impact on the durations of prison terms. As noted earlier, in 2012 to 2014 the average recommended executed-prison duration for blacks was 1.11 times the average for whites; but for actual executed-prison sentences the average recommended black duration was 1.23 times higher. This further increase in recommended-duration disparity is caused by the patterns of dispositional departures across the Minnesota guidelines grids: downward dispositional departures tend to occur in higher-duration grid cells for whites than for blacks (thus lowering average recommended terms more for whites), and upward dispositional departures tend to occur in lower-duration cells for whites than for blacks.

e. Racial Differences in Sentences Imposed

The racially disparate impacts of criminal history on guidelines sentence recommendations and dispositional departure decisions carry over into sentencing practice: there are substantial racial differences in the frequency of executed-prison sentences, in the durations of those sentences, and in overall severity on a measure that reflects both the frequency and duration of prison sentences. Indeed, racial disparity in the latter measure is greater than at any previous stage of the process.

In 2012–2014 the percentage of blacks receiving an executed prison term (both grids combined) was 1.45 times greater than the percentage for whites—33.3 percent for blacks, versus 22.9 percent for whites. Black-white differences in the duration of imposed executed prison sentences are smaller but still substantial: the average black prison duration was 1.18 times the average white duration—48.8 months for blacks, 41.2 months for whites.[14]

When the higher average black executed-prison duration is combined with the higher black prison-commitment rate, the overall racial disparity, as measured by average prison months imposed per offender, is very substantial—in 2012 to 2014 the average number of prison months imposed on blacks was 1.73 times the average for whites: 16.70 months for blacks, versus 9.67 months for whites (in this comparison a non-prison sentence is coded as zero, so the averages for each race are much lower than the prison durations reported in the previous paragraph, which were only for cases receiving an executed prison sentence).[15]

Again, much of this overall racial difference is due to blacks being convicted at higher severity levels. But higher black criminal history scores also play a major role, as can be seen by examining prison months imposed by race within each offense severity level. In 2012 to 2014 average prison months were higher for blacks than for whites in over two-thirds of the 19 severity levels on Minnesota's two grids.[16] Overall, within-severity-level factors accounted for almost half of the 73 percent higher black prison-months measure described in the previous paragraph.[17]

Of course, other factors besides criminal history also operate within severity levels, in particular: mandatory-minimum and other special sentencing rules, and judicial findings of aggravating and mitigating circumstances justifying departure. Mandatories and special rules accounted for about 6 percent of the difference between average black and white prison-months in 2012–2014, while 42 percent was caused by criminal history enhancements and departures (the remaining 52 percent was caused by higher black offense severity). With respect to departures, we noted in Section B.2.d that durational departures actually tend to favor blacks, but that dispositional departures worsen racial disparities in the duration of recommended prison sentences; we also reported that dispositional departures are heavily influenced by offender criminal history. Thus, it appears that criminal history is the predominant cause of within-severity-level black-white differences in average prison months imposed.

To summarize: black offenders in Minnesota (and probably in many other jurisdictions) pay again and again for their prior crimes. Higher black criminal history scores are the most important cause of the much higher black recommended executed-prison rate (1.46 times the white rate, in 2012 to 2014), and also contribute to higher average black recommended prison durations. Higher black criminal history further contributes to lower rates of mitigated dispositional departure, which, given racial differences in conviction offenses, has the indirect effect of increasing black-white disparity in the recommended duration of executed-prison sentences. That disparity is somewhat reduced through durational departures, but the end result is still much higher black averages for executed prison duration and on a combined measure of prison commitment and prison duration (counting non-prison as zero months). On that combined measure, the average for blacks was 1.73 times the average for whites. Almost half of that overall racial difference in punitiveness was accounted for by within-severity-level factors—primarily criminal history.

C. Our Proposals

Given the substantial contributions of criminal history enhancements to racial disparities in prison populations, and the serious moral and practical consequences of those disparities, it is imperative to evaluate and, wherever possible, reduce the racially disparate impacts of these sentencing rules. That can be done in several ways: (1) by eliminating or de-emphasizing components of criminal history scoring that have strongly disparate racial impacts, (2) by reducing the proportions of offenders who are recommended for prison terms solely because of their elevated criminal history scores, (3) by reducing the degree to which criminal history increases the duration of recommended prison terms, and (4) by discouraging judges from giving an offender's elevated criminal history score a major role in guidelines departure decisions. Of course, disparate impacts in any of these areas could conceivably be justified on policy grounds, in particular: by assumptions that offenders with higher criminal history scores or with particular score components have a higher risk of further offending, or that such offenders are more blameworthy and thus deserve more severe punishment. But as we have stressed throughout this book, in most jurisdictions such assumptions are untested, and often have not even been clearly articulated. Particularly when sentencing rules have major racial disparate impacts, it is essential to clarify the sentencing policies sought to be achieved and ensure that the rules are closely tied to defensible policies.

1. *Criminal History Score Components*

Commissions or outside researchers in each guidelines jurisdiction should examine the racial/ethnic impacts of that system's criminal history score, and each score component. Systems that have good data on sentences imposed should begin with an audit, similar to what was done for Minnesota as described in Section B.2, to determine the overall magnitude of racial disparities, the portions caused by criminal history enhancements, the specific decision points where this occurs, the components of that system's score that cause the most disparity, and the policy rationales underlying those components. If a particular score component is found to have a strong disparate impact on nonwhite offenders the commission should carefully evaluate the rationales for including that component, to ensure that the degree of added enhancement is narrowly tailored to meet the chosen goals without unnecessary severity and disparate impact. In particular, researchers should compare the disparate impact of each criminal history component to the added recidivism-predictive value of that component (as well as the added crime-preventive value of sentence enhancements that result from including that component). Any score component that has substantial racial/ethnic disparate impact and no more than moderate added recidivism-predictive and crime-preventive value should be eliminated or at least given lesser weight. Here are examples of score components that are likely candidates for such pruning:

- Prior convictions for offenses (e.g., drug crimes, loitering, minor traffic violations) as to which the disproportionate nonwhite representation in criminal justice caseloads does not reflect racial differences in the frequency of offending but instead reflects police decisions about how, where, and against which offenders to enforce those laws (including the effects of racial profiling and implicit bias). This is likely to be particularly true for drug convictions. Much of the racial difference in the frequency of drug arrests results from police decisions to focus on open-air, inner-city drug markets (O'Hear 2009; Tonry 2011), causing blacks to be stopped, searched, and arrested more often than whites who engage in the same behaviors indoors or in areas with lower enforcement levels. In addition, the number and severity of drug charges is heavily dependent on police decisions about when to make an arrest and stop engaging the offender in additional transactions. Moreover, many drug convictions reflect addiction and lack of access to effective treatment programs.

- Heavy weighting of prior convictions for offenses with higher severity ranking. The in-depth Minnesota analysis found that felony weighting produced greater racial disparity in criminal history scores than unweighted scoring would have.

2. *Prison-Commit Recommendations*

As was shown for several states in Section B.1, and in more detail for Minnesota in Section B.2, criminal history enhancements are the most important cause of higher black recommended-prison rates, which then translate into higher black prison-commitment rates. In all jurisdictions where this is true, policymakers should give serious consideration to reducing the proportion of medium- and low-offense-severity offenders recommended for prison because of their elevated criminal history scores, that is, the proportion of offenders falling into what we have labeled grid zone 2 (or its counterpart in systems using worksheets rather than grids). This can be done by relocating the "disposition" line defining the start of zone 2, and/or by changes that lower the proportions of offenders with high criminal history scores. Even if equal proportions of blacks and whites are moved out of recommended-prison grid cells, the result will be to lower the number of blacks recommended for and receiving prison sentences.

3. *Duration of Recommended Prison Terms*

Section B.2 showed that higher black criminal history scores in Minnesota accounted for about half of the difference between the average severity of black and white sentences. This disparate impact can be reduced by lowering the numbers of offenders with high criminal history scores (which can be done by eliminating some score components and/or reducing the weighting of some components). Even if such a change were to produce equal reductions in black and white scores, blacks would benefit more since they tend to be convicted at higher offense severity levels, where added history points add relatively more prison time.

4. Departure Decisions

As noted in Section B.2, analysis of Minnesota sentencing practices has found that the offender's criminal history score is negatively associated with the odds of receiving a downward dispositional departure and positively associated with the odds of receiving an upward dispositional departure. Although criminal history is not, by itself, a legal basis for granting or denying departure in Minnesota, it appears that judges are strongly influenced by this factor. Similar patterns probably exist in other jurisdictions and, given the generally higher criminal history scores of black offenders, contribute to racial disparities in sentencing and prison populations. This source of racial disparity can be reduced in at least two ways. First, guidelines should discourage judges from treating the offender's criminal history score as an important factor when making departure decisions; instead, judges should be encouraged to consider the underlying rationales for granting or denying departure, asking, for example, what it is about the offender's more extensive conviction record that increases his or her blameworthiness and/or recidivism risk (and, in the latter case: whether a validated and race-neutral risk and needs assessment or other evidence could be employed to provide a more accurate measure of current and future risk). Second, the racially disparate impact of criminal history on departure decisions can be indirectly addressed by eliminating or de-emphasizing score components with demonstrated disparate impact, as was suggested earlier. Indeed, even a race-neutral lowering of criminal history scores may help to reduce disparity in departure decisions, since relatively greater numbers of blacks will be shifted out of the high-history categories that have higher upward dispositional departure rates, and lower downward rates.

Conclusion

Criminal history enhancements are a major contributor to racially disproportionate prison and jail populations. Sentencing commissions and outside researchers should study the ways in which guidelines criminal history scoring and enhancement rules produce this undesirable result, and propose appropriate changes in those rules. Similar problems can probably also be found in many non-guidelines jurisdictions, although there is usually less available data to document them.

8 IMPACTS OF CRIMINAL HISTORY ENHANCEMENTS ON PRISON BED NEEDS AND COSTS

Co-author: Rhys Hester

In the previous three chapters we presented data on various impacts of criminal history enhancements, including: how powerful enhancements affect sentence severity through prison commitment and duration decisions (chapter 5), how they undercut conviction-offense proportionality and prison-use priorities (chapter 6), and how they contribute to racially disproportionate prison and jail populations (chapter 7). This chapter shows how sentencing data can be used to quantify the prison bed impacts and resulting fiscal costs of high-magnitude criminal history enhancements, overall and with respect to the particular problematic aspects of those enhancements that were identified and discussed in previous chapters. We use data from Minnesota and several other states as examples because of the excellent sentencing data available for those states.

In Part A we examine the total added bed needs and costs (hereafter collectively referred to as fiscal impacts) that result from the sentence-enhancing effects of criminal history on prison commitment and prison duration decisions. Part B quantifies the fiscal impacts of imposing disproportionately severe prison durations on high-history offenders. In Part C we discuss the fiscal impacts of imprisoning large numbers of nonviolent offenders who are recommended for prison solely because of their elevated criminal history scores. Part D focuses on fiscal impacts associated with the imprisonment of aging offenders recommended for prison due to their high history scores. Part E shows that racial disparity in criminal history enhancements has fiscal as well as individual and social costs.

Since prison bed impacts are discussed throughout the rest of this chapter, here is a brief explanation of the formula we use to estimate such impacts. In general, if X number of offenders receives an average executed-prison sentence of Y years, this will require at least X times Y prison beds. We say "at least" because, in our estimates, we conservatively assume that all offenders will receive the maximum allowable credit for good conduct in prison; for instance, Minnesota offenders can earn up to one-third off of their prison sentence, so we multiply the average prison sentence for the applicable offender group by two-thirds.[1] Our bed-impact estimates also do not include additional prison time that many offenders serve after their probation or post-prison release is revoked (as with good-conduct credits, there is very little reliable data on the frequency and timing of such release revocations). To give a concrete albeit simplified example: suppose that, each year, 100 Minnesota offenders are sentenced to prison, all of them on July 1st, and they each receive a sentence of exactly three years (which, assuming maximum good-conduct credits, means they each will serve two years). For each year's batch of offenders, at least 200 prison beds will be required (100 offenders, times two years in prison). Of course, in the first year only 100 beds are needed. But since those offenders will still have a year to serve on the following July 1st when the next batch of 100 offenders is sentenced, 100 additional beds will be needed at that point. (On the third July 1st sentencing date, the next 100 offenders can take the places of the first group, who on that date will have completed their two-year minimum terms.)

Our estimated budget impacts are likewise simplified and conservative. We use state-specific average per-prison-bed operating costs as of 2015, reported in a nationwide survey (Mai and Subramanian 2017, table 1). The survey did not report data on initial construction costs, so we do not include such costs; we also make no adjustment for post-2015 increases in operating costs. Moreover, the use of average per-bed costs does not take into account the higher costs of imprisoning certain groups of offenders who are particularly likely to be imprisoned due to their elevated criminal history scores: aging offenders, and offenders believed to pose higher security risks.

A. Total Fiscal Impacts due to Increased Prison Commitments and Longer Prison Terms

This Part shows how sentencing data can be used to assess the prison bed impact and cost of high-magnitude criminal history enhancements, looking separately at the effects those enhancements have on prison-commitment and prison-duration decisions. We use Kansas, Minnesota, and North Carolina as examples because of the extensive sentencing data available for those three states.[2]

1. *Impacts due to the Effects of Criminal History on Disposition Decisions*

In chapter 5 we used an on-paper measure (percent-of-grid-cells), and an in-practice measure (percent-of-sentenced-offenders), to show the extent to which an elevated criminal history score changes the recommended sentence from probation to prison—low- and medium-offense-severity offenders with higher criminal history scores are pushed across the guidelines grid into "Zone 2," where grid cells carry an executed-prison sentence; at lower criminal history, those offenders would be recommended for probation. In table 8.1 we use sentencing data from three states to show how Zone 2 offenders contribute to prison commitments and the prison beds required to accommodate those commitments. Column A of the table shows the percentage of all prison commitments in 2014 that were from Zone 2 in each jurisdiction. Minnesota has the highest dispositional impact of prior record, with over half of executed prison terms coming from Zone 2; Kansas has a smaller percentage of prison commitments from Zone 2, and North Carolina has the lowest percentage. Column B of the table reports the proportion of the total prison beds required to house offenders sentenced in 2014 that is attributable to Zone 2, reflecting not just prison disposition decisions but also

Table 8.1. Prison-admission and bed impacts of Zone 2*

	Column A Zone 2's % of total Executed-Prison sentences	*Column B* Zone 2's % of total Prison Bed needs
Kansas	36%	20%
Minnesota	51%	36%
North Carolina	18%	13%

* In each state, Zone 2 offenders are those convicted of medium- or low-severity offenses who are recommended for prison rather than probation because of their elevated criminal history scores. Figures are based on 2014 sentencing data from each state.

average prison durations. As one might predict, in all three jurisdictions Zone 2 accounts for a lower percentage of total beds needed than the percentage of all prison commitments that is attributable to that zone. Since offenders convicted in Zone 2 have committed low- and medium-severity crimes that are generally punished with shorter prison terms than the high-severity offenders in Zone 1, the Zone 2 bed impact is comparatively lower.

Table 8.2 extends this bed impact analysis by showing the fiscal impact of the 2014 Zone 2 bed needs for each of these states. The one-year dollar impact attributable to Zone 2 ranges from almost $38 million in Kansas to over $160 million in Minnesota. These are substantial and direct monetary costs associated with criminal history enhancements; the one-year figures shown in the table mean that, over the course of a decade, Minnesota and North Carolina will each spend well over 1 billion dollars on operating costs associated with Zone 2 offenders (plus the additional constructions costs for these additional prison beds).

The fiscal impact figures reported previously are not directly comparable across the three jurisdictions, due to substantial differences in state populations (Minnesota has about half as many residents as North Carolina, and twice as many as Kansas). Accordingly, the second column of table 8.2 shows the 10-year fiscal impacts expressed in per capita terms (per state resident).[3] Even with this adjustment, fiscal impact varies remarkably: the Zone 2 per capita prison cost for Minnesota citizens is over twice the cost incurred by North Carolina and Kansas citizens.

Table 8.2. Fiscal impact of Zone 2 prison sentences

	One-Year Fiscal Impact	10-Year per Capita Impact
Kansas	$37,881,639	$130
Minnesota	$160,372,433	$293
North Carolina	$132,512,513	$132

Note: Fiscal impacts are derived by multiplying the estimated average annual cost per prison bed in 2015 (Mai and Subramanian 2017, table 1) by the number of prison beds required by Zone 2 executed-prison sentences imposed in 2014.

2. *Fiscal Impacts due to Enhanced Prison Durations—Minnesota as an Example*

Criminal history enhancements also greatly increase the durations of prison terms recommended and imposed. This effect applies not only to the offenders examined previously, whose history pushes them into the recommended-prison zone (Zone 2), but also to several other groups of offenders: presumptive-probation offenders sentenced to prison by upward dispositional departure, offenders sent to prison after revocation of probation, and high-offense-severity offenders subject to recommended executed-prison terms regardless of their criminal history score. The overall impact of criminal history enhancements is more difficult to estimate for prison duration than for prison commitment; the latter impact depends on a simple dichotomy (at medium and low offense severity levels, a given offender either is or is not recommended for prison, depending on the criminal history score), whereas criminal history's impact on prison duration is felt across the entire guidelines grid.

However, the impact of criminal history enhancements on executed prison durations and on prison populations can be illustrated by an example comparing offenders in two adjoining cells on the main Minnesota grid. In this analysis, we compare actual bed and cost impacts to a counterfactual in which every offender in the higher-history cell has one less criminal history point, and thus is shifted over to the next-lower criminal history cell. In 2014 there were 74 offenders convicted at offense severity level eight who had a criminal history score of three and received an executed prison term; if all of these offenders had had one less criminal history point, and as a result had received the average prison term given to the offenders with a criminal history score of two at that severity level, their average prison term would have been over 10 months shorter (55.3 instead of 65.6 months) and 42 fewer prison beds would have been required. But that is surely an underestimate, since offenders with lower criminal history scores are more likely to receive a downward dispositional departure, and thus escape prison entirely. If we assume that level-eight offenders who are shifted over one cell, from criminal history three to two, would benefit from the lower prison rate observed for 2-point offenders,[4] we can estimate that an additional 21 prison beds would not be needed, for a total of 63 fewer beds—all from reducing criminal history scores by 1 point in a single cell on the grid.

If we extend this counterfactual durational and dispositional analysis to all 522 severity level eight offenders who received an executed prison sentence in 2014—subtracting 1 point from their criminal history scores and thus shifting all of them over one cell—at least 300 fewer prison beds would be needed, at an annual operating cost saving of almost $13 million (based on 2015 prison costs, source previously cited). Since this example only applies to one of the 19 offense severity levels on the two Minnesota guidelines grids that were in effect in 2014, the overall impact of criminal history enhancements on executed prison durations and bed needs in that year was, of course, much greater.[5]

B. Fiscal Impacts of Disproportionately Severe Recommended Prison Durations

Criminal history enhancements have a great potential to undercut the proportionality of punishment relative to crime seriousness, because these enhancements cause many high-history offenders to have recommended and imposed prison terms that are longer than the terms given to lower-history offenders convicted of more serious crimes. As was shown in chapter 6, less than one-quarter of the cells on Minnesota's main guidelines grid are fully proportionate in the sense that the recommended prison duration is less than in all cells at higher offense severity levels, and greater than in all cells at lower levels. Moreover, only 2 percent of main grid offenders sentenced in 2014 were convicted in fully proportionate cells. If these violations of offense proportionality were eliminated, sentencing in that year would have been more proportionate, and also much less expensive. For example: if all recommended prison durations for high-history offenders in presumptive-prison cells had been capped at the recommended duration for lowest-history offenders one offense severity level higher on the grid, we estimate that almost 1,900 fewer prison beds would have been required to accommodate all recommended-prison sentences for offenders sentenced in 2014,[6] which would cost $78 million less per year to operate. If offenders sentenced on the sex-crimes grid are included, over 2,300 fewer beds would be required, costing $95 million per year less to operate.

Admittedly, capping high-history prison terms in this manner might be objectionable on policy grounds, since at several offense levels the same cap would apply to three or four of the seven criminal history categories, thus making no distinction between offenders with medium versus high criminal history scores. This capping exercise also assumes no change in existing prison durations for lowest-history offenders. But as we suggested in chapters 1, 2, and 6, there are sound reasons, based on both retributive and crime control sentencing purposes, to substantially reduce first-offender sentences and then apply only modest increments in recommended sentence severity as offenders acquire higher criminal history scores. A hypothetical guidelines grid, incorporating this sort of inverted-ice-hockey stick enhancement curve, was provided in chapter 6 (see figure 6.2): recommended severity rises sharply between the first two criminal history categories (0 points and 1 point), but then rises more slowly across the remaining criminal history categories (2 points and higher). On that grid, the highest criminal history category (6 or more points) is capped at (does not exceed) the recommended severity for offenders in the second category (1 point) who are convicted one severity level higher; thus, except for first offenders, there is no overlap, in the ranges of recommended prison duration, between adjoining offense severity levels.

If the grid displayed in figure 6.2 had been in effect in 2014, and all offenders sentenced to prison from recommended-prison cells had received the revised recommended prison durations, about 1,200 fewer prison beds would have been needed compared to the prison durations these offenders actually received, saving almost $50 million in annual operating costs. If we also count offenders convicted in recommended-probation cells who were sent to prison by upward departure, an additional 140 beds would not be needed compared to the prison terms these offenders received, saving another $6 million per year.

C. Impacts of Imprisoning Many Nonviolent, Medium- and Low-Severity Offenders

As was discussed in chapter 6, reserving limited and expensive prison beds for violent and other serious offenders is often a policy goal of guidelines reforms; yet in the three state systems examined, many nonviolent offenders convicted of medium- or low-severity offenses were recommended for and received executed-prison sentences. Moreover, these offenders required a substantial number of prison beds. For example, in 2014 in Minnesota, 1,700 offenders convicted of a medium- or low-severity crime but recommended for prison because of their elevated criminal history score ("Zone 2" offenders) were convicted of a non-"person" crime (mostly property and drug crimes), and over 1,300 of these offenders received an executed prison sentence, requiring over 2,200 prison beds that cost over $90 million per year to operate. Moreover, these estimated fiscal impacts would be even higher if low-severity "person" offenses were also counted as nonviolent, and if bed impacts included any or all of the following: offenders initially receiving probation who were later revoked to prison, offenders released from prison who were revoked back to prison, and initially committed or later-revoked prisoners who did not earn the maximum good-conduct credit.[7]

D. Impacts of Imprisoning Many Aging High-History but Lower-Severity Offenders

Many states have recently experienced a growing population of aging inmates whose risk of recidivism is falling while the costs of holding them are increasing. In Minnesota, the average prison inmate was almost 37 years old at year-end 2014, and one out of every seven inmates was 50 or older (Minnesota Department of Corrections 2018a). Of offenders sentenced in 2014, 9 percent were 50 or older, and one-quarter were 40 or older. As was shown in chapter 6, many of these offenders were sent to prison, or sent for longer, because of their elevated criminal history scores, even though these aging offenders were convicted of low- and medium-severity crimes. The fiscal impact of imprisoning these offenders is quite substantial. In 2014, offenders convicted in Zone 2 (medium or low offense severity, elevated criminal history) accounted for over half of all prison commitments in Minnesota, and almost one-third of those imprisoned Zone 2 offenders were 40 or older at the time of sentencing. At least 1,160 prison beds were required to house these aging offenders, at a total cost of almost $50 million per year as of 2015, not including original construction costs. Moreover, the latter figure is surely a substantial underestimate, since it is based on average costs per prison bed; the cost (especially, for medical care) to hold older inmates is much higher than the average per-inmate cost (Fellner and Vinck 2012).

Table 8.3 reports older-offender data from our three states, Kansas, Minnesota, and North Carolina. In each jurisdiction, offenders aged 40 and older make up about a quarter of all offenders sentenced (not reported in the table). Columns A and B of the table, examining offenders sentenced in all zones of each state's grid, demonstrate that older offenders are somewhat more likely to be imprisoned compared to offenders of all ages; this difference appears to reflect the higher average criminal history scores of older offenders, not higher average offense severity.

As noted previously, many offenders aged 40 and older were convicted of low- and medium-severity crimes, and were given an executed prison sentence, or a longer sentence, because their elevated criminal history scores pushed them across the grid into a recommended-prison grid cell in Zone 2 of that state's grid. Column C of table 8.3 (which repeats data reported in table 8.1), shows that the proportion of total prison bed needs attributable to Zone 2 is higher in Minnesota than in the other two states. But as shown in Column D, the Minnesota-Kansas difference is even more pronounced when we focus on Zone 2's contribution to aging-offender bed needs. Column D

Table 8.3. Imprisonment rates by age and zone

	A prison rate for all offenders (all zones)	*B* prison rate for 40+ offenders (all zones)	*C* % of total bed needs attributable to Zone 2	*D* % of 40+ bed needs attributable to Zone 2
Kansas	27%	31%	20%	19%
Minnesota	26%	28%	36%	39%
North Carolina	41%	45%	13%	19%

Note: Estimated prison rates and bed needs are based on 2014 sentencing data from each state.

Table 8.4. Fiscal impacts of age 40+ Zone 2 offenders

	1-Year Fiscal Impact	10-Year Fiscal Impact per Capita
Kansas	$11,145,071	$38
Minnesota	$47,978,931	$88
North Carolina	$63,197,863	$63

Note: Fiscal impacts are derived by multiplying the estimated average annual cost per prison bed in 2015 (Mai and Subramanian 2017, table 1) by the number of prison beds required by Zone 2 executed-prison sentences imposed in 2014.

also shows that, in Minnesota and North Carolina, Zone 2's contribution to aging offender bed needs is even greater than that zone's contribution to total bed needs (Column C). These differences suggest that, in these two states, aging inmates are particularly likely to receive a prison term because their elevated criminal history score pushed them into Zone 2.

The Zone 2 aging-offender bed impacts previously reported impose significant fiscal costs, as shown in table 8.4; moreover, it is very doubtful that these substantial expenditures are cost-effective in crime control terms since, for most aging offenders, their criminal careers (and thus their overall risk levels) are declining (see, e.g., Piquero et al. 2007; Sampson and Laub 1995; Hirschi and Gottfredson 1983). The one-year fiscal impacts shown in the first column of the table are not directly comparable across jurisdictions, since the states have different underlying general populations, so for better comparability table 8.4 also provides per capita data. However, absolute dollar-impact data is useful for each jurisdiction to consider. The one-year data in table 8.4 mean that, over the course of a decade, the prison beds allocated for these aging offender populations in Minnesota and North Carolina will cost half a billion dollars or more to operate. And again, these dollar estimates are understated since they are based on average operating costs per prison bed, not the substantially higher costs to house older offenders, and also exclude initial construction costs.

E. Fiscal Impacts of Racially Disparate Criminal History Enhancements

As discussed in chapter 7, one of the most important adverse impacts of criminal history enhancements is to increase racial disproportionality in prison populations. Of course, that is a very troubling outcome for reasons unrelated to fiscal impact, but added cost provides one more reason to reduce the disparate impact of these enhancements. And those added costs can be quite substantial. For example, in 2014 almost 1,500 more prison beds were required in Minnesota than if black offenders had received similar disposition and duration decisions as whites did that year; over 600 of those additional beds were due to the effects of criminal history, costing over $25 million per year to operate (at 2015 rates, not including original construction costs).

Conclusion

Sentence enhancements based on the offender's prior convictions send more offenders to prison, and lengthen their prison terms; as was shown in Part A, these more severe penalties greatly increase prison bed needs and prison operating costs.

Prior record enhancements also have a number of effects that are not only undesirable from a policy perspective but also, viewed individually, very expensive—each of the negative consequences discussed in Parts B to E has a substantial bed and fiscal impact. For example, the estimated Minnesota main-grid bed impacts of each of these consequences were as follows: 1,900 more beds needed due to offense disproportionality of recommended high-criminal-history prison terms (or 1,340 more beds, comparing the existing Minnesota grid to one incorporating our nonlinear (inverted-ice-hockey-stick) enhancement curve); 2,200 beds needed to imprison non-person offenders convicted in Zone 2 (elevated criminal history but medium- or low offense severity); 1,160 beds needed for offenders aged 40 or more convicted in Zone 2; and 600 more beds required to house black offenders than if those offenders had received the same average prison-commitment rates and prison durations as white offenders committing the same crimes. Of course, the total bed impact from these four negative consequences is less than their sum (5,860 beds, costing about $240 million per year to operate as of 2015). But the total is undoubtedly much higher than the highest single figure (2,200 beds, costing over $90 million).

In addition to changes in criminal history rules to address these specific policy concerns, further substantial bed and cost savings could be achieved by reducing the impacts that criminal history has on prison-disposition decisions (shrinking Zone 2, thus moving some offenders into the recommended-probation zone), and by revising criminal history scoring rules so that more offenders have lower total scores, thus moving them to grid cells with lower recommended prison durations and higher probation rates.

9 THE LONG ARM OF THE LAW

LOOK-BACK PROVISIONS

How long should a conviction remain alive for the purposes of subsequent sentencing? Even if a prior conviction is deemed relevant for sentencing a fresh crime, does it remain relevant for the rest of the offender's life? If not, where should the line be drawn—how old does a prior crime have to be before it is disregarded as an aggravating factor? And should temporal, "look-back" limits depend solely on the amount of time that has passed since the prior offense, on the offender's conduct during that period, or on some combination of these factors?

Look-back limits can be justified on both of the principal rationales for record-based sentencing enhancements. An offender's risk level will often decline over time, and that may remain true even if some re-offending has occurred between the older crime and the one now being sentenced. Mere aging will explain much of this declining risk: given the well-established age-crime curve discussed in chapter 3, the likelihood of recidivism will steadily decline as offenders grow older, especially after they move out of the high-crime years of their late teens and early twenties. In addition, events correlated with the passage of time will also affect risk levels; these may include such critical life-course events as entry into marriage or a relatively long-term relationship, the birth of a child, or the securing of stable employment, all of which can trigger or facilitate desistance (Farrington 2014). Likewise, to the extent that retributivists regard prior crimes as relevant to current sentencing severity, they will also see significance in temporal gaps between offenses. An individual who achieves eight years of crime-free living before reconviction is less culpable than one who has re-offended within a year of his previous offense. For example, under Lee's (2009) culpable omission theory, discussed in chapter 1, we should give an offender who has a substantial gap in offending credit for having partially addressed his criminogenic lifestyle.

Sentencing guidelines and other laws have recognized the declining significance of prior convictions in a variety of ways. Some look-back limits are unconditional—the passage of time is all that matters. A narrower type of look-back rule requires that there be a specified crime-free gap following a prior conviction, in order for that conviction (as well as earlier convictions) to be excluded from consideration at sentencing. However, both kinds of rules often still count many convictions that are much older than the specified look-back or gap period. That is because the period does not begin to run until an event that may occur long after the entry of the prior conviction—for example, the date on which the offender completes her probation or post-prison supervision.

Look-back limits are often referred to as "decay" rules, although that term is a misnomer (Parent 1988; Roberts 1997). Decay implies that the prior conviction (analogous to a radioactive element) has a steadily declining power to influence the current sentence. But as will be shown in this chapter, almost all look-back rules actually operate in a dichotomous fashion: a prior conviction counts fully up to a certain point, and then it abruptly ceases to affect sentencing. For example, guidelines using a 15-year look-back rule will assign the same weight to a 1-year-old and a 14-year-old prior crime. Other terms applied to such look-back limits—"washout" or "lapse"—do a better job of capturing this on/off quality. As discussed later in the chapter, a system that gradually reduced the weight accorded a prior conviction over time would be more consistent with the underlying punishment rationales for prior record enhancements. Of course, a fully graduated approach would be more complex and difficult to administer, but a simplified, stepwise decay rule is feasible and that is what we propose. We will also argue that judges should be given discretion to ignore or give less weight to older priors that have not yet triggered the guidelines look-back limit. Such an approach may be foreign to U.S. guidelines systems, but is the norm in other common law jurisdictions (Roberts and Pina-Sanchez 2015).

Although many guidelines systems do have look-back limits, almost half of the systems have no limits for any prior adult felony convictions, and almost three-quarters of the states have no limit for at least some felonies. Under that kind of "eternal criminal record" approach (see Jacobs 2015), an offender's prior convictions never go away; for example, a 65-year-old defendant will have his current sentence enhanced by a conviction that was recorded when he was 19 years old. This results in over-punishment on a massive scale: enhancing sentence for 10-, 20-, and 30-year-old crimes cannot reasonably be justified on grounds of either risk or retribution. In addition, as we discuss later in this chapter, such an unforgiving policy is also inconsistent with public opinion. The central message of this chapter is that the eternal-record approach is wrong: prior convictions should be subject to look-back limits. We also argue that those limits should be much shorter than those currently found in guidelines jurisdictions that have limits.

The presence or absence of look-back limits has important practical consequences. The absence of any such limit allows the individual's criminal history score to keep growing throughout her life, interfering with her efforts to move on from her earlier criminal phase and greatly raising the cost and other adverse impacts of criminal history enhancements. Unlimited look-back also causes older offenders to receive some of the largest criminal history enhancements. That result raises important issues of punishment theory as well as practical impact—imposing more severe sentences on older offenders makes little sense if such enhancements are designed to target the highest risk offenders, given the well-documented decline in criminality in later decades of life. Apart from the aging-offenders problem, unlimited look-back enhances sentences based on old convictions that may tell us very little about the offender's current recidivism risk.

In the absence of a convincing risk-management rationale, continually growing criminal history scores and life-long enhancements would have to be justified on other grounds, such as retribution (the view that offenders steadily become more culpable and blameworthy with each further crime), or deterrence of future crimes by this or other repeat offenders. But as discussed more fully later in the chapter, neither of these punishment rationales supports an unlimited look-back policy.

The organization of this chapter is as follows. Part A surveys the widely varying look-back rules found in American guidelines systems, while also noting which jurisdictions have no limits for some or all offenders. This Part also examines the important policy issue of when the look-back period "clock" starts to run, in applying each of the existing rules. Part B considers the ways in which different approaches to look-back relate to various punishment purposes that are thought to justify criminal history enhancements. We also present a summary of recent research surveying public opinion about the desirability and formulation of look-back limits. Part C presents our proposals for addressing the policy issues raised in Parts A and B.

A. Survey of Existing Look-Back Limits and Related Rules (and Non-rules)

In this Section we survey the various look-back and starting-point rules found in American guidelines systems, and also identify systems that have no look-back limits for all or many offenders.

1. Look-Back, Gap, and Other Rules Limiting the Counting of Older Priors

In the descriptive survey below, and in the remainder of this chapter, the following terminology will be applied:

- An "unconditional look-back limit" is one that stops counting a prior conviction after a defined period of time, regardless of whether the offender has incurred further convictions during that period—the passage of time is all that matters.
- A "recent-gap" rule no longer counts any of the defendant's prior convictions if he or she had no new convictions during a specified period immediately preceding the date of commission of the current offense. (Some versions of this rule are stricter, requiring that no part of any prior sentence have extended into the specified gap period preceding the current offense.)
- An "any-gap" rule gives offenders credit for crime-free (or prior-sentence-free) periods of living at any time in their past, and washes out all convictions prior to that gap—even if the current offense was not immediately preceded by an equivalent gap.
- A "true decay" rule gradually reduces the weight given to a prior conviction with the passage of time (which may or may not be conditioned upon the absence of new convictions); this process can continue until the prior conviction is completely erased, or it can end with the prior still being counted but given a reduced weight.
- A "juvenile cut-off" rule no longer counts juvenile court adjudications after the offender has attained a certain age (which might or might not require the offender to have had a crime-free gap immediately preceding the attainment of the specified age).

Some guidelines systems have more than one type of rule (for example, Minnesota has unconditional look-back limits for adult felonies and misdemeanors, plus a juvenile cut-off rule for juvenile adjudications).

a. Unconditional Look-Back Limits

Guidelines systems that apply this approach to some or all offenses include Arkansas (for some crimes),[1] Minnesota,[2] and the U.S. federal courts.[3] The applicable look-back period for most prior convictions in these systems is either 15 years or 10 years, depending on varying measures of prior crime seriousness, and applies regardless of whether the offender had any new convictions during that period.[4]

b. Recent-Gap Rules

This kind of rule, conditioning the lapse of prior convictions on a crime-free (or prior-sentence-free) period immediately preceding the current offense, is applied in the District of Columbia,[5] Florida,[6] and Maryland.[7] In each system the required crime-free period is 10 years. In the District (and apparently also in the other two systems), previously lapsed crimes that were not counted in an earlier sentencing (because of a 10-year gap preceding the offense then being sentenced) can be revived if, at a later sentencing, there was not a new 10-year gap preceding the most recent offense.[8] Thus, in these three systems, the absence of the specified recent 10-year gap means that all prior convictions are counted, no matter how old they are, and even if some of those older priors were followed by a 10-year or longer crime-free gap.

c. Any-Gap Rules

Delaware[9], Michigan[10] and Washington[11] disregard all or some prior convictions that preceded a 10-year conviction-free period, and that period may have occurred at any time in the offender's criminal career—it could be immediately before the current offense, or it could be at some earlier point in time. These rules are more favorable to defendants than recent-gap rules because older convictions can be washed out even if the offender has one or more recent convictions—every 10-year gap helps the defendant, no matter when it occurred. But an any-gap rule will still result in lengthy or even unlimited look-back for offenders who rarely or never go a full 10 years without a new sentence.

d. True Decay Rules

No jurisdiction has such a rule, but Maryland's look-back rule has a decay-like feature in that older priors effectively carry less weight if the 10-year recent-gap requirement is met (the offender's criminal history category is reduced; however, convictions preceding the gap are still part of the offender's prior record and are not erased entirely).

e. Virginia's Unique Approach

Rather than using look-back or gap rules expressed in some number of years, Virginia's guidelines provide that only the five most recent sentencing events (adult convictions, juvenile adjudications, and release revocations) will be counted.[12] For an offender with more than five recent convictions, this approach effectively excludes all of the older convictions. But there is no limit on the age of the five counted convictions, nor is there any limit if the offender has a total of five or fewer convictions. Thus, Virginia's rule can result in counting some very old convictions, even those that were entered decades earlier.

f. Juvenile Cut-Off Rules

Four states disregard juvenile adjudications after the offender attains a designated age.[13] Minnesota excludes juvenile adjudications when sentencing for crimes committed after the offender has attained the age of 25.[14] Kansas applies the same rule to non-serious juvenile offenses.[15] In Maryland the juvenile priors washout age is 23.[16] In Pennsylvania the age is 28, but the offender must have been crime-free for the 10 years preceding his or her 28th birthday.[17] (We shall discuss juvenile prior crimes in more detail in the next chapter).

g. No Look-Back Limits

Of the 19 American state and federal jurisdictions that currently have some form of sentencing guidelines, 13 have no look-back limit for some or all types of prior convictions:

- Look-back limits are absent for all adult crimes in nine states: Alabama, Kansas, Massachusetts, North Carolina, Ohio, Oregon, Pennsylvania, Tennessee, and Utah.[18]
- Look-back limits are absent for the most serious crimes in three states: Arkansas,[19] Delaware,[20] and Washington.[21]
- Virginia's rule, counting the five most recent prior sentencing events,[22] does not exclude older convictions if the offender has a total of five or fewer convictions.

2. When Does the Look-Back or Gap Clock Start to Run?

The number of prior convictions excluded by the operation of a look-back limit or gap rule depends not only on the nature and length of the specified elapsed time period but also on when that period starts to run. In theory, the broadest exclusion (earliest start point) would start the clock on the date when the prior crime was committed, but in practice no system takes this approach; instead, the broadest rule we have found starts the clock at the time of sentencing for the prior offense. The latter rule is most likely to be applied where the prior sentence did not include incarceration—the clock starts when the offender is sentenced and allowed to remain free in the community. Other rules count a larger number of prior convictions (reaching convictions entered further back in time) by not starting the clock until the offender is finally released from custody in connection with the prior conviction, or when he or she completes or is discharged from probation. For offenders sentenced to prison, some systems delay starting the look-back clock (thereby counting more prior convictions) until the offender is discharged from post-prison supervision.

Given that probation terms, prison terms, and periods of post-prison supervision often last for many years, such final-release and final-discharge rules cause criminal history scores to include many crimes sentenced much farther back in time than the specified look-back or recent-gap period. For example, Minnesota has a 15-year look-back period for all adult felonies, but uses a date-of-final-discharge clock-starting rule. Lengthy probation terms are frequently imposed in this state (averaging about 5.5 years in 2014), while the average term of imprisonment plus post-prison supervision is almost four years.

The combined effect of these rules and sentencing practices is that some Minnesota convictions continue to be included in criminal history for decades. Here are the periods of time that convictions entered in 2014 will be counted in those offenders' criminal histories:[23]

- 52 percent of the convictions will continue to be counted in criminal history for 20 or more years after the date of sentencing;
- 12 percent of convictions will be counted for 25 or more years;
- 4.5 percent of convictions will be counted for 30 or more years.

These figures run from the prior sentencing date, but the crimes themselves were committed even farther back in time—in 2014, an average of one year before sentencing. Thus, each of the above figures should be increased further by an average of one year. To put these numbers into perspective: a date-of-offense look-back of 26 or more years means that a crime committed when the offender was 24 years old will be counted in his or her criminal history until he is 50.

B. Rationales for Look-Back Limits and Gap Rules

In order to assess whether and how to apply look-back, decay, and similar rules, we must examine the possible rationales for having such rules. Those rationales are, in turn, closely related to the rationales for criminal history enhancements generally (although practical concerns, such as the availability of necessary information at the time of sentencing, must also be considered in designing look-back rules, particularly those related to when the "clock" starts). As we have stressed throughout this book, offender recidivism risk is the most convincing and widely accepted rationale for criminal history enhancements, so we will address that rationale first. We then consider how the design of look-back and gap rules might be affected by considerations of retributive and deterrent punishment goals.

1. Recidivism Risk

An unconditional look-back limit might plausibly (but with limited research support) be based on the lower assumed risk-predictive value of very old convictions—such convictions may date from a very different social environment and/or phase of the offender's life, and in any case they reflect the higher propensity to crime found in younger persons; indeed, look-back limits are sometimes intended as proxies for current offender age.[24] As was noted in earlier chapters, advancing age is a well-documented low-risk factor, albeit one that is seldom recognized in guidelines rules.

With regard to recent-gap rules, a recent period of desistance suggests that, despite the offender's relapse (by committing the crime for which he is now being sentenced), his criminal career is tapering off and may soon end entirely. The risk-predictive relevance of earlier crime-free gaps (for which offenders receive credit under the any-gap rule) is perhaps less intuitively plausible. But such a gap shows that the offender is capable of temporary desistance, which, if not too far in the past, may suggest that he can achieve it again. As we noted in chapter 3, risk is a continuum, and desistance from crime (like abstinence from addictive substances) is often a relapsing process; for many offenders, progress is measured not by sudden and complete cessation but rather by increasingly frequent and longer periods of desistance.

Assuming a risk-prediction rationale, further questions arise: How far back should prior convictions be counted? When should the clock begin to run? And when should crime-free gaps be required or credited? Research on the crime-predictive value of older convictions suggests that prior convictions should be disregarded after a recent crime-free gap of approximately seven years.[25] And since it appears that most of the offenders in these studies were not incarcerated at any time during that period, the start point for the seven-year period should be when the offender's period of uninterrupted liberty began --that is, when the offender was last sentenced if no custody was immediately or later executed for that crime, or when he or she was last released into the community, if such custody did occur.

2. *Retributivism*

Although retributive rationales for criminal history enhancements are highly contested, some theorists and policymakers assert this justification for prior record enhancements (see generally, Roberts and von Hirsch 2010). Even if one accepts that theory, however, a good argument can be made that an offender's desert for her latest crime is increased less by the fact that she has an old prior conviction than it is by a recent conviction, especially if there has been a crime-free gap since the older conviction. But the form and strength of this argument will depend on which version of heightened-desert one accepts as underlying criminal history enhancements,[26] and which kind of look-back rule is being examined.

With respect to recent-gap rules, it can be argued that a crime committed after many years of crime-free living is more easily seen as an uncharacteristic "lapse"; the latest crime is deemed less indicative of an antisocial character, and more likely to reflect the offender's current life circumstances or environmental factors. There is also an argument for gap requirements that returns to the early formulation of the retributively based, progressive loss of mitigation model noted in chapter 1. That perspective on prior convictions argues that the first offender is entitled to mitigation, and that successive reconvictions increasingly disentitle him to the same level of mitigation. Thomas (1970, 197) described this principle as the "progressive loss of credit" (see also Ashworth 1983)—an offender's law-abiding life to the point of first conviction establishes good character credit which is then progressively eroded by subsequent offending and conviction. When the offender has succeeded in living without a conviction for a sustained period of time, this in effect restores his credit with the result that he goes a long way towards re-establishing his status as a first offender. Failing to acknowledge the offender's efforts in this respect would thus violate the spirit of an important retributive account of prior record enhancements.

Alternatively, if we apply Lee's culpable-omission PRE rationale (2009, 2010), discussed in chapter 1, the passage of many years with no new convictions suggests that the offender has at least been trying to control her criminal tendencies; even if she has not yet succeeded in achieving complete desistance, such efforts may make her less culpable. To some extent the same argument might be made in favor of an any-gap rule—any period of desistance, even if not recent or permanent, is worthy of praise and makes the offender less culpable for later crimes.

The retributive rationales for unconditional look-back limits are less clear. Under theories that are based on the repeat offender's assumed defiance of the law, greater notice of the law's requirements, or culpable omission to address the causes of his criminal behavior, very old convictions tell us less than recent convictions about the offender's increased culpability for his current crime. On the other hand, if one adopts the highly contestable character-based retributive account, then older convictions would, if anything, be more probative—they suggest that the offender has an antisocial disposition and consistently chooses to do wrong; he is not someone who, for example, has simply had the misfortune to periodically find himself in circumstances posing strong temptations or pressures to commit crime.

Under any retributive rationale, however, it is difficult to justify the repeated and escalating enhancement of penalties with each new crime, and this problem gets worse and worse the farther back in time we count prior crimes. Even the first time a prior offense is used to enhance a later punishment, we are, in effect, punishing the offender again for that crime. But at each subsequent sentencing until the look-back limit is reached, we punish the offender *yet again* for her prior crime—*a crime for which she has already been repeatedly punished.*

With respect to the starting-point question, some desert-based arguments (e.g., those based on defiance, State notice, or culpable omission) would start the clock at the time of sentencing for the prior crime; other retributive theories (e.g., those based on lapse, gap-credit, or character) would seem to require that the look-back clock begin with the *commission* of the prior crime. Even under those theories, however, for ease of administration it may be necessary to use the dates of conviction or sentencing for the prior crimes.

But under any of the various retributive theories, a practical problem arises—how is the precise look-back or gap period chosen? Retributive rationales do not seem capable of generating any particular rule stated in years (although public opinion research, of the kind discussed later on in the chapter, might provide at least some empirical validation of specific desert-based look-back limits). In this respect, another advantage of taking a risk-based approach is that assumptions of reduced recidivism risk after the passage of time (with or without a crime-free gap) can more readily be validated with empirical evidence.

3. *Deterrence*

A third potential rationale for criminal history enhancements, and thus also for the application and scope of look-back and gap rules, is deterrence. Such enhancements may be designed to discourage repeat offenders, and those like them, from continuing to commit crimes, by threatening that such crimes will incur escalating punishment. As was noted in chapter 4, deterrence rationales have intuitive appeal but little empirical support—for a variety of general, situational, and psychological reasons, increased penalty severity, whether based on prior record enhancements or other grounds, seems to have very little effect on aggregate crime rates or re-offending rates. Deterrence is particularly implausible as a rationale for unlimited (perpetual) look-back: we would have to assume that younger offenders will commit fewer crimes if we threaten them with life-long escalating enhancements, and/or that older offenders will never desist unless we keep raising the penalties they receive.

Nevertheless, repeat offenders as a group are more likely to commit future crimes than persons with no convictions, and thus some policymakers may believe it is worthwhile imposing additional punishment in hopes of deterring them and other, similarly risky offenders. Under this theory, however, it should probably be assumed (subject, as always, to empirical research), that the deterrent benefits of prior record enhancements will decline the farther in the future such enhancements are threatened; most offenders are focused on the present, so it seems unlikely that a threat of lifetime penalty enhancement will add much deterrent value above the threat of enhancement for crimes committed sooner.

Again, however, this rationale provides little or no guidance as to the choice of a specific look-back or gap period; it does suggest, however, that sheer passage of time, even without a crime-free gap, might be enough to undercut the continuing deterrent value of counting older convictions in criminal history. As for the choice of starting point, passage of time would seem to begin at sentencing—the point at which future penalty enhancement is or could be specifically threatened—not some later date on which the offender was released from custody or discharged from the sentence.

This discussion assumes a traditional, threat-based deterrent model, but sentencing rules can create positive as well as negative incentives. From this perspective, an any-gap rule, especially one with no possibility of later "revival" of older convictions, could have a positive-incentive rationale. We say to the offender at sentencing: if you can manage to stay crime-free for the next X years, we will stop including this conviction in your criminal history. Such a rule allows us to focus the offender's attention on the near term, unlike a recent-gap rule that may not definitively benefit the offender until sometime in the distant future. Compared to recent-gap rules that permit revival of lapsed priors, a no-revival any-gap rule provides a particularly attractive offer: the current conviction will be erased permanently if the offender remains crime-free during the designated near-term period.

4. *Public Attitudes toward Look-Back Limits*

Reforms along the lines of those advocated in this book stand little chance of adoption if there is strong public opposition. The U.S. public has often been portrayed as being highly punitive, particularly regarding repeat offenders. Yet there is another side to public attitudes, one that is more forgiving of past offending (except for the most serious crimes) and more supportive of rehabilitation. Would the U.S. public support stricter limits on sentence enhancements for crimes committed many years ago? A number of state and federal commissions have conducted public opinion research and revealed sensitivity to community attitudes (see, e.g., Rossi et al. 1997), but the issue of look-back limits has been ignored. In order to test public reactions, we conducted a national survey of U.S. residents, examining opinions about prior adult and juvenile crimes.[27]

A. Support for Look-Back Limits on Prior Adult Convictions

In this study, respondents were asked the following general question:

> *Imagine your state is considering passing a separate new law related to criminal sentencing [. . .] [J]udges would not be allowed to count an offender's prior criminal convictions against him if the crimes were*

committed long ago. Those in favor of the policy argue that society shouldn't count past crime against a person forever. Those against it stress that even old crimes continue to be relevant for determining punishment for a newly committed offense. Which of the following best describe your position on such a proposal?

- *I would be in favor of limiting the offenses used to increase punishment to more recent convictions.*
- *I would be in favor of allowing all offenses, new and old, to count against an offender.*

Two-thirds of respondents were in favor of the policy to limit old convictions, while one-third preferred to count them all, regardless of the age of the prior conviction.

The respondents who were in favor of a temporal limit were then asked how long they thought a prior conviction should remain relevant for the purposes of enhancing subsequent sentences. The potential responses were 5, 10, 15, and 20 years, with an option for "other." As shown in table 9.1, approximately one-quarter of the subsample chose 5 years and one half chose 10 years; thus, three-quarters supported look-back of no more than 10 years. Look-back limits vary considerably across the United States, but this pattern of responses is more forgiving than under most guideline systems (especially since, as was noted earlier, existing look-back limits often run from discharge or some other date long after the date of conviction, whereas the latter starting point (or even the date of the prior offense) was implicit in the survey questions and responses). These responses demonstrate clear public support for look-back limits on prior crimes.

Table 9.1. Number of years after which a prior conviction should be disregarded (proportion of respondents favoring each rule)

5 years	23%
10 years	53%
15 years	12%
20 years	4%
Other	7%

Source: Data reported by Hester et al. 2017.

Respondents were also asked to consider a series of case vignettes, beginning with a version in which the offender has no prior record:

> *Sam Davis is 45 years old and currently employed as an accountant. He is married and has one teenaged daughter. He has just been convicted of possession of stolen property. He bought some expensive electronic equipment knowing that it was stolen. The usual sentence for a crime of this nature is about 15 months in prison. Sam has no previous convictions of any kind. This is his first criminal conviction. Until now he has not been in any trouble with the law. What effect, if any, should the fact that this is his first conviction have on the 15-month sentence? Should it:*
>
> - *Have no effect on the sentence?*
> - *Increase the sentence by ____ months?*
> - *Decrease the sentence by ____ months?*

Once respondents gave an answer to this no-priors scenario they were told to assume that Sam has a one-year-old auto theft conviction, and were again asked whether that should have no effect, increase, or decrease the sentence (and if an increase or decrease, by how many months). The question was repeated two more times with the age of the prior auto theft changing to 9 years, and then 14 years. As figure 9.1 reveals, slightly more than half

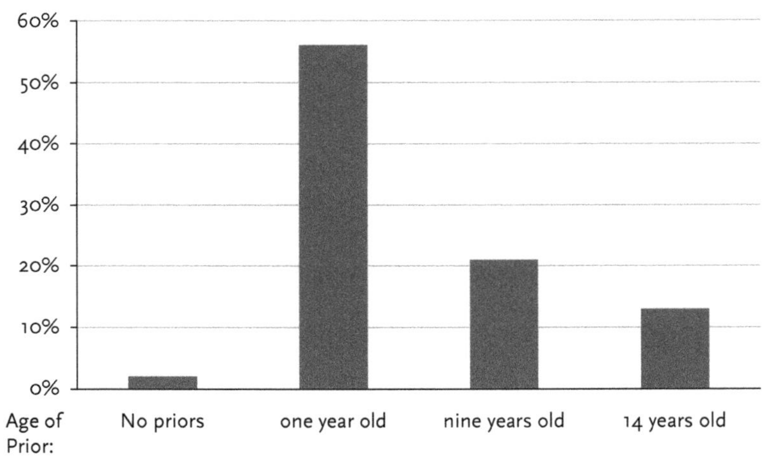

FIGURE 9.1: Respondents indicating that an offender's prior record should increase the sentence, by age of prior

Age of prior: No priors—1 year old—9 years old—14 years old

Source: Data reported by Hester et al. 2017.

would have increased Sam's sentence for the one-year-old prior. But when respondents were asked to assume the prior conviction was 9 years old the percent increasing the sentence fell to 21 percent; and when the conviction was 14 years old, the percentage favoring an increased sentence was only 13 percent. The public were clearly less punitive as the age of the prior offense increased.

B. Attitudes toward Counting Prior Juvenile Offenses

To explore public attitudes on this subject, we first asked the following general policy question:

> *Imagine your state is considering passing a new law related to criminal sentencing. Under the new law, judges would not be allowed to count an offender's prior criminal convictions against him if the convictions were committed while the offender was a juvenile. Which of the following would best describe your position on such a proposal?*
>
> - *I would support the proposal that offenses committed as a juvenile should no longer count against an offender.*
> - *I would not support the proposal; I believe judges should be allowed to increase punishment for offenders who committed crimes as juveniles.*

In response, 71 percent were in favor of a policy barring sentencing enhancements for prior offenses committed while a juvenile, and 29 percent were against.

Next, respondents were asked to consider a case vignette involving an adult offender with one prior juvenile conviction when he was 17; all respondents were given the same basic facts about the case, but were randomly assigned to four test groups with different details about the offender's prior record and current age. The juvenile prior was described as occurring 23, 18, 13, or 8 years ago, with the corresponding offender ages being 40, 35, 30, and 25. Here are the basic case facts:

> *Jay Williams is now [___] years old. He has just been convicted of tax evasion. When filing his tax return he failed to report $7,000 of extra income he had earned as a home renovator. The usual sentence for this crime is around 12 months in prison. At sentencing, his lawyer informed the court that although Williams has one prior conviction, it occurred [___] years ago. When Williams was 17 years old and finishing high school he*

was convicted of a minor robbery. He was sentenced to a term of juvenile probation that he completed successfully. Since then, and until now, he has led a law-abiding life. Should this previous juvenile conviction from [___] years ago affect the sentence that should be imposed now for this crime?

- *No, the offense should not be considered for sentencing the current tax evasion offense because it was committed years ago when he was a minor.*
- *Yes, because of the prior juvenile offense, the current sentence should be increased by ____ months.*

The object of the experimental design was to test whether the public would view a juvenile prior as less relevant the longer ago it occurred. But what we found was that almost all respondents deemed the offender's juvenile offense irrelevant even when it was only eight years old—in all four test groups, over 90 percent of respondents opposed counting the prior conviction. Yet many jurisdictions would count this prior conviction in at least some adult sentencing hearings (Mitchell 2015b, table 5.1)

Taken together, our findings suggest that the public would support stricter look-back limits on prior convictions, especially for juvenile offenses.

C. Our Proposed Model

Based on the survey of existing rules in Part A, and the discussion of sentencing-purpose rationales and public opinion in Part B, our model contains the following look-back and gap rules and related procedures.

1. 10-year Unconditional Felony Look-Back Limit

All guidelines systems should adopt an unconditional look-back limit of 10 years applicable to all felonies (with shorter periods for misdemeanors and juvenile offenses, if they are counted at all—see further discussion in the next chapter). A felony should no longer be counted in sentencing a new crime committed 10 or more years later, regardless of whether the offender remained crime-free or was incarcerated during some or all of that period. If a jurisdiction wishes to exclude serious prior crimes from the 10-year limit, this should require very clear and strong justification. The 10-year unconditional limit is based on our view that prior record enhancements are primarily justified by their correlation with offender recidivism risk, and on research suggesting that older convictions add little additional risk-predictive value to the criminal history score. This diminished predictive value most likely results from the fact that older convictions typically reflect an earlier, more crime-prone phase of the offender's life. Strict look-back limits also find support in the results of our public opinion research—three-quarters of respondents favored an unconditional look-back limit of 10 years or less. The public apparently does not view older convictions as relevant under either a risk-prediction or a retributive theory.

Given the declining risk rationale, the starting point for this rule would ideally be the date of commission of the prior crime; however, it may be necessary to use the date of conviction or sentencing for that crime, if information on prior offense dates is often not available or sufficiently reliable. The 10-year unconditional look-back limit can be expressed in absolute terms or as a strong presumption permitting the prosecution to argue for an exception (based, for example, on evidence of a steady stream of further offending during the intervening period, or that the offender was incarcerated for most of that time and shows no signs of having changed his or her criminal ways). An absolute limit is easier for courts to apply, but has the defects of any absolute rule.

2. Seven-Year Any-Gap Rule

In addition to the unconditional look-back rule stated previously, all guidelines systems should also adopt a seven-year any-gap rule with no possibility of later revival, for all prior felony convictions (again, with shorter gap periods for misdemeanors and juvenile offenses, if they are counted at all). If an offender manages to remain crime-free for that many years, the conviction and all earlier convictions should no longer be counted in any later sentencings. This rule is likewise based on a risk prediction rationale, and finds support in research showing that offenders with a crime-free gap of seven or more years have much lower recidivism risk than offenders with shorter gaps. The starting point for this rule could be either the date of sentencing or the point at which the offender is free in the community and at risk of committing further crimes. The former rule allows the seven-year clock to run while the offender is serving time in prison, instead of starting when he or she is released. The arguments for this more generous gap rule are, first, that aging alone predicts a decline in the offender's risk level, and second, that he could have offended while in prison. Moreover, if we are to assume that his risk level is unchanged after 10 years of detention, the state has as much to answer as the offender.

We recommend the any-gap rule, rather than a recent-gap rule, for several reasons that were discussed at greater length in earlier Sections, all of which have to do with the former's broader exclusionary scope (an any-gap rule is triggered by any qualifying gap, whether that gap immediately preceded the current sentencing or occurred between two crimes committed years earlier). First, in comparison to a rule limited to recent crime-free gaps, an any-gap rule with no possibility of later revival gives offenders a stronger incentive to remain crime-free in the years following each conviction. Second, if an offender succeeds in remaining crime-free for a lengthy period following a conviction, she deserves to be rewarded by having that conviction permanently erased. Third, a recent-gap rule that permits revival of previously lapsed convictions will inevitably allow many very old convictions to be counted.

The different ways in which any-gap and recent-gap rules apply can be illustrated with the following case, which, for simplicity, assumes that for each type of look-back rule the clock starts to run on the date that each offense was committed. Our hypothetical offender commits crime #1, goes *eight years* crime-free before committing crime #2, goes another *eight years* before committing crime #3, and then goes *six years* before committing crime #4. These four crimes can be diagrammed as follows:

Crime-1 ---------------- Crime-2 ---------------- Crime-3 ------------ Crime-4
8-year gap 8-year gap 6-year gap

Under a seven-year any-gap rule without the possibility of revival, the offender has no prior record at his sentencings for crimes #2 and #3, and one prior conviction when sentenced for crime #4. Under a seven-year recent-gap rule subject to later revival, the offender likewise has no prior record when sentenced for crimes #2 and #3; but at his sentencing for crime #4, all three of his prior crimes would be counted, including a crime committed 22 years earlier!

3. *Gradual Decay Rules in Place of All-At-Once Washout*

Guidelines should adopt one or more true "decay" rules that gradually reduce the weight of prior convictions with the passage of time, in order to more precisely match the size of criminal history enhancements to the declining risk-predictive value (and perhaps, the declining culpability relevance) of older convictions. Of course, a literal "decay" rule would be more difficult to apply than the simple all-at-once washout rules that are currently in place, under which a prior conviction counts fully and then suddenly ceases to count at all. Accordingly, in order to simplify application of the decay concept, a step-wise rule could be adopted, for example: a prior conviction receives half its normal weight when half of the 10-year unconditional look-back period has elapsed, or half of the seven-year crime-free gap period.

4. *Judicial Power to Disregard Old but Not-Yet-Lapsed Priors*

Guidelines systems should expressly give judges discretion to depart downward from the recommended sentence, and/or ignore specific older convictions, in cases where the inclusion of such convictions in criminal history under generally applicable look-back and gap rules overstates the offender's current degree of risk and/or current culpability.[28] An example would be a case in which the offender's life has changed so radically that the earlier conviction(s) have no material significance with respect to her current level of recidivism risk or her level of blameworthiness for the current crime. Even without such a change in the offender's life, judges should have authority to waive or discount criminal history enhancements when the offender offers substantial evidence of progress toward desistance (even though that progress has been interrupted by commission of the current offense). Otherwise ex-offenders have less incentive to reform, and reformation is, after all, a desired outcome of any sentence.

5. *Empirical Validation of Look-Back and Starting-Point Rules*

Each guidelines system should use empirical data to validate the assumptions of declining risk or whatever other rationale that system has adopted to justify its criminal history enhancements, look-back, and/or gap rules, as well as the applicable clock-starting points. Validation research for risk-predictive value, based on recidivism data, is fairly straightforward; as we discussed in chapter 2, similar research (albeit not addressed to look-back rules) has been done for several guidelines systems. Validation for retributive value will be more difficult to design and defend, but perhaps could be based on public opinion research. Validation based on deterrence will be the most difficult of all (and may be impossible given the inherent difficulties and meager past results of such research, as discussed in chapter 4).

Conclusion

Most U.S. guidelines systems replace individualized determination of sentencing factors with relatively rigid counting rules.[29] With respect to criminal history, offenders with potentially very different risks of re-offending are assigned to the same criminal history category, and the absence of look-back limits in many guidelines systems compounds this over-aggregation problem. The problem is worsened by the absence, in almost all American guidelines systems, of rules expressly allowing judges to depart based on the imperfections of criminal history scoring as applied in the particular case.

To prevent the offender's criminal history score from overstating his current recidivism risk and/or culpability, guidelines systems should adopt unconditional or at least presumptive look-back limits based solely on the passage of time, combined with additional washout rules triggered by shorter periods (gaps) with no new convictions. Both absolute limits and gap rules should incorporate some form of true "decay" principle, reducing the weight of a prior conviction over time, rather than the all-at-once washout approach used in existing rules. Judges should also be given discretion to ignore a prior conviction and/or depart downward from the recommended sentence when one or more older convictions, even though not yet washed out under that system's look-back and gap rules, cause the criminal history score to overstate the offender's current risk and/or culpability, or when mitigation is appropriate in order to recognize and reward progress toward desistance.

10 PROBLEMATIC COMPONENTS FOUND IN MANY CRIMINAL HISTORY FORMULAS

Criminal histories can be complex in nature. Offenders with multiple prior convictions will often have a mix of offenses, differing in timing, seriousness, their relationship to each other, and other variables. Courts in jurisdictions without guidelines must interpret the dimensions of criminal record in order to determine the magnitude and nature of any enhancement (Wasik 1987). Guidelines do much of the work for courts by stipulating counting rules that define and assign weight to different dimensions or components.

The focus of this chapter is upon components of existing criminal history scores that are problematic from the perspective of risk, retribution, or both rationales. Under most guidelines an offender's criminal history score reflects multiple components including the number, seriousness, and age of prior convictions, and sometimes other elements. According to point-based guidelines, each criminal history component attracts one or more criminal history points, and these in turn trigger a more severe sentence: a higher score usually increases the recommended prison duration, and the offender may also be pushed into the recommended-prison zone of the sentencing grid. When the latter occurs, the offender is being imprisoned solely because of his prior crimes, without which he would have received a community-based penalty for his current offense.

Each criminal history component should have demonstrated relevance to the offender's risk of re-offending and her level of blameworthiness. And even if this has been demonstrated, the relative weight assigned to each dimension remains to be determined. For example, should a previous conviction similar to the current conviction carry more weight than a dissimilar prior? Should prior juvenile court adjudications receive the same weight as adult crimes, or even be considered at all?

This chapter explores five common criminal history score components whose inclusion is questionable or that carry too much weight. By "questionable" we mean that their inclusion cannot be justified on grounds of heightened risk or blameworthiness. Part A examines the common practice of counting juvenile court adjudications in an adult offender's criminal history score. We document the ways that different guidelines jurisdictions incorporate juvenile priors, as well as the retributive and preventive justifications for considering juvenile offenses when sentencing an adult. Part B considers the inclusion of misdemeanor priors in criminal history, and the problems this raises. Part C turns to the offender's "custody status" when he committed the offense being sentenced—whether he was incarcerated or on some form of criminal justice release. We examine the role that custody status plays across the jurisdictions examined in this book, and evaluate the significance of this factor from retributive and risk-based perspectives. Part D addresses the practice of according extra weight to prior offenses that were similar to the offense being sentenced—what we will refer to as a "patterning" premium. Again, we describe existing rules and evaluate the relevance of patterning from retributive and preventive perspectives. In Part E, we examine the common practice of weighting prior felony convictions according to their seriousness, with an emphasis on the problems associated with substantial upweighting of more serious priors. Part F presents data from a state, Minnesota, in which four of these problematic components (all except patterning) are potentially included in every offender's criminal history score. We show how these components, individually and together, greatly increase the duration of recommended prison terms, and the proportion of offenders recommended for an executed-prison sentence.

For all five of these aspects of prior and current offending, we conclude that routine inclusion in guidelines criminal history scores lacks strong justification in terms of offender culpability, crime prevention, or both, and thus results in over-punishment of the offender while also producing a number of adverse effects. Accordingly, all five are excluded from our model outlined in the next chapter. However, we will suggest some more limited ways in which each of these components might properly be taken into account.

A. Juvenile Court Adjudications

Throughout this volume we have identified reasons to restrict the influence on sentencing outcomes of certain prior convictions or dimensions of prior offending. Sometimes the reason is that the given conviction or dimension of offending is insufficiently related to risk or culpability to justify its weight in the sentencing equation. Other reasons relate to the adverse consequences of counting certain priors, even if they do help predict re-offending and/or increase culpability. With respect to juvenile adjudications, the reasons to restrain the aggravating effect of prior convictions are particularly compelling. Some would argue that if a prior conviction carries some predictive or retributive significance it should be counted—regardless of whether the offender was a juvenile at the time of the crime. On this view, the inclusion of a given juvenile prior would be determined by its strength as a predictor, and that prior would no longer be considered in adult sentencing hearings as soon as it ceased to predict re-offending. A conflicting view holds that juvenile priors should automatically expire when the offender reaches the age of adulthood. In our view, there are strong reasons to adopt the latter approach, which we shall shortly explore. First however, we describe the varying ways that juvenile priors are considered in guidelines systems.

1. *Current Practices*

American guidelines systems generally steer a middle course between the two views described previously, neither counting all juvenile priors nor excluding them all. Only one jurisdiction (North Carolina) makes no use of juvenile convictions in its criminal history calculation; all of the 17 other state and federal guidelines systems with some sort of criminal history score count juvenile priors but, in various ways, circumscribe their influence relative to adult prior convictions. Mitchell (2015b) reports that the varying approaches to this policy issue include the following:

- Limiting juvenile adjudications by offense type: eight jurisdictions (e.g., Washington) count only prior felonies; others count only the more serious prior adjudications or only offenses for which the juvenile could have been tried as an adult (e.g., Arkansas).
- Capping the number of criminal history points that can be assigned for juvenile priors (e.g., the federal guidelines).
- Under-weighting juvenile priors—for example by assigning half the criminal history points scored for a similar adult crime (e.g., Utah).
- Applying shorter look-back (decay, lapse, washout) periods for juvenile offenses (e.g., Washington, DC).
- Counting juvenile priors only until the adult offender reaches a certain age, after which juvenile priors will no longer count. In Maryland for example, juvenile priors cease to count when the individual turns 23.

2. *Retributivism and Juvenile Priors*

As was noted in chapter 1, only a few retributive scholars consider *any* previous conviction relevant at sentencing. And although retributive scholarship does not often separately address the issue of juvenile priors, it would appear that any retributive justification for PRE is even weaker in this context than for adult prior convictions. As the Supreme Court has recognized in several cases, juveniles are categorically less culpable than adult offenders due to their incomplete cognitive and emotional development, vulnerability to peer pressure, and limited control over their living arrangements.[1] This judicial recognition of diminished juvenile culpability raises serious questions about the fairness of using juvenile priors to enhance adult sentences. Those doubts are particularly strong when the offender makes his first appearance in adult criminal court. Many scholars believe that first offenders are less culpable than recidivists, and that therefore less censure is warranted at the first sentencing (e.g., Roberts 2010a). An adult offender with only juvenile priors can argue that upon attaining adulthood he should be able to reclaim his first offender status. In addition, the more limited procedural due process afforded in most juvenile court proceedings raises issues of reliability as well as fairness, when juvenile priors are used to enhance adult sentences. Finally, as reported in chapter 9, recent opinion research shows very little public support for the practice of considering juvenile adjudications when sentencing adults, even adults still in their twenties.

3. *Juvenile Priors as Predictors of Adult Offending*

Although some long-standing risk assessment tools include all juvenile court adjudications (see chapter 3 for further details), research casts doubt on this practice. Studies of criminal careers have found that the strongest juvenile-record risk factor is "early onset," as measured by the age of the first recorded delinquency (see, e.g., Piquero et al. 2007, 73, noting that offenders with a first conviction prior to age 14 had longer criminal careers, with many more convictions). Yet guidelines criminal history scores generally either include juvenile adjudications regardless of the age at which they occurred, or include only *later* adjudications (e.g., those entered at age 14 or older). Two sentencing commissions have recently examined the risk predictive value of counting juvenile priors, and appeared to reach opposite conclusions. The Pennsylvania Sentencing Commission found that, for most offenders, prior juvenile court adjudications were associated with higher adult recidivism risk; accordingly, all but one of the Commission's 10 proposed risk prediction tools includes a point for this factor (2018b, §§ 305.7(a), 305.7(b)).

In contrast, a project to validate the risk-predictive value of each component of the Minnesota guidelines criminal history score found that the score was equally predictive of recidivism with and without inclusion of juvenile court adjudications (Laskorunsky 2018). The latter finding is consistent with a major premise of the Supreme Court decisions, cited previously: that juveniles are more likely than adults to change due to maturation. On the basis of risk, then, juvenile priors represent an uncertain criminal history score component, and one that may be outweighed by the normative objections noted previously. As discussed later on in the chapter, it is also important to apply adult sentencing rules that encourage, rather than undercut, the capacity for change by youthful offenders.

4. Desistance and a Fresh Start

The importance of a fresh start in life is well-recognized in the literature on the processes of desistance from crime. One of the principal impediments to moral and personal transformation is continued stigmatization of the individual. All jurisdictions provide a mechanism by which ex-offenders may establish themselves as persons with full standing in the community. Juvenile prior convictions should be set within this conceptual framework. The transition to adulthood permits ex-offenders to shake off their juvenile transgressions, and to start life afresh as an adult.

A second conceptual framework engages the psychology of human behavior. There are important limitations on the effectiveness of punishment as a means to achieve lasting behavioral change. Put simply, punishment alone is an ineffective way of changing people. This is true as a general proposition, but carries particular resonance in the domain of juvenile offending. Young offenders are generally insensitive to threats of punishment; much of their criminal behavior is a failure to adequately consider the future consequences of offending. Punishment is most effective when the cause of the behavior is wholly a function of the individual decision-maker. Yet environmental factors such as peer pressure and substance abuse play such an influential role in the etiology of juvenile offending that in many cases even very stringent punishments prove ineffective in achieving compliance.

The existence of a separate criminal justice and sentencing regime for young offenders also argues against considering juvenile priors in adult sentencing proceedings. The conditions prevalent when the individual was a juvenile have often changed; the legal framework in which the offender is prosecuted and punished has also changed. Counting juvenile priors against the adult offender flies in the face of this separation of sentencing regimes.

Summary

The policy arguments summarized in this Part help to explain the ambivalent approach of American guidelines, with most schemes counting juvenile priors while limiting their impact. This compromise should be rejected, however. When an individual attains adulthood, juvenile court adjudications should be expunged for the purposes of future sentencing. Excluding juvenile priors from the criminal history score will cause little if any loss in the score's predictive efficacy, and the reduced-culpability, reduced-procedural-safeguards, and desistance-based critiques are compelling. For these reasons we generally exclude juvenile priors from our model criminal history scoring rules. In exceptional cases, a court might be accorded the power to aggravate the adult sentence to reflect juvenile priors. However, any such power should be narrowly tailored to ensure that only the most serious juvenile priors are considered, and only when they suggest an unbroken course of criminal conduct into adulthood. Moreover, this exceptional power to enhance based on juvenile priors should only apply to the sentencing of young adults.

B. Adult Misdemeanor Convictions

Much of the description and policy discussion above also applies to the inclusion of adult misdemeanor convictions in adult criminal history scoring (for a more detailed discussion, see Mitchell 2015c). Sixteen guidelines systems (all but Delaware and Tennessee) count at least some misdemeanor priors, but only three systems count all of them; the other 13 systems exclude minor traffic crimes or all minor crimes. In addition, 13 of the 16 systems weight misdemeanors less than felonies; 9 systems "cap" criminal history points added for misdemeanors; some systems do not count them when deciding which offenders fall into the highest criminal history categories; and most systems that count misdemeanors and have rules excluding older priors, apply shorter look-back periods than are applied to felonies.

As with juvenile priors, however, these compromises should be rejected. By definition, misdemeanor offending is less culpable than felony-level criminality, and like juvenile courts, procedural safeguards (e.g., appointed counsel, jury trial, pretrial discovery rules) are often weak or entirely lacking when misdemeanor convictions are pled to or proved at trial. Nor does a prior misdemeanor conviction or even several of them indicate an elevated risk of serious future crime—the Minnesota recidivism study mentioned above found that adding misdemeanor priors to that state's criminal history score only slightly increased the score's risk-predictive power (Laskorunsky 2018). This result is consistent with self-report studies (see, e.g., Baxter 2017; Gilman et al. 2014), showing that most people commit minor criminal violations at some point (and almost everyone violates traffic laws). For all of these reasons, prior adult misdemeanors should be excluded from adult criminal history scoring in all but the most exceptional cases (for example: when serious misdemeanor-level offending is related to one or more proven felony crimes).

C. Custody Status

Many guidelines systems add one or more points to the criminal history score if the offense being sentenced was committed while the defendant was in a post-conviction release status such as probation or post-prison release (parole); some jurisdictions also count pretrial release, and/or various incarceration or escape statuses. A substantial portion of sentenced offenders fall into one of these categories. According to the Bureau of Justice Statistics (BJS 2013, table 6), almost one-fifth of felony offenders prosecuted in large urban counties in 2009 were on probation or parole at the time of their arrest. In the federal system, about one-quarter of offenders sentenced in fiscal year 2016 had additional criminal history points added based on custody status (USSC 2017c, table 20). Sentencing data for Minnesota in recent years show that about 40 percent of sentenced felons have one or two custody status points in their criminal history scores.

Common law jurisdictions outside of the United States also impose a severity premium to reflect the fact that the offender was under some form of judicial order (bail, probation, parole) when the crime was committed. For example, in England and Wales, section 153(3) of the Criminal Justice Act 2003 states that "in considering the seriousness of any offense committed while the offender was on bail, the court must treat the fact that it was committed in those circumstances as an aggravating factor." As well, the English sentencing guidelines include "offense committed while on licence" (i.e., post-prison release) as a factor "increasing seriousness" (Sentencing Guidelines Council 2004, 6). However, in 2014 (the most recent year for which data were available) committing an offense while on bail had a negligible effect on actual sentence severity, and the aggravating effect of committing the offense while on licence was modest.[2]

Comparable analyses derived directly from judges' decisions have rarely been conducted in the United States, but the available evidence suggests that custody status carries significantly more weight in American guidelines sentencing. This appears to be a continuation of pre-guidelines practices, under which American courts imposed a more severe sentence when the offender was under some form of judicial order.[3] Several features set American guidelines systems apart, and cause custody status to have greater weight in these systems than in other common law jurisdictions. First, many American guidelines define custody status broadly, including pretrial release and/or crimes committed while the offender was incarcerated or in escape status (Roberts 2015a, table 9.1). Second, under some guidelines, custody status carries the same weight as some or all prior felony convictions; it is very doubtful that this equivalence of weight can be justified in terms of desert or dangerousness.

Third, most American guidelines include custody status in the criminal history calculation, rather than treating this circumstance as an aggravating factor at sentencing that courts may apply in their discretion. Thus, custody status under guidelines automatically triggers an increase in the offender's score and recommended sentence severity; in other common law systems courts may disregard this circumstance if there are sound reasons it should not be considered.[4] Presumably American guidelines jurisdictions adopted a points-based approach to promote greater consistency of application. We shall argue, however, that this consistency comes at a price, namely of a loss of individualization and a degree of over-punishment.

In short, custody status under American guidelines affects more offenders and has a greater sentence-enhancing effect than in non-guidelines systems. We see principled and practical objections to the inclusion of custody status in the criminal history equation. The principled objection concerns the assumption that committing an offense while under court order *always* enhances the offender's culpability for the current crime and/or his or her level of recidivism risk, and does so to the same degree in all circumstances—if this factor is included in the criminal history score, all offenders in this category will have their recommended sentences enhanced. We argue that a better approach is to treat custody status as an aggravating circumstance that courts may consider along with other relevant circumstances. As indicated in Section C.1, several American guidelines systems have taken the aggravating-factor approach, in lieu of added criminal history points or other rigid formulas.

1. *Custody Status in Guidelines Systems*

The majority of American guidelines jurisdictions incorporate custody status in the criminal history calculation, although these 11 systems display significant variation in terms of two key issues: the *categories* of court order included, and the *weight* that custody status attracts as a component of the criminal history score (Roberts 2015a, table 9.1). Six other jurisdiction treat custody status as an aggravating factor or as a basis for required consecutive sentencing,[5] and two jurisdictions (Oregon and Pennsylvania) have no explicit custody status enhancement provision.

Jurisdictions that include custody status in their criminal history calculation define such status and assign additional criminal history points in a variety of ways, for example:

- In Florida, four additional sentence points are added if the defendant was under any form of pretrial intervention or diversion program, or court-imposed or post-prison release community supervision.[6]
- Washington State assigns one extra criminal history point if the offense was committed while the offender was under post-conviction community supervision.[7]
- Under the federal guidelines, two criminal history points are assigned if the instant offense was committed while under any criminal justice sentence, including probation, parole, supervised release, imprisonment, work release, or escape status (USSC 2016a, Section 4A1.1(d)).

In some jurisdictions custody status carries the same or almost as much weight as a prior adult felony conviction. In Minnesota, for example, prior felonies are assigned different numbers of criminal history points depending upon their severity level (MSGC 2017a, Section 2.B.1). For offenders sentenced on the main grid, .5 point is added for a prior felony at seriousness level 1 or 2, 1 point at levels 3 to 5, 1.5 points at levels 6 to 8, and 2 points at levels 9 to 11. Custody status generally adds 1 point, but adds 2 points for some repeat sex offenders. One point is equivalent to the weight of a prior felony at main grid level 5 (e.g., unarmed robbery), and sometimes (since half points are disregarded in the total point score) it is the equivalent of a prior felony ranked as high as level 8 (armed robbery). Two points is equivalent to the weight given to some forcible rapes. This level of enhancement for custody status is hard to justify—the enhanced risk or culpability arising from committing a crime while on probation is surely not the equivalent of a prior felony deemed to be of medium or medium-high seriousness. In other guidelines systems custody status carries significantly less weight than a prior felony. For example, in North Carolina custody status adds a single criminal history point, whereas prior felonies add 2, 4, 6, 9, or 10 points—in that state, custody status never carries more than half the weight of a prior felony, and compared to most felonies it carries a small fraction of the weight (North Carolina Sentencing and Policy Advisory Commission 2014).

2. *Custody Status and Retributivism*

An offender who commits an offense while still serving a previous sentence might strike many people as being more blameworthy, but this is an example of penal intuitionism. That is, it seems appropriate to impose additional punishment, although the specific ground for doing so remains unstated.

A leading authority on the Minnesota guidelines has asserted that an offender "deserves greater punishment if he committed a new crime before completing service of a previous sentence" (Parent 1988, 70). But the reasons underlying this conclusion remain unclear. Ashworth (2015, 166) notes that custody status (e.g., released on bail) "does not increase the harm caused by the offense, nor does it increase the culpability of the offender in relation to that crime." He ascribes the use of this factor as an aggravating circumstance to perceived defiance of the court that imposed the order, or a breach of trust placed in the offender who was allowed to remain in the community on bail, probation, or parole. Alternatively, there may be a desire to punish the offender for being the kind of person who violates criminal laws. But these cannot be deemed retributive considerations unless they can somehow be related to the seriousness of the current offense. Under any of these rationales, it is very questionable whether additional punishment is justified on desert grounds, particularly when the offender's custody status carries as much weight as a previous felony (see previous discussion).[8]

In some cases a crime committed in custody status may indeed seem more serious in light of the previously imposed court order. An offender who while serving a community sentence for assault commits a fresh assault is arguably more blameworthy for his latest assault than, for example, if the same offender were to commit tax evasion while on probation for assault. In the former case, committing a crime while on probation for the same type of offense violates the conditions of a judicial order; it is a serious form of breach, and the offender may be sanctioned by revocation of probation or tightening of release conditions. But in the latter case, why should the fact that the offender was on probation for assault enhance the sentence for a new offense of tax evasion? As noted previously, the harm of the latest offense is unaffected by custody status, and it is hard to see how the offender's culpability for the tax violation is affected.

3. *Custody Status and Crime Prevention*

Sentence enhancements based on custody status could also be justified if being on probation or parole at the time of the current offense indicates an increased likelihood of future crime. An assumption of higher risk is plausible, given that the offender was unwilling to obey the law even when under official supervision; in addition, custody status usually means the offender has at least one recent conviction, which, in turn, suggests that the offender's criminal career is still "active." If there is a link between custody status and risk, then further questions arise as to the *weight* that this factor should carry, and whether different forms of custody status should all attract the same level of sentence enhancement. To answer these questions we need to examine the empirical research into recidivism. We first explore the role that custody status carries in existing risk prediction scales. Most of these instruments were developed after years of validation research, using multiple, independent samples of cases. For this reason, one might expect custody status to be included as a variable, yet it often is not. Second, we review the limited empirical research that has explored the relationship between custody status and subsequent re-offending.[9]

a. Custody Status as a Component of Recidivism Risk Instruments

Given that well over half of guidelines systems include custody status as a criminal history factor, it is surprising to find that several of the most well-known risk assessment scales do not include this variable.[10] The Level of Service Inventory Revised [LSI-R], perhaps the most widely used actuarial risk assessment tool in sentencing, contains 54 items relative to all domains relevant to re-offending. Several versions of this instrument have been developed and validated over the past 30 years. The latest version of the LSI-R—the Level of Service/ Case Management Inventory (LS/CMI)—contains eight criminal history items in its criminal history subcomponent but custody status is not included, although a related factor, prior violations of release conditions, is included (Andrews et al. 2004).[11] The California Static Risk Assessment (CSRA) is one of the more recent risk prediction instruments, and it also omits custody status (although, again, it includes a measure of prior sentence or release condition violations). Since the search for risk-related variables has generated a great deal of research, the omission of custody status from widely used predictive devices raises questions about the validity of this component of the criminal history score.

b. Limited Validation Research by Commissions or Outside Researchers

As noted previously, the U.S. Sentencing Commission has attempted to validate the risk-predictive value of all components of the federal guidelines criminal history score, including custody status (U.S. Sentencing Commission 2005). The guidelines custody status factor emerged as a much weaker predictor of re-offending than other dimensions of criminal history (such as the number of prior convictions).[12] To our knowledge, the only other guidelines system with data on the risk predictive value of custody status is Minnesota, where it was found that adding custody status to the state's criminal history score only slightly increased the score's ability to predict recidivism (Laskorunsky 2018). Thus, while most guidelines use custody status as a criminal history component, this usage remains largely unsupported by validation research in guidelines jurisdictions.

4. *Categories of Custody Status*

Perhaps for the sake of operational simplicity and consistency, custody status enhancements are insensitive to important variations between offenders, and between categories of legal status. Yet fresh offending may vary in its significance depending upon the nature of the custody status.

An important distinction is whether *any* form of court order should be included, or whether only post-conviction custody status should count. Jurisdictions that include custody status as a criminal history factor are relatively evenly divided on this point: about half (e.g., Arkansas) consider pretrial custody status and half (e.g., the federal system) exclude it (Roberts 2015a). Both retributive and risk-based justifications for a custody status premium could plausibly distinguish between pre- and post-conviction statuses. As we noted in chapter 1, culpability-based justifications for *any* prior record enhancement seem unconvincing. But if increased culpability is the rationale, it is arguably appropriate to assign a sentencing premium based on the custody status of being on probation or parole, but not when the offender was under pretrial supervision. When an offender is serving a sentence in the community, committing a fresh offense seems naturally aggravating; this justification does not apply to defendants on bail, for whom the presumption of innocence remains in effect.[13] It also seems likely that convicted offenders who commit crimes while on probation or parole are at higher risk of recidivism than charged but unconvicted offenders who commit crimes while on bail; however, that is a matter that must be resolved by empirical research, which, to our knowledge, has not been done in any jurisdiction.

Guidelines jurisdictions also differ as to whether incarceration is a qualifying status. Again, pretrial detention seems distinguishable, since the offender is still presumed innocent. Indeed, even if the offender's current offense was committed in post-conviction detention, this is arguably not an indicator of either heightened culpability or higher risk, given the stressful and artificial nature of incarceration (and, in the case of crimes committed against another inmate, problems of proof). Finally, to the extent that custody status enhancements are intended as a further deterrent, crimes by prison and jail inmates can be sanctioned sooner and more directly through denial of privileges, good-conduct credits, and/or parole release.

5. *Timing, Seriousness, and Similarity of the New Offense*

The timing of an offense committed while in a release status is important—the current offense may have been committed very early, or very late, in the supervision period. An offender who commits an offense shortly after commencing a community sentence is arguably more blameworthy and/or a higher risk than one who re-offends near the end of that sentence, particularly if the period of supervision was very long or the offender's new offense occurred after almost completing a community sentence.[14] In the latter case, courts should be allowed to mitigate the impact of custody status or even disregard this element. If consideration of the timing of the current offense within the release period is viewed as unduly complicating criminal history calculations it would be better to exclude this factor from the criminal history score. Similarly, the seriousness of the current offense may call into question the imposition of a custody status enhancement. For example, conviction of a low seriousness crime while on parole may trigger a custody status enhancement that is excessive relative to the offender's culpability for the latest offense and his risk of future crime. Custody status formulas are insensitive to this important distinction.

In each of the ways discussed, the inclusion of custody status in criminal history computations results in an undifferentiated approach that assigns the same additional punishment no matter which legal status was infringed, how soon the violation occurred, how serious the current offense is, and how similar it is to the prior offense.

Summary

The manner in which custody status is incorporated in many U.S. guidelines—by the addition of one or more criminal history points—is too rigid, too broad, and inevitably results for some offenders in the imposition of more punishment than can be justified. At a minimum, pretrial custody statuses should be disregarded because of the presumption of innocence. As to post-conviction custody statuses, this component is unlike other dimensions of criminal history and there are compelling reasons to treat it differently. First, it is a *single application* enhancement. A prior felony conviction counts against the offender at all subsequent sentencing decisions (as long as the conviction remains within the "look-back" period); custody status applies only to the current sentencing, which suggests that it should be treated as an *offense-related* aggravating factor. Second, even if custody status is deemed to enhance offense culpability (which is contestable) and/or to predict higher risk (for which there is limited research validation), the categorical imposition of additional punishment fails to distinguish between different forms and circumstances of the custody status, which is inconsistent with an individualized determination of culpability and risk factors by a sentencing court. When other aggravating offense and risk factors are considered, their relevance and weight are determined by the court on an individual basis.

Another reason to avoid the use of routine, formulaic custody-status enhancements is that they may duplicate, or prevent, other more appropriate sanctions. Violating conditions of probation or post-prison release is generally subject to revocation or other sanctions independent of any sentencing enhancement for subsequent offending; crimes committed while incarcerated or after escaping from custody, are likewise subject to other sanctions. Similar considerations led the Pennsylvania guidelines commission to exclude custody status from its criminal history calculations: first, defendants who had already had their probation or parole revoked would be penalized twice for the same conduct, and second, including custody status in the criminal history calculation for a fresh offense may inhibit prosecutors from pursuing revocation sanctions when those might be more appropriate (Pennsylvania Commission on Sentencing 1988, 48).

Removing custody status as a categorical criminal history enhancement may result in less consistent application of this potentially aggravating factor. Yet the inclusion of custody status in criminal history promotes a false consistency, disregarding individual circumstances and important variables such as the nature of the prior court order and the timing of the status violation. The degree of additional punishment should be calibrated to reflect important differences between forms of custody status and relevant offender characteristics. For example, the court can consider the extent to which this circumstance increases the offender's culpability (however, we would favor keeping any such enhancement within strict limits, for example, within the applicable guidelines grid cell or other non-departure sentencing range). This leaves it open to the court to withhold any additional punishment—for example, because the fresh offense was committed very close to expiry of the previous court order, following a protracted period of compliance with the conditions attached to the previous order. If custody status is excluded from the criminal history score, this circumstance can still be taken into account at sentencing. The offender committing an offense while on probation or parole may be revoked to prison, or the offender can be sentenced more harshly for the current offense by treating this factor as an aggravating circumstance at sentencing. Custody status involving a violation of prior release conditions would seem to be a particularly relevant factor when deciding whether the offender should be given a community-based sentence.[15]

D. Similarity of Prior to Current Offending

Imagine two co-accused, convicted of burglary, both of whom have one previous conviction. Offender A has a prior burglary while Offender B has a prior felony conviction for a very different type of crime. Should these two criminal history profiles be treated the same? As discussed later on in this Section, some guidelines systems overweight prior convictions for the same crime or offense category as the current conviction. Is this appropriate?

When the current offense is the same as, or similar to the prior convictions, sentencing schemes around the world sometimes impose a harsher sentence. Courts in non-guidelines jurisdictions are often given statutory directions to consider the relationship between the current and prior convictions when deciding whether and how much to aggravate the sentence. For example, in England and Wales courts are told to consider the relationship between the previous and current offenses (Criminal Justice Act 2003, Sec. 143(2)), although this leaves unanswered the question of why and how similar prior convictions are more relevant than dissimilar priors. Wasik (1987, 107) cites the similarity of previous offenses to the current offense as one of eight dimensions of criminal record "likely to be perceived by the sentencer as relevant." More recently he describes the similarity of prior to current offense as one of the "main dimensions of a record" (Wasik 2010, 181), and it appears that the courts do treat similar previous convictions as more relevant to sentencing. But the reasons for seeing them as more relevant are not articulated.

When guideline systems impose greater sentence enhancements for the repeat offender who commits the same or similar offense than when the prior and current crimes are of different types, we refer to this as a "patterning" premium. We will first summarize the different patterning rules found in American guidelines systems, then consider the punishment rationales such rules might serve, and the adverse consequences.

1. *Patterning in American Guidelines*

Considerable variability exists in the way that patterning rules apply; many guidelines jurisdictions lack any formal rule based on the similarity between prior and current offending, and no guideline system applies patterning across all offense categories (Roberts 2015c).[16] Six of 19 guidelines jurisdictions—Arkansas, District of Columbia, the federal courts, Maryland, Massachusetts, and Michigan—recognize no patterning premium of any kind. In eight states—Alabama, Kansas, Minnesota, Ohio, Oregon, Pennsylvania, Tennessee, and Utah—patterning rules are defined in very broad terms, usually providing enhancement when the past and the current offenses are both "person," "violent," high-severity, property, or sex crimes. For example, in Pennsylvania, the two highest criminal history categories are reserved for offenders with designated combinations of violent or very serious prior and current offenses. Three states—Florida, Virginia, and Washington—have patterning rules that only apply to specific crimes (for example: grand theft auto, in Florida; burglary, in Washington).[17] Under the North Carolina guidelines, one additional criminal history point is added if all elements of the current offense are included in any prior offense (which means that the enhancement only applies when the current offense is identical to or *less serious*[18] than the prior offense). In Delaware, if the offender has two or more prior convictions or juvenile adjudications for the same or a similar crime, this is listed as an aggravating factor but is not included in criminal history scoring.

2. *Offense Similarity and Retributive Perspectives*

Some retributivists may see similarity between prior and current offending as an indication of higher culpability. A pattern of similar crimes arguably suggests that the offender is particularly indifferent to, or acting in defiance of, the prior sentence(s) of the court, thus increasing his level of blameworthiness for the current offense—despite having previously been formally censured for this very behavior, he has gone and done it again! But this rationale is contestable; as was noted in chapter 1, defiance theories are incompatible with the core principle that an offender is punished for his culpable criminal acts, not for his bad "attitude."

Patterning enhancements may also find support in retributive justifications for PRE based on the repeat offender's heightened "notice" of illegality—an offender cannot claim she didn't know her behavior was wrong or illegal if she has previously been convicted and sanctioned for that very behavior. But as previously discussed, notice theories are implausible when applied to serious crimes, and they are also inconsistent with the general principle that citizens (including first offenders) are assumed to know the law.

A patterning premium might also be justified under Youngjae Lee's culpable-omission theory of PRE (2009, 2010; see chapter 1 for further details). Lee argues that repeat offenders are more blameworthy for having failed to address the causes of their offending. For example, an offender convicted of fraud who has a previous fraud conviction is arguably more culpable than an offender who is also now convicted of fraud but whose prior conviction was for assault. The former offender has evidently failed to address his tendency to commit a particular type of crime; moreover, his duty to address that tendency is stronger because the State has called attention (by the prior conviction and sanction) to the crime and, perhaps the specific causes of that crime. But again, there are problems with this rationale. How can courts reliably determine that similar crimes had similar underlying causes? Also, can the court find or simply assume that the offender *could have* overcome those causes if he had made more strenuous efforts? And can offenders be punished for omission to address crime causes when the law has declared no express legal duty to do so?

Andrew von Hirsch's "lapse" theory (discussed in chapter 1) may also ascribe some relevance to the question of offense similarity. It will be recalled that unlike Lee and other theorists, von Hirsch's theory does not relate to culpability. Rather, he sees the reduced punishment extended to first offenders as a way of treating the offender as a moral agent "by giving him the opportunity to make the requisite effort of will [to desist]," while also showing some tolerance for "the human tendency to err" (2010, 10, 11). Such mitigation is then progressively withdrawn, so that offenders with a few prior convictions may receive a mitigated punishment but to a lesser degree than the first offender: "If he does not [desist], he (gradually) loses the discount, depending on the frequency of his subsequent offending" (2010, 10). Although von

Hirsch does not explicitly address the issue of offense similarity, it could be argued that the offender who commits exactly the same offense on the second and third occasions should lose his mitigation more rapidly than another offender who commits different offenses. In other words, under von Hirsch's model society may properly be less tolerant if the offender repeats the exact same conduct. But why? Is there any greater "human tendency to err" in diverse ways, than in consistent ways? Moreover, as with notice arguments, the "lapse" concept is unconvincing when applied to serious crimes.

To summarize: Patterning premiums find support in some retributive rationales for PRE. But each of these rationales is contestable, or at least strongly dependent on the nature and particular circumstances of the offenses. Moreover, as we argue throughout this book, more severe punishment must not only be deserved, it should also serve a useful purpose, the question to which we now turn.

3. *Offense Similarity and Recidivism Risk*

As with other dimensions of prior record, the more compelling justification for sentencing enhancements is related to risk rather than retribution.[19] The similarity of past and current crimes may suggest that the offender specializes in a particular form of offending (e.g., auto theft, drug dealing, burglary, armed robbery, or rape). Such specialization may then provide insight into the *seriousness* of any future offending, in particular: if an offender is convicted of a violent felony and has a prior violent crime conviction, we might assume that she is more likely (than an offender without such a pattern) to commit another violent offense. Alternatively, the commission of two or more similar crimes might suggest that the offender is a career criminal, thus indicating a greater *frequency* of future criminal behavior of all kinds.

There is surprisingly little research on offense patterning and risk. As discussed later on in the chapter, criminal careers research has found that most offenders commit a variety of crimes and do not specialize in a certain crime or type of crime. But such research has generally not sought to quantify the extent to which an offender with at least two convictions for a given crime or crime type is statistically more likely to commit that crime (especially, another violent crime) in the future, or a higher number of crimes of all types, compared to an offender with no such patterning. In addition, it may be significant that none of the widely used risk assessment tools discussed in chapter 3 includes any kind of patterning factor, nor has the relationship between past-current offense patterning been examined in the extensive recidivism risk research conducted by several sentencing commissions.[20] The limited research on patterning and risk is summarized in the next two Subsections, addressing the two kinds of predictive value that patterning might have: (a) Does similarity between past and current offenses help predict the *nature* of any future offending, especially with respect to violent crime? (b) Do offenders displaying a pattern of the same kind of offending have higher *rates* of future offending overall, compared to offenders with no such pattern?

a. Does Patterning Predict Similar Future (Violent) Offending?

The answer to this question depends in part upon the extent to which offenders tend to specialize in particular crimes or types of crime: if such specialization is fairly common, then an offender with at least two convictions for crime X is likely to be one of the specialists in that crime, and therefore likely to commit the same crime in the future. On the other hand, if specialization is relatively rare then such an offender may just be a "generalist" who happens to have been caught more than once for crime X. Criminal careers research has found evidence of specialization for certain categories of offending; but most offenders have heterogeneous offending histories, and the nature of one offense is often not a strong predictor of the next (see, e.g., BJS 2018, Table 7; Laskorunksy 2013; Owen and Cooper 2013; Piquero et al. 2007; Simon 1997; Washington Sentencing Guidelines Commission 1992; Bottomley and Pease 1986).

A recent study of criminal history and offender recidivism in Minnesota compared offenders' offense types when sentenced in 2003 with the offense types of their first subsequent conviction, if any. Evidence of patterning was found for each of the broad offense types examined (person, property, drug, other). For example, 42 percent of offenders convicted of a person offense in 2003 who recidivated within three years of release were reconvicted for a person offense, while only 19 percent of all recidivating 2003 offenders had a new person offense (Laskorunsky 2018). On the other hand, the overall three-year recidivism rate for 2003 person offenders was lower than the recidivism rate for offenders convicted of other offense types. But evidence of patterning is still present when new person-offense convictions are expressed as a percent of all defendants who were convicted of person offenses in 2003 (including those who did not recidivate): 8.7 percent of 2003 person offenders were reconvicted of a person offense, whereas only 4.5 percent of all 2003 offenders had a subsequent conviction for a person offense.[21] These findings thus lend some support to a patterning premium for person offenders. As noted in chapter 6, however, "person offense" in Minnesota is a very broad category, including many low-severity crimes that involve neither serious injury nor use of a weapon.

One limitation of all of the studies described previously is that they usually only examine the extent to which the nature of a given conviction offense predicts the nature of the offender's next crime; the more precise question, in assessing patterning and risk, is whether an offender with *at least two convictions for the same crime or crime type* is significantly more likely to commit that crime or crime type yet again. Another limitation is that some studies do not control for the varying base rates of different types of offending—if drug offenses only constitute 25 percent of recidivism convictions, then a 35 percent proportion of drug offending, among offenders with an earlier drug-offense conviction, provides some evidence of specialization, even if 65 percent of subsequent offenses are not for drug crimes. Yet another limitation of conviction-based (as opposed to self-report) studies is what might be called the "usual suspects" bias—convicted offenders who later commit the same or a similar offense are more likely to be viewed by police as likely perpetrators of that new offense and thus are more likely to be arrested and convicted for that offense, in comparison to offenders whose latest crimes are very different from their prior crimes.

To summarize, the limited empirical research has generated inconsistent findings, but overall it suggests that similarity or patterning premiums carry only limited benefits in terms of enhanced prevention of particular kinds of crime.

b. Does Patterning Predict More Frequent Future Crime?

With respect to the second question identified previously, specialization is seldom a reliable indicator of a generally higher risk of re-offending. Several studies have found that past offense frequency rather than offense patterning is a better predictor of the frequency of future offending (Piquero et al. 2007; Laskorunsky 2013); similarity between current and prior offenses is not itself a strong predictor. This research, along with studies of offense specialization by crime or crime type, described previously, calls into question the use of formulaic patterning rules based on assumptions of higher recidivism risk. Such rules are even more questionable in light of their adverse impacts.

4. Potential Adverse Impacts of Patterning Premiums

The use of a patterning premium can have adverse consequences, at least if the premium is applied broadly. For example, property and other nonviolent offenders generally have higher recidivism rates than violent offenders, and also appear somewhat more likely to specialize in nonviolent crime. A robust, broad-scope patterning premium therefore escalates punishment more rapidly for this profile of offender. Over time, such a premium will change the profile of admissions to custody, and increase the proportion of nonviolent offenders in prison populations. Strong patterning premiums can also disturb offense-based proportionality; an offender with several prior similar offenses may attract a more punitive sentence than an offender convicted of a more serious current offense but with dissimilar prior crimes. Even a patterning rule limited to repeat violent crimes can easily result in over-prediction of violence, given the limited degree of offender specialization in violence (Piquero 2000; Farrington 1998), combined with the especially marked decline in violent offending as offenders grow older.

We conclude that there is little merit to including patterning premiums in criminal history scores or other rigid formulas, especially premiums that apply broadly (e.g., to all "property" or all "person" offenses). Unless further research can identify types of offense patterning with a strong link to future serious offending types and/or frequency, formulaic patterning enhancements are likely to impose additional punishment costs that outweigh their preventive benefits. As with custody status, however, there may be cases in which the pattern of offending clearly indicates a career criminal. For example, an individual convicted repeatedly of trafficking juvenile prostitutes or fencing stolen goods may have made a conscious choice to earn his living in this manner. Imposing a patterning premium in a particular case such as this may be justified on risk-reduction grounds. But the premium must still respect proportionality limits relative to the seriousness of the specific offense for which the offender is currently being sentenced. There is little to be gained by imposing a patterning premium on persistent offenders convicted of minor crimes such as theft, or on more serious offenders with only limited patterning in their criminal histories.

E. Weighting of Prior Felony Convictions according to Their Seriousness

Just as prior juvenile adjudications and adult misdemeanor convictions are usually given less weight in criminal history scoring than even the lowest level adult felony, most guidelines systems also give reduced weight to less serious than to more serious adult felonies (for more detailed discussion, see Hester 2015). The most common weighting scheme is based in whole or in part on the severity ranking of the prior crime (on most guidelines grids these rankings place an offense higher or lower on the vertical axis of the grid).[22]

Weighting rules vary substantially, and it is difficult to compare them directly since some systems employ a broader range of point values. For example: in Minnesota the highest criminal history category is for offenders with 6 or more points, and on this state's main grid prior felonies receive from .5 to 2 points each. But on the North Carolina felony grid the highest category is 18 or more points, and prior felonies receive from 1 to 10 points each. One way to compare felony weighting across jurisdictions, independent of such scaling differences, is to ask: How far across the grid—across what proportion of the higher criminal history categories (grid cells) beyond the zero or lowest category—can a single prior felony push the offender? The answer is: from 13 to 75 percent of the way across the grid (Hester 2015, table 8.1). Can such felony weighting rules be justified, especially when they assign high numbers of criminal history points to a single prior crime?

Giving heavier weight to more serious prior crimes might seem like an obviously right thing to do, but it is doubtful that such enhancements are either deserved or justified by higher recidivism risk. As discussed more fully in chapter 1, retributive accounts provide weak support for prior record enhancements of any kind, although the culpable-omission theory may provide the best general account. In the context of prior felony weighting, the argument would be that the more serious an offender's prior felonies are (and the more numerous they are), the more the offender is on notice of his serious criminal tendencies, and thus, the more culpable he is for not taking effective steps to control those tendencies. This theory seems strongest when the offender's latest crime is also very serious; yet almost all felony weighing schemes apply even when the new crime is minor—even though the offender has *succeeded in reducing the seriousness of his offending*, his prior high-severity crimes still receive extra weight! Conversely, when an offender is "going in the wrong direction," from less to more serious crimes, his lower-severity prior crimes receive reduced weight.

The risk-based rationale for high-weighting of prior serious crimes is even weaker. Research consistently shows that the severity level of prior crimes is not a good predictor of either the frequency or the severity of later offending (Laskorunsky 2018; Hester Forthcoming; USSC 2016b, 20). Moreover, a comparison of the Minnesota guidelines criminal history score with and without upweighting of more serious adult felonies found that both scores were equally good predictors of recidivism (Laskorunsky 2017).

At the other end of the severity continuum, however, reduced weight for very minor prior felonies makes sense. Even if we accept some version of the omission theory, noted previously, failure to address criminal tendencies is less culpable following conviction for a minor felony than after a more serious one. And even if offenders with multiple low-severity prior felonies have higher recidivism rates, another valid justification for down-weighting such priors is to reduce the number of nonviolent and other minor offenders recommended for and sent to prison. This was one of the reasons in 1989 Minnesota reduced, to a half point, the weight given to low-severity felonies—too many repeat property offenders were ending up in state prisons (MSGC 1989; see further discussion in chapter 6).

F. How Much Difference Do These Problematic Components Make?

To put these policy issues in practical perspective, here is some data from Minnesota, for 2015, showing how often the problematic components discussed in Sections A through E, individually and collectively, move an offender to a higher criminal history category, increasing recommended prison durations and the proportion of offenders recommended for an executed-prison sentence. (We do not present data on patterning since Minnesota has only one such rule, and there is no available data on how often it applies.)

First, how often is an offender's criminal history category (and thus, the recommended prison duration) increased by the presence of one of these problematic components?[23] Custody status has the strongest impact—38 percent of offenders had their criminal history score raised for this reason (and 43 percent had their recommended prison duration increased, if we also count offenders subject to a special "add three months" rule for custody status when the offender is already in the highest criminal history category). The proportions with raised criminal history scores for the other three components were: juvenile points, 2 percent (but 7 percent of eligible offenders—those aged less than 25 on the offense date); misdemeanor points, 7 percent; and upweighted felonies, 5 percent.[24] Overall, almost half of the offenders sentenced in 2015 had their recommended prison duration raised due to the presence of one or more of these four components.

Second, how often does one or more of these components push an offender convicted of a medium- or low-severity crime over the "disposition line," into the grid zone where the recommended sentence is an executed rather than a suspended prison term? (In previous chapters we have referred to this as "Zone 2.") Again, custody status has the greatest impact—in 2015, 22 percent of main-grid, Zone 2 offenders would not have been in that zone without the inclusion of custody status points. The proportions for the other four components were: juvenile points, 1 percent; misdemeanor points, 6 percent; and upweighted felonies, 4 percent. Overall, over one-quarter of main-grid, Zone 2 offenders were pushed into that zone due to the presence of one or more of these four components.

Conclusion

At sentencing, courts must consider and apply a wide range of aggravating factors. Guidelines formalize this exercise by identifying relevant factors for judges to consider. With respect to criminal history, guidelines quantify the impact of various dimensions of a prior record by specifying the number of criminal history points to be added. But guidelines drafters need to justify all aggravating factors, and all dimensions of variables such as criminal history, in terms of increased culpability and the prevention of re-offending.

With respect to juvenile and adult misdemeanor priors, we conclude that their utility as a predictor of later adult offending is often overstated, and in any case is outweighed by competing considerations, in particular, the reduced culpability associated with juvenile and misdemeanor priors, and the more limited procedural protections in courts handling those cases. Under our model, we therefore exclude both types of priors from criminal history calculations for adult sentencing. With respect to custody status, offense patterning, and upweighting of prior serious felonies, the evidence suggests that these factors are overused in most guidelines systems that include these factors. We therefore also exclude those dimensions from our model scheme. In light of the high proportion of offenders affected by the custody status premium, and the potentially high proportion affected by any broad-scope patterning or upweighting premiums, eliminating those components from the criminal history calculation would result in significant cost savings in terms of prison places.

11 THE MODEL REGIME

Throughout this volume we have documented the failings of current prior record enhancement regimes across the United States. These may be summarized in the following propositions:

- Most guidelines fail to articulate a clear justification for prior-record-based enhancements, leaving defendants and other interested parties unaware of the reason for the additional punishment.
- The most common justifications for such enhancements are elevated risk (crime prevention goals) and elevated culpability (retributive rationales). But the current magnitudes of enhancement are excessive and cannot be justified on either ground, thus unnecessarily punishing offenders and increasing the size and expense of prison populations.
- Prior record enhancement formulas suffer from overreach in several ways, including counting prior crimes that carry little or no significance in terms of risk or culpability.
- Prior record enhancements are too simplistic and rigid. They ascribe the same level of enhancement to offenders who vary greatly in terms of risk and culpability, while preventing or discouraging courts from individualizing record-based enhancements to reflect individual variations in levels of risk or culpability.
- Prior record enhancements are also unconditionally punitive, imposing additional punishment without regard to any actions by the offender to desist.
- The current high magnitudes of enhancement impose punishment that is disproportionate relative to the seriousness of the crimes being sentenced.
- Prior record enhancements fail to consider factors such as advancing age that diminish an offender's risk, even in cases of high criminal history scores.

- Such enhancements also send many property and other nonviolent offenders to prison, thus undercutting efforts to reserve expensive prison beds for violent offenders.
- Prior record enhancements contribute substantially to racial disproportionality in prison populations.

Many of these deficiencies have existed since the creation of the guidelines—40 years ago in the case of Minnesota and Pennsylvania. Their continued existence suggests a lack of awareness of the problems, on the part of commissions, or an indifference to the need for reform. The current volume does not claim to provide a definitive and lasting set of remedies. Rather the reforms are offered in the hope of encouraging more critical reflection on this important and overlooked element of sentencing guidelines in the United States. More importantly, we advocate continual scrutiny of prior record enhancements. Crime prevention through deterrence and incapacitation is used to justify these enhancements in most systems. This being the case, prior record enhancements should change in response to our evolving awareness of the causes of re-offending, and the effectiveness of different penal interventions. Two examples illustrate. Forty years ago, when the Minnesota Commission was devising its grid, researchers were only beginning to understand the long-term consequences of lengthy custodial sentences. Imprisonment was generally seen as the deprivation of time; the punishment ended with the sentence. Today we much better understand the complex and long-lasting effect of imprisonment on the life chances, health, and welfare of ex-prisoners and their dependents. We also have much more realistic expectations of the preventive efficacy of imprisonment as a deterrent. If the commissions in the 1980s had had the knowledge about imprisonment and deterrence that we have now, guideline structures might have evolved differently. If commissions had known then what we know now about racial disproportionality, prior record enhancements might look very different too.

There is a better way. This concluding chapter outlines the principal elements of our model set of sentencing provisions to regulate the use of prior convictions. The model is conceived with U.S. state and federal guideline schemes in mind, but the fundamental principles and approach may be applied to discretionary sentencing systems such as those found in non-guidelines states and in other common law jurisdictions. In Part A we state our underlying normative principles to limit the application and magnitude of prior record enhancements. Part B applies these principles and lays out the specific counting and scoring rules in our model. Part C concludes.

A. Normative Principles

The extensive literatures on punishment theories and punishment practices in Western countries leads us to endorse the following fundamental principles.

1. *Rationale and Justification for Enhancement*

Prior record sentence enhancements are only justified if there is reason to believe that:

- the offender's prior convictions indicate an elevated risk of further crime;
- the enhancement will prevent or reduce re-offending by this offender; and
- the enhanced penalty does not exceed the offender's deserved punishment for the offense or offenses being sentenced.

In terms of punishment theory, our underlying assumptions are as follows:

1) Prior record enhancements must be both deserved and useful—they must be justified both by principles of desert and by crime prevention goals.
2) For any given offense, first offenders are less culpable and generally pose a much lower risk of recidivism than previously convicted offenders. However, as offenders acquire further convictions their levels of culpability and risk increase at a much slower rate. Accordingly, recommended typical-case sentences (and the average of sentences actually imposed) should not steadily increase as criminal history scores increase; the rate of increase should be greatest between the lowest- and second-lowest categories (reflecting substantial mitigation for first offenders), with much slower rates of increase through the third and higher categories.
3) Although recidivism risk generally increases as offenders acquire more substantial records, and offender risk has important relevance to crime-control punishment goals, the specific criminal history scale or scoring rules must be validated with empirical evidence—each component of the score must be shown to improve the risk-predictive accuracy of the score. If a component fails the validation test, it should be discarded.
4) Even if a jurisdiction's criminal history formula has been validated and shorn of components that add no predictive value, increased punishment severity based on that formula can only be justified in pursuit of crime-control goals if such severity is designed to achieve incapacitation

or closer supervision; it cannot be justified on grounds of individual or general deterrence.[1] Moreover, the actual crime-control value (through the mechanisms of incapacitation or closer supervision) of imposing enhanced punishment by means of the validated criminal history formula must be demonstrated with empirical evidence, not simply assumed.

2. *The Proportionality Constraint*

In light of the importance of offense-based proportionality, prior convictions should never carry more weight at sentencing than the offense or offenses for which the offender is being sentenced. Indeed, in most cases prior offending (for which the offender has already been punished) should carry much less weight than the current crime. Accordingly, within each group of similarly serious crimes (e.g., each guidelines offense severity level) the recommended typical-case sentence[2] for offenders in the highest criminal history category should not be more than double the sentence given to offenders in the lowest history category. In addition, to further ensure conviction-offense proportionality, the range of recommended typical-case sentences for crimes of a given level of severity should not overlap with the range of penalties for crimes of greater or lesser severity, except to the extent needed to permit substantial mitigation of first-offender penalties (as discussed previously).

3. *Efficiency, Cost-Effectiveness, And Competing-Values Constraints*

Prior record enhancements—even if they are deserved, likely to prevent or reduce further crime by this offender, and offense-proportionate—are unjustifiable if:

- the same crime-control effects can be achieved with a shorter period of incarceration, or with a noncustodial disposition; or
- the crime-control benefits are outweighed by their fiscal and human costs, or by undesirable countervailing effects of the prior-record-enhanced penalty, including the substantial disparate impact of the penalty on nonwhite offenders.

These are general requirements in pursuing all utilitarian/consequentialist goals. But these essential precepts have been particularly neglected in the design and application of prior record enhancements.

Intrusive government measures must be no more severe than necessary to achieve their valid purposes (this is sometimes referred to as the principle of parsimony, narrow-tailoring, or applying the least restrictive means).[3] Furthermore, even if no less severe alternative would be as effective to control crime, the benefits of prior record enhancements must not be outweighed by their costs and other negative consequences.[4] Prior record enhancements in the United States have many serious negative consequences, including the following:

- Increased prison populations, and resulting private and public costs, as a result of more offenders being sent to prison and/or longer prison sentences;
- Reduced cost-effectiveness due to imprisonment of aging low-risk, high-cost offenders;
- Reduced cost-effectiveness due to imprisonment of larger numbers of offenders who have only been convicted of nonviolent and other less harmful offenses;
- Reduced cost-effectiveness due to the documented criminogenic effects of imprisonment on some offenders—not only are they not rehabilitated, or even allowed to simply "age out" of their criminality, they are actually made more crime-prone;
- Reduced cost-effectiveness due to the inclusion of criminal history score components that are not shown to correlate with increased risk, yet increase the sentence severity;
- Increased minority overrepresentation in prison admissions and populations;
- Greater impairment of offenders' life chances arising from spending more time in custody; this in turn adversely affects subsequent re-entry as well as third parties such as relatives and dependents.
- Interference with and failure to give credit to the offender's efforts to desist, as measured, for example, by the offender's enrollment in and completion of ameliorative programming, preference for prosocial over antisocial companions, and a substantial crime-free interval between the offender's last offense and the current one.

4. *Balance between Rule and Discretion*

Sentence enhancements for prior convictions must strike a reasonable balance between, on the one hand, the values of consistency across cases as well as the overall greater accuracy of actuarial (group-based) risk assessments, and on the other hand, the need to permit a measure of individualized judicial determination based on case-specific factors. Criminal history scoring and application rules promote consistency by giving all judges a common starting point based on typical-offender patterns. And actuarial risk assessment tools have often been found to be more accurate than entirely "clinical" (individualized) assessments.[5] But judges must be allowed to depart from the group-based assessment where appropriate. Indeed, courts should be *directed* to consider, in all cases, whether the ascribed level of risk based on the assigned criminal history score is appropriate to the specific individual being sentenced. If not, the court should depart from the guideline recommendation. Such departures are allowed under all sentencing guidelines systems, when there are atypical facts related to the crime or crimes being sentenced; there is no reason an offender-based criterion such as prior record, or offender risk generally, should not likewise be subject to exceptional case-specific adjustments.

B. Prior-Record Counting Rules

Our model addresses two aspects of the construction and use of criminal history scores: the rules governing which prior crimes are included and with what weights; and the rules that determine how particular scores are translated into recommended and imposed sentences.

1. Which Prior Crimes Count, and How Much?

Criminal history scoring formulas should only include components that increase an offender's culpability, that are associated with higher risk of further criminal conduct, and that produce crime-control benefits that are cost-effective and not outweighed by negative consequences such as substantial racial disparate impact. As discussed in prior chapters,[6] many existing criminal history formulas include components that fail one or more of these requirements. Accordingly, our model criminal history scoring system excludes or gives less weight to the following components found in many existing guidelines systems:

a. Offenses Committed When the Offender Was a Juvenile

As is recognized in recent Supreme Court decisions,[7] juvenile offenders are less culpable than adults, and are also more likely to change even without system intervention. In addition, juvenile court adjudications are entered with fewer procedural protections and this makes their underlying "facts" less reliable. That problem, along with widespread belief in the reduced culpability of juveniles, increases the perceived unfairness of enhancing adult sentences on this basis. We therefore exclude all juvenile-age priors.

b. Adult Misdemeanor Convictions

By definition, such offenders are less culpable than those who commit felony-level crimes, and they may be no more risky than offenders who lack a misdemeanor conviction record—as a descriptive matter, minor offending is "normal" behavior: almost all people have committed some minor crime in the past.[8] Moreover, misdemeanor convictions, like juvenile adjudications, are often entered with limited procedural safeguards, thus reducing adjudicative accuracy and increasing the perceived unfairness of using these convictions to enhance sentence severity in later proceedings. For all of these reasons, prior adult misdemeanors should be excluded from adult criminal history scoring in all but the most exceptional cases (for example: when serious misdemeanor-level offending is closely related to one or more proven felony crimes).

c. Adult Convictions from Many Years Earlier

As was discussed in chapter 9, many guidelines systems have no look-back limits at all, or have limits that formally or in practice do not exclude convictions entered many decades earlier. Moreover, most systems do not give offenders credit for substantial periods of crime-free living. Under our model, felony-level offenses are no longer counted 10 years after the entry of the conviction.[9] In addition, in order to both reward efforts at desistance and reflect the lower risk of these offenders, our model includes a seven-year "gap" rule for felony convictions: if an offender remains crime free for seven years following any felony conviction, that conviction and all prior convictions are no longer counted. Finally, as to both the 10-year outer limit and the shorter seven-year "gap" rule, guidelines systems should enact a true "decay" policy under which the prior conviction is still counted but assigned less weight after a shorter period has elapsed (for example: assign half the normal weight when five years have elapsed since the conviction, or when the offender has been crime-free for three years following the conviction).

d. Upweighting of Prior Felonies according to Severity

In many guidelines systems some prior felonies are very heavily weighted, which means that one or two such crimes can move an offender most or even all of the way across the grid and into the highest criminal history category or categories. Yet there is little evidence tying high prior-offense severity to elevated recidivism risk; indeed, the opposite is often the case (Hester forthcoming; Laskorunsky 2018; USSC 2016b). Nor is there a clear basis to posit increased culpability. Moreover, if the current offense is less serious, we should praise the offender for committing less serious crime; yet felony upweighting schemes apply regardless of the nature and severity of the current offense. Finally, like most of the problematic components we have identified, felony upweighting has a disparate impact on nonwhite offenders. Thus, our model rejects upweighting unless it has been shown to improve the prior-record score's risk prediction accuracy; we also recommend that, if such weighting is used, it should not (as some systems do) allow a single prior conviction to move the offender more than halfway across the guidelines grid. Our model does, however, permit down-weighting (e.g., to .5 point) of minor felonies, as a means of reducing the numbers of minor, repeat offenders who are recommended for prison terms. The same result can also be achieved by specifying, as several guidelines systems do (Hester 2015), that an offender cannot move into the highest criminal history categories unless there are convictions for one or more very serious crimes. We would go further, however: offenders should not be recommended for the highest categories unless the current and at least one prior crime were violent.

e. "Patterning" Enhancements for Offenders Previously Convicted of the Same Crime

As we discussed in chapter 10, there is only limited evidence suggesting that such offenders pose significantly higher risk of further crimes of the same type (e.g., violent crime), and no evidence that they pose a higher risk generally. Perhaps for this reason, most guidelines systems do not include many patterning rules, and no system applies such rules to all forms of patterning. We do recognize that in exceptional cases this is a valid factor for courts to consider; however, temporal and other variations do not support the use of routine, formulaic patterning enhancements.

f. Custody Status Points

This form of enhancement[10] is found in almost all guidelines systems, and it applies to a high proportion of offenders, thus greatly increasing the frequency and duration of custodial sentences. Again, there is little empirical evidence to support an assumption that all such offenders pose a higher risk of recidivism. Some may, but custody status rules sweep too broadly in a number of respects: they include custody status violations no matter how long the preceding period in which the offender had complied with all custody or release conditions, they apply no matter how serious the release violation or the current offense (in some systems, they even apply to released offenders who are awaiting trial and thus presumed innocent), and they apply without regard to whether the offender has or will receive other punitive consequences (e.g., revocation of probation; loss of prison good-conduct credits) because of the violation. Some would argue that a custody status violation makes the current offense more culpable; yet such a violation has nothing to do with the harm of the current offense itself, or the offender's criminal intent, motives, or role in that offense.

We therefore exclude this factor from our model criminal history scoring system. We also do that to avoid perceived unfairness. Since the prior conviction giving rise to the custody status is also being counted, custody status enhancements essentially double-count the prior conviction. And when the offender's release is revoked because of the current offense, the current offense is essentially being triple-counted (it causes revocation; it is punished as a new offense; and it receives enhanced punishment). We wish to add, however, that although our model does not routinely include custody status in criminal history scoring, judges can still consider such status in other ways. In particular, an offender who has just violated probation by committing the current offense is, for that reason, a less promising candidate to be given a probation sentence for the new offense.[11]

2. *How Does a Higher Score Affect Recommended and Imposed Sentences?*

Just because an offender has an elevated criminal history score, that does not necessarily mean that the offender should be sent to prison, or receive a much longer prison term. Nor should recommended sentence severity increase in a steady, linear fashion, although that is what most existing guidelines systems do. Here are the ways in which our model structures the process of translating criminal history scores into recommended and imposed sentences:

a. "Slope" of the Prior Record Durational Enhancement Curve

As noted previously, our model recognizes a greater difference between first offenders and second offenders than between successive groups with higher criminal history scores (e.g., second versus third, third versus fourth, etc.). Our recommendation can be visualized in the form of a graph of recommended custody durations (vertical axis) by criminal history scores (horizontal axis): instead of a straight (or uniformly curving) upward-sloping line, we propose a two-stage "bent" line, rising sharply at first, then rising much more slowly (roughly in the shape of an ice hockey stick, held with the blade pointing down). For example, in a system with seven criminal history categories running from zero to six or more points, the recommended custody duration might increase by 40 percent from zero to one point, after which it would rise by only 5 percent with each added history point.

b. Proportionality Cap on Prior Record Aggravation

As previously discussed, our model places two absolute limits on the degree to which criminal history may enhance durational sentence severity, in order to preserve offense-based proportionality. First, the model stipulates that highest-history offenders cannot be recommended for prison sentences that are more than twice as severe as sentences recommended for lowest-history offenders committing crimes at that level of offense severity; this rule ensures that prior record will not receive more weight than the offense being sentenced. Second, our model permits only a limited degree of overlap in the sentences recommended for adjoining offense severity levels; recommended sentences for highest-history offenders in any given offense severity level should not exceed the recommended sentences for any offenders in the next most severe offense severity level (except for first offenders at that higher level, to recognize the special mitigation we allow for first offenders; see chapter 6, figure 6.2, for an example of this limited-overlap approach). Of course, both of these proportionality-preserving rules may be overridden if there are case-specific aggravating circumstances of a high-history offender's current offense, or mitigating circumstances of a low-history offender's offense.

Our model further promotes offense-based sentence proportionality by stipulating that typical-case sentence recommendations for offenders in the highest criminal history category should be well below applicable statutory maximum penalties, in order to ensure that judges have authority to enhance sentence durations of highest-history offenders based solely on aggravating circumstances of the current offense. Criminal history enhancements should not "use up" the entire legislatively authorized sentencing range.

c. Alternate Approach: Criminal History and Other Risk Factors Forming a Single Scale

Rather than categories of criminal history within a two-dimensional grid, our model also recognizes an alternative approach that places offenders in broad categories of low, medium, and high risk, each with an associated durational Enhancement Coefficient (EC). Assignment of the case to a risk category is determined by the number and nature of prior convictions as well as other relevant risk-related circumstances (e.g., substance abuse, advancing age):

Low recidivism risk (Enhancement Coefficient < .3)
Medium risk (Enhancement Coefficient .3 < .5)
High risk (Enhancement Coefficient .5 to 1.0)

It should be noted that the highest EC value, 1.0, has the same effect as the earlier no-more-than-doubling rule—the offender's risk level cannot receive more weight than the crime being sentenced.

Here are two examples of how this approach would work for an offense with a first-offender sentence of 24 months:

For an offender in the Low recidivism category (minimal prior conviction record, very few other risk factors), if EC = .1 the total sentence is 26.4 months (24 months times 1.1).

For an offender in the High category (serious criminal history and/or major risk factors), if EC = .7 the total sentence equals 40.8 months (24 months times 1.7).

d. Disposition Rules

Our model also seeks to reduce the sentence-enhancing effects of higher criminal history scores on disposition decisions (prison versus probation), while increasing the mitigating effects for first offenders. As to the former, we showed in chapter 5 that many offenders convicted of low- and medium-seriousness offenses are recommended for prison due to their higher criminal history score, who would otherwise (at a lower score) be recommended for probation. Moreover, as shown in chapter 7, this type of prior record enhancement is a major cause of racial disproportionality in prison populations. Furthermore, as shown in chapter 4, imprisonment appears to make many offenders *more* crime-prone and less able to reintegrate into society. For these reasons, we believe that such cases of criminal history "push-in" to prison should be restricted to offenders with the most serious criminal histories; even then, prison should be the recommended disposition only where the current offense is of at least a medium level of severity, and where the current and at least one prior crime involved actual violence or potential for serious harm.

As for first offenders, our model expressly authorizes additional mitigation in the form of what some guidelines systems call downward "dispositional" departure—the recommended prison term is never imposed and executed if the offender remains law-abiding and otherwise satisfies the conditions of probation or other community-based sanctions. Again, first-offender mitigation has the strongest retributive rationale, and also a strong crime-control basis—these offenders deserve a second chance, and most of them will not be seen again in criminal court. At least one guidelines system (Washington) expressly recognizes the special status of these offenders: when the "first offender waiver" provision applies, a non-custodial sentence or a shorter term is not deemed to be a "departure" from the recommended custody sentence for that crime.[12]

e. Judicial Power to Depart from or Otherwise Modify Applicable Enhancements

Under our model, sentencing judges are given express authority to adjust the recommended sentence upon a finding that the offender's criminal history score does not accurately reflect the risk of serious recidivism. Judges already have authority to depart based on atypical offense facts, and the same should be true for offender-related factors. Such adjustments are permitted in several guidelines systems (Frase 2015a). Consistent with the Parsimony principle, upward adjustments should be used sparingly, and they may also require special fact-finding procedures under *Blakely v. Washington* (2004); downward adjustments pose no such problems.

A particularly strong basis to mitigate prison duration and/or disposition, even for offenders with a number of prior convictions, would exist where the court finds that, notwithstanding her most recent crime, the offender has made substantial efforts to address the causes of her offending. Such mitigation should always be recognized if the current offense is not very serious. In point-based schemes offenders should also be allowed to earn "negative" criminal history points.[13] These may then be used to wash out conventional points. Examples of ways to earn negative criminal history points would include: the offender has successfully completed treatment programing in prison or on probation, or the offender has maintained employment or full-time education for a protracted period of time. Sentencing systems should recognize that desistance from crime, like abstinence from addictive substances or behaviors, is often a relapsing process in which progress is measured by longer and longer periods of desistance, rather than permanent, all-at-once cessation.

As further discussed in Appendix C, several other categories of offenders will often justify more or less severe punishment than their prior conviction record, and the limits of our model, would otherwise prescribe. High-frequency serious violent offenders, and some repeat nonviolent offenders, may require more severe punishment; repeat drug offenders, aging offenders, and offenders experiencing major life-course changes, will often require less severe punishment. Most of the offenders falling into these groups can be dealt with by means of the expanded judicial departure power we propose. But, for at least some of these offender groups, the reasons supporting enhanced or mitigated punishment may be consistent enough to merit the development of specialized presumptive rules and departure standards.

C. Conclusion

Prior record is a major determinant—sometimes the primary determinant—of the form and severity of punishment in contemporary sentencing systems, especially under the kinds of numerical guidelines systems found in the United States. Yet this aspect of sentencing has been largely ignored by researchers and policymakers; prior record enhancements have been seen as "obviously" justified.

In this volume, we have shown that such enhancements are often not justified at all, and are almost always excessive relative to their supposed justifications. There is substantial agreement that first offenders are less culpable, and substantial evidence that they are less likely to recidivate than offenders with a prior conviction; indeed, first-offender mitigations should be even greater than they are at present. But the degrees of culpability and risk rise only modestly, as offenders acquire additional prior convictions; moreover, research has repeatedly documented the meager crime-preventive benefits of penalty enhancements. As a result, the penalties recommended for and imposed on repeat offenders are unjustified and often counterproductive, wasting public resources and burdening offenders' efforts to desist and move on with their lives.

We have also documented many other adverse consequences of such enhancements: besides the greatly increased costs to build and operate prisons, current prior-record enhancements cause sentences to be disproportionate to the seriousness of the crimes being sentenced; disrupt prison-use priorities by sending large numbers of nonviolent and aging offenders to prison; and increase racial disproportionality in prison populations.

To lessen these adverse consequences, and ensure that prior record enhancements are deserved, fair, and a cost-effective means of preventing crime, in this final chapter, we have proposed a model system containing guiding principles and specific rules governing which prior crimes to count, how much, for how long, and with what effects on the form and severity of the sentence.

Reform of prior record enhancements is long overdue in all jurisdictions. The need is probably greatest—or at least, it is easier to document and address—in jurisdictions with numerical guidelines, containing criminal history formulas that directly affect the form and severity of recommended and imposed sentences. We therefore strongly encourage researchers, sentencing commissioners, and others interested in sentencing reform to tackle these issues in all guidelines systems. But our work also has important implications in sentencing systems without guidelines. Studies of sentencing in all systems, with or without guidelines, find that most sentenced offenders have at least some prior record, and that prior record has a strong effect on sentence severity. So the broader challenge we pose, to researchers and policymakers in non-guidelines systems, is this: *Do you know how much weight prior record has in your system, with what justification, what crime-control benefits, and what adverse consequences?*

APPENDIX A

REPRESENTATIVE CRIMINAL HISTORY PROVISIONS IN U.S. GUIDELINES

In American guidelines systems,[1] the manner in which prior convictions are translated into sentence enhancements depends on the structure and format of each system, in particular: Does it use a grid format? If not, what kind of worksheet or other non-grid system is used? Grid systems display further variations, in particular: Are there separate grids for certain offense types? Is the criminal history axis of the grid or grids scaled according to a specific number of criminal history points? By a range of points within each criminal history category? By categories that depend on types of prior crimes, such as violent versus nonviolent? By a combination of points and offense types?

Here is a summary of how criminal history provisions in the 19 existing American guidelines systems are structured (systems described in more detail below are shown in bold type):

- Fourteen systems use a grid or grids; Arkansas, Massachusetts, Oregon, Tennessee, and the federal system have a single grid; the District of Columbia, Kansas, Maryland, Michigan, Minnesota, North Carolina, Pennsylvania, Utah, and Washington have multiple grids.
- Nine grid systems define criminal history with either single-point categories (**Arkansas**, Maryland, Minnesota, and Washington) or with point-range categories (**District of Columbia**, Michigan, North Carolina, Utah, the federal system). In four grid systems (Kansas, Massachusetts, Oregon, Tennessee), criminal history categories are determined not by points but by the number and type of prior convictions; for example, in **Kansas** the third-highest category is for offenders with prior convictions that include one "person" felony and at least one non-person felony. **Pennsylvania** takes a mixed approach: the first six criminal history categories are for offenders with zero, 1, 2, 3, 4, or 5 points while the two highest categories are defined according to prior crime types (repeat felony and repeat violent).

- Three of the five non-grid systems (**Alabama**, Florida, and Virginia) use worksheets to compute recommended sentences, and prior convictions add a designated number of points to a total point score. **Delaware**'s guidelines provide recommended, typical-case sentence ranges, which may be increased by application of prior-offense-type (not point-based) rules somewhat akin to those used in Kansas and several other states (see above). Ohio's statutory guidelines consist mostly of general standards and principles (some of which relate to prior record) that are designed to help judges decide whether to impose a prison sentence and if so, for how long.

The criminal history provisions found in six U.S. guidelines systems are described below. Each system represents one of the structural variations summarized above.

1. *Arkansas—Grid Format with Single-Point Criminal History Categories*

There are six criminal history categories on Arkansas's single grid, corresponding to scores of 0 to 5 or more points (Arkansas Sentencing Commission 2018). An offender's criminal history score includes the following components: (1) felony convictions, (2) Class A misdemeanor convictions, (3) juvenile court adjudications for crimes for which the offender could have been tried as an adult and which the sentencing court deems relevant, and (4) custody status at the time of the offense being sentenced, in connection with a prior felony charge (pre- or post-conviction incarceration or supervision). High-severity felonies count 1 point each, and lower-severity felonies .5 points; custody status adds 1 point; misdemeanors and most juvenile priors count .25 points each. No more than 1 point may be accrued for misdemeanor convictions, and generally no more than 1 point for juvenile priors (up to 2 points can be scored if any juvenile adjudication was for capital murder, murder in the first degree, murder in the second degree, kidnaping in the first degree, aggravated robbery, rape or battery in the first degree). High-severity felony convictions are counted no matter how long ago they were entered; lower-severity felonies are not counted if a period of 15 years has elapsed since the date of discharge from or expiration of the prior sentence to the date of the current offense (this is an absolute look-back limit; the defendant need not have remained crime-free during the 15- year period). Juvenile and misdemeanor priors are excluded if the prior-offense date was more than 10 years before the date of the offense(s) being sentenced.

2. *District of Columbia—Grid Format with Point-Range Criminal History Categories*

The District has a separate Drug grid, and a Master grid for all other felonies (District of Columbia Sentencing Commission 2018). Each grid has the same six criminal history categories, defined by the following ranges of total criminal history points: category A = 0 to ½ points; B = ¾ to 1¾ points; C = 2 to 3¾ points; D = 4 to 5¾ points; E = 6 or more points. An offender's criminal history score includes the following components: (1) adult felony convictions, (2) adult misdemeanor convictions if the maximum penalty was 90 days or more, and (3) juvenile court adjudications for drug offenses and for crimes that would be a serious felony for an adult offender. There are no points for custody status, but judges may consider the offender's pre- or post-conviction release or incarceration status as an aggravating factor at sentencing; moreover, the sentence for the current offense must be imposed consecutively to any sentence the defendant was serving when that offense was committed. Except for older priors that lapsed but have been revived (explained below), adult felony priors count from ¾ to 3 points each, depending on their guidelines severity ranking, and adult misdemeanors count ¼ point each; juvenile adjudications count from ½ to 1½ points each. Misdemeanors are capped at one point; juvenile adjudications are capped at 1½ points except for offenses weighted at 1½-points. Felonies and misdemeanors lapse and are no longer counted 10 years after completion of the sentence. However, all lapsed felonies are revived if any part of any adult felony sentence falls within the 10-year period preceding the commission of the present offense. Except for 3-point priors, revived felony priors generally receive less weight (from ¼ to 1 point, depending on their severity ranking; slightly different weightings apply to lapsed prior convictions for being an accessory after the fact). Lapsed misdemeanors can never be revived and cannot revive other lapsed convictions. Juvenile adjudications lapse after 5 years and can never be revived.

3. *Kansas—Grid Format with Prior-Offense-Type Criminal History Categories*

Both of Kansas's two grids (Nondrug grid and Drug grid) use the same criminal history categories, defined by prior offense types rather than by points (Kansas Sentencing Commission 2017). The nine lettered categories are as follows: category A = three or more person felonies; B = two person felonies; C = one person felony and one or more non-person felonies; D = one person felony and no non-person felonies; E = three or more non-person felonies (and no person felonies); F = two non-person felonies; G = one non-person felony; H = two or more misdemeanors, no more than two of which are person misdemeanors; I = no prior record, or one misdemeanor (of any type). Prior adult convictions and juvenile adjudications are treated the same, within the subcategories of prior "person" and "nonperson" offenses. Class A and B person misdemeanors and Class C assaults (if committed within the past three years) are converted to person felonies; three such misdemeanors equals one person felony. Except for Class B "select" (weapons) misdemeanors, Class B and Class C non-person misdemeanors are not scored. It should be noted that if an offender has not been convicted of a person offense, his or her criminal history score can be no higher than the E (fifth-highest) category; on the other hand, a single person felony moves an offender more than halfway across the grid (to category D). Custody status does not raise an offender's criminal history category, but one of the recognized grounds for upward departure is that the offender was incarcerated when he or she committed the current offense. Adult convictions from many years past are always counted and do not decay or lapse. Juvenile adjudications are no longer counted if the current offense was committed after the offender reached the age of 25, and that offense (if committed by an adult) would be a nondrug felony ranked in the lower part of the Nondrug grid (levels 5 through 10), a drug felony, a non-grid felony, or a misdemeanor. A broader lapsing rule, waiving the after-age-25 requirement, applies if there has been a five-year period since the juvenile court adjudication during which the offender has had no new adjudications or adult convictions.

4. Pennsylvania—Grid Format with a Combination Of Point- and Offense-Type Categories

This state uses a combination of six single-point categories (Prior Record Score categories 0 to 5), plus two higher categories defined by types of prior crimes (Pennsylvania Commission on Sentencing 2012a). Points are determined as follows: adult felony and juvenile felony-level adjudications receive from 1 to 4 points each, depending on their degree of seriousness; DWIs and designated class-1 misdemeanors count 1 point each. If the offender has two or more other misdemeanor convictions, he or she receives 1 to 3 points (1 point is scored if there are two or three such convictions; 2 points, if there are four to six such convictions; and 3 points if there are seven or more such convictions). No points are added for custody status, nor is this listed as an aggravating factor. The second-highest criminal history category (Repeat Felony/ RFEL), is for offenders who have previous convictions or juvenile adjudications for felony 1 and/or felony 2 offenses that total 6 points or more (per the point system described previously), and who do not fall within the highest criminal history category. That category (Repeat Violent/ REVOC) is for offenders who have two or more previous 4-point offenses and whose current conviction offense is ranked at level 9 or higher (e.g., robbery). Thus, as was noted previously with respect to the Kansas guidelines, a Pennsylvania offender is not eligible for either of the two highest criminal history categories unless he or she has multiple serious and/or violent prior convictions. Prior adult convictions are always counted, no matter how old they are. Prior juvenile adjudications may "lapse" and not be counted if the offender was 28 years of age or older at the time the current offense was committed, and was crime-free for 10 years immediately prior to his or her 28th birthday (or, during that time, only committed summary offenses and/or one misdemeanor offense with a statutory maximum of one year or less). However, prior juvenile offenses worth 4 severity points are always included in the prior record score; moreover, the guidelines expressly allow judges to consider lapsed prior adjudications when exercising their sentencing discretion.

5. *Alabama—Non-grid, Worksheet Format with Points Added for Criminal History*

Each major type of offense (drug, property, and person) has its own worksheets to derive recommended sentences and, for each of these offense types, there are separate worksheets to guide prison in/out and prison-duration decisions (Alabama Sentencing Commission 2016). On both the in/out and prison-duration worksheets, points are scored for offense-related factors as well as prior record factors. As to the latter, points may be allocated for: number of prior adult felony convictions and misdemeanor convictions, prior custody sentences, number of prior felony probation or parole revocations, number of prior juvenile delinquency or youthful offender adjudications, and (on the property crimes worksheet only) similarity of past and current offenses. The specific scoring of each component depends on the offense type being sentenced and the applicable decision. For example, on the property crimes *prison-in/out worksheet* the number of prior adult felony convictions receives up to 3 points (1 point for one or two priors; 2 points for three or four priors; 3 points for five or more priors). Additional points are added for the number of prior felonies that are identical in type and degree to the current offense (1 to 4 points); prior criminal misdemeanors and serious traffic misdemeanors such as DWI (3 points for 10 or more); prior unsuspended custody sentences of less than one year, or of a year or more (3 and 6 points, respectively); prior juvenile adjudications (4 points for five or more, applying the same limits on traffic misdemeanors as for adult priors, described previously); and any prior felony probation and parole revocations (2 points). Offenders scoring 15 or more points are recommended for prison commitment. On this worksheet the maximum number of points for criminal history factors is 25, and the maximum for offense factors is 17. In contrast, on the property crimes *prison-duration* worksheet offense factors predominate: the maximum number of points for criminal history factors is 192 and the maximum for offense factors is 324. On this worksheet, criminal history points are scored for: additional felony conviction offenses currently being sentenced (15 points for three or more), prior adult felony convictions (121 points for 10 or more); prior adult felony property convictions (34 points for five or more, some prior felonies are thus counted twice), any prior unsuspended custody sentence of one year or more (15 points), and any prior felony probation and parole revocation (7 points; inmate or supervision [custody] status at the time of the current offense does not add points, but this is listed as an aggravating factor that may justify departure). The total score on this worksheet is plugged into a separate table that, for each point total, shows the recommended "low," "middle," and "high" prison term, as well as the shorter recommended custody term if the judge chooses to impose a split sentence of prison followed by probation. Prior adult convictions and juvenile adjudications do not decay or contribute less to an offender's score on either the prison- in/out or the prison-duration worksheets.

6. *Delaware—Non-grid format with Extended Sentence Ranges Based Partly on Prior Record*

This system uses neither grids nor worksheets. Instead, the guidelines provide typical-case recommended sentence types and ranges for each felony and misdemeanor class, usually with separate recommendations for statutorily designated violent and nonviolent crimes within that class (Delaware Sentencing Accountability Commission 2018). Specified mitigated sentence types and/or ranges are provided for offenders who show acceptance of responsibility by pleading guilty at least 30 days before the scheduled trial; specified aggravated sentences apply when certain factors are present. For most crime types those factors include commission of the offense with exceptional cruelty, custody status (on release or awaiting trial or sentencing), and three categories of prior record: two or more prior nonviolent felonies; one prior violent felony; and two or more prior violent felonies. A different set of factors is provided for nonviolent class C, E, F, and G felonies; those factors are "repetitive criminal history" (previously convicted twice of the same or a similar crime), and "lack of amenability to lesser sanctions." Repetitive criminal conduct, custody status, and lack of amenability are also included in the general list of aggravating factors. The general list of mitigating factors includes "no prior convictions." Recommended sentences invoke one or more of five defined Levels of Supervision: Level I is limited to fines and administrative (not face-to-face) supervision; Level II requires 1 to 50 hours of supervision per month. Level III involves intensive supervision (from 1 hour per day to 56 hours per week); Level IV requires partial confinement in a halfway house, restitution center, residential treatment facility, re-entry program facility, and/or by electronically monitored house arrest); Level V consists of full-time confinement by the Department of Corrections (which runs all jail as well as prison facilities in the state). For example, a Class B Nonviolent felony carries a presumptive range of 2 to 5 years at Level V, but the top end of that range rises to 10 years for custody status, two or more prior nonviolent felonies, or one prior violent felony; with two or more violent felonies, or with exceptional cruelty, the top end rises to 25 years. For some crime classes and types the recommended sentence requires a period of time at one of the five levels followed by more time at another level; a sentence may also involve simultaneous combinations, for example: two years at Level V, suspended, with two years of supervision at Level II. If 10 years have passed conviction-free since final release from prison, or from date of sentence if only probation at Levels I to IV was ordered, all Felony C or lesser convictions prior to that date are "washed." (Felony A and B convictions are always counted.)

APPENDIX B

REPRESENTATIVE PROVISIONS FROM OTHER COMMON LAW SYSTEMS

1. ENGLAND AND WALES

The sentencing statute in this jurisdiction explicitly notes the aggravating effect of prior convictions and, unusually, relates these to the seriousness of the current offense. The statute further specifies two key dimensions for courts to consider: the degree of recency of the prior conviction, and its relatedness to the current offense. Finally, the statute recognizes judicial discretion to ignore prior convictions if it would be unreasonable to consider them in aggravation. In addition to the statute, there are definitive offense-specific guidelines; prior convictions are found in Step Two of the guidelines methodology, where they have less impact on sentence severity than the offense-based factors applied in Step One.

Coroners and Justice Act 2003, Section 143: Determining the seriousness of an offence

(1) In considering the seriousness of any offence, the court must consider the offender's culpability in committing the offence and any harm which the offence caused, was intended to cause or might forseeably have caused.

(2) In considering the seriousness of an offence ("the current offence") committed by an offender who has one or more previous convictions, the court must treat each previous conviction as an aggravating factor if (in the case of that conviction) the court considers that it can reasonably be so treated having regard, in particular, to—

  (a) the nature of the offence to which the conviction relates and its relevance to the current offence, and

  (b) the time that has elapsed since the conviction.

2. NEW ZEALAND

There are no formal sentencing guidelines at present, although the Law Reform Commission has proposed a guidelines scheme similar to the English guidelines mentioned in Section 1 of this Appendix.

Sentencing Act 2002, Section 9: Aggravating and mitigating factors

(1) In sentencing or otherwise dealing with an offender the court must take into account the following aggravating factors to the extent that they are applicable in the case: . . .

(j) the number, seriousness, date, relevance, and nature of any previous convictions of the offender and of any convictions for which the offender is being sentenced or otherwise dealt with at the same time.

3. QUEENSLAND, AUSTRALIA

This jurisdiction's sentencing provision is unique because it directs courts to consider prior crimes in aggravation, but to also consider any attempts at rehabilitation on the part of the offender.

Penalties and Sentencing Act 1992, Part 2: Governing Principles

(3) In sentencing an offender to whom subsection (2A) applies, the court must have regard primarily to the following—

. . .

(g) the past record of the offender, including any attempted rehabilitation and the number of previous offences of any type committed;

4. CANADA

This jurisdiction lacks any statutory provision stipulating prior convictions as an aggravator, although prior convictions constitute a judicially recognized aggravating factor. The case law clearly supports the use of prior crimes, but as Manson (2001, 151) notes, "It is important to consider the similarity of offences to determine whether there is any relevance to the offence before the court. An impaired driving conviction has no relevance to a charge of theft but would be directly relevant to a charge of dangerous driving." There are no formal sentencing guidelines at present.

5. ISRAEL

The sentencing statute stipulates a guiding principle of proportionality and also sets out a series of steps for courts to follow at sentencing. Sentencing factors fall into two categories. The factors that carry the most weight are related to the commission of the crime. In addition, the law provides for factors unrelated to the crime but which should affect sentence severity. This provision implies that the existence of priors aggravates and the absence of priors mitigates, without offering any additional guidance. There are no formal sentencing guidelines at present.

Sentencing Law of 2012, Section 40k: Circumstances unrelated to the commission of the crime

(a) In deciding the defendant's sentence within the *Proportionate Sentencing Range*, pursuant to article 40c(b), the Court may consider circumstances unrelated to the commission of the offence, as delineated below, and the degree to which they occur, if the Court believes that it is appropriate to take them into consideration, and so long as the sentence does not deviate from the *Proportionate Sentencing Range*.

...

(11) the defendant's criminal past or lack thereof.

APPENDIX C

SOME OFFENDER GROUPS THAT MAY REQUIRE SPECIAL TREATMENT

Certain groups of repeat offenders may require exceptional treatment, outside the standard terms of our prior record model. In this Appendix we briefly address the reasons this is so, and sketch some ways of handling these offenders. The first two groups discussed involve offenders who may require penalties more severe than are allowed under the limits of our model. The third and fourth groups of repeat offenders pose the opposite problem—prior record enhancements will frequently overstate the risk and/or culpability of these offenders. The higher and lower levels of risk and culpability found in these four groups of offenders can often be adequately addressed by means of the expanded judicial departure power we proposed in chapter 11. Alternatively, some of these specialized risk patterns may be consistent enough to merit the development of specialized guidelines criminal history scoring, sentence presumptions, and/or departure standards. The use of specialized rules would make the guidelines more complex, but would promote more frequent and more consistent consideration of important differences between offenders.

1. High Frequency Serious Violent Offenders

The limits our model places on prior record enhancements are perhaps too strict in cases of repeat serious violent offending. If an offender is now being sentenced for his third armed robbery, his third forcible rape, or his third unprovoked vicious physical assault causing serious injury, why should he not be given a sentence at or close to the statutory maximum penalty, based on his evident high risk, even if there is nothing particularly aggravated about his most recent crime? In a sense, these offenders (and perhaps the next group) represent the mirror image of the first offenders for whom our model proposes systematic (rule-based) mitigation. Should repeat serious violent offenders therefore be recommended for systematic sentence enhancement, beyond the upper limits of enhancement permitted by our model?

Many of these offenders can reliably be identified as posing an elevated risk of further, very serious crimes (some offenders simply are very violent people, just as other offenders rarely or never engage in acts of violence). But what about the requirement of enhanced culpability? Are these offenders, as a group, *more than twice as culpable* as offenders committing one of these serious offenses for the first time, so that our normal "doubling" limit should not apply? Is there something *qualitatively* different about their culpability, or about culpability analysis as it applies to this pattern of repeat offending? We are not sure but perhaps the answer is yes, particularly if the offender's crimes often involve a serious potential for irreparable physical and/or psychological harm. Even though the repeat armed robber or rapist has already been punished for his prior serious crimes, perhaps his proper degree of blame for the latest crime is enhanced by his evident total lack of respect for others' rights to physical and emotional security. This is a variant of Youngjae Lee's (2009, 2010) theory of heightened culpability based on the repeat offender's violation of a duty to take steps to control his criminal tendencies, after he has previously been sanctioned for crime. In chapter 1 we expressed doubts about whether this theory can adequately justify prior record enhancements across the board. But in extreme cases, perhaps it can, even if there is no basis for the court to find aggravating circumstances directly related to the latest crime being sentenced.

One way to protect the public from such offenders, while retaining the core principle that no one may be punished in excess of his or her desert, would be to expand the use of civil commitment (Frase 2013a). But any such expansion must be kept within strict limits. And the overuse of this alternative in some states, to civilly detain large numbers of sex offenders, raises serious doubt that such limits will be respected (Frase and Mitchell 2017).

2. *Career Offenders Committing Numerous Serious Property and Other Nonviolent Crimes*

A second group of offenders (e.g., career burglars, fraud artists, polluters, etc.) are not as scary as the first group, described in Section 1, and their crimes are not as likely to cause irreparable harm. Except in unusual circumstances (e.g., when a homeowner happens to be home or come home during a burglary), these offenders are more of a nuisance than a terror. Thus, annoying as they may be, and even though many of these "frequent flyer" offenders do pose a high risk of repeating their crimes, we do not believe they deserve more severe punishment than our model enhancement rules would allow, that is, more than twice the punishment we would give them for a first offense.

There may be other options for dealing with these cases, however. One way to provide scope for greater punishment within the model's prior record enhancement limits is to use consecutive sentencing—which is often available for these kinds of offenders since they are very likely to be charged with multiple counts of similar crimes. But that sentencing tool must be much more strictly limited than it currently is in most U.S. jurisdictions where, even under guidelines, judges usually have broad discretion to sentence consecutively (Frase 2013a, 2015c, 2017). Another option available under some criminal laws is to aggregate the losses or harms of the various charged counts, combining them into "one big crime" that then triggers a higher statutory and guidelines recommended sentence even if none of the individual crimes was particularly aggravated.[1] But such treatment is easier to justify if the multiple crimes were committed in a single course of conduct or pursuant to a common scheme; if the crimes are unrelated, the offender should be seen as having chosen to commit a number of small crimes, not one big crime. A third way to deal with more or less "physical" crimes such as theft and burglary, while respecting our prison-duration doubling limit, is to make more effective use of increasingly sophisticated surveillance tools, such as GPS monitoring, that allow us to more credibly threaten detection and punishment for further offending (Frase 2013a).

3. *Repeat Drug Offenders*

Offenders in this group and the next raise the opposite problem—standard prior record enhancements may so often be excessive that special mitigation rules are needed. The reasons this is true of drug crimes relate to the ways in which such crimes are typically investigated and enforced, and to the nature of many such offenders. On the enforcement side, this is a type of crime as to which the police can often generate as many separate offenses as they like, simply by continuing to buy from or sell to the same offender, thereby steadily increasing the number of charges and the total drug amounts. Such police-driven repeat offending is very troubling, even when it does not rise to the level of legal entrapment: granted, the offender agreed to commit the crime again and again when given opportunities to do so, but the police can and do decide which willing offenders to target, and to what extent. The police discretion factor is made measurably worse by the tendency for such "controlled buy" and "controlled delivery" tactics to be most heavily used in low-income, inner-city neighborhoods where the arrested defendants are mostly nonwhite, thus strongly contributing to the racial disproportionality problems that were discussed in chapter 7.

A further distinctive feature of repeat drug offending is that many of these offenders are chemically dependent, and are selling drugs to support their own habit. This means that their culpability, although legally sufficient for purposes of criminal liability, is significantly diminished for purposes of sentencing, particularly when it comes to attributing enhanced culpability based on their prior crimes. Moreover, to the extent that addiction was the cause of their repeat offending, this is a criminogenic factor that can be, and often is, successfully treated or otherwise overcome. Yet prior record enhancements pay no attention to that; an offender's addiction-motivated crimes continue to count against him, even long after he has overcome his addiction.

Case-specific mitigation can resolve many of these problems. But since the special features of drug offending are so often present—and so difficult for courts to reliably identify case by case—a systemic (presumptive-rule) solution may be better. Our recommendation would be, at a minimum, to either limit the number of minor police-initiated drug crimes that can be included in criminal history, or better yet, exclude all of them. Any prior drug crimes should certainly be excluded if they were the product of an addiction that the offender has subsequently overcome by treatment, religious belief, or life-course change (see further discussion in Section 4).

4. *Aging and Altered-Life-Course Offenders*

Advancing age, particularly if the offender is also infirm, will often provide another strong basis for sentence mitigation, notwithstanding the offender's substantial prior conviction record.[2] As was noted in chapter 3, one of the best documented findings of criminological research is the "age-crime curve"—the odds of further crime steadily diminish with age, and this is true even for offenders who at earlier ages had a very active criminal career resulting in a substantial record of convictions. One of the most serious limitations of criminal history enhancements in guidelines systems is that they take no account of the offender's current age, and thus result in the confinement of large numbers of aging prisoners whose risk of re-offending is dropping while the cost of holding them, especially medical costs, is rising. Sentencing judges should therefore give careful consideration to whether an older offender's criminal history score overstates his or her current level of recidivism risk. Indeed, this is such a strong and consistent mitigating factor that it may be preferable for sentencing commissions to formally recognize it. This could be done in a number of ways, for example, by shortening the decay (washout or look-back) period for older offenders, or by downward adjustments to the total criminal history score based on a formula tied to advancing age, at least for offenders who are middle-aged or older. Judges would still have power to depart up or down from the mitigation formula—departing down if additional case-specific factors (including the kinds of life-course changes noted later in this section) indicate an even lower risk than the average person of that age, departing up if case-specific factors indicate higher-than-average risk (for example: recent serious crimes; a steady, unbroken record of offending despite aging; other indicia that the offender's criminal career is still very "active").

An important reason older offenders display declining risk (other than from sheer loss of energy due to aging) is that such offenders are likely to have experienced major life-course or lifestyle changes that diminish their interest in or need for criminal behavior. However, such changes can occur at any age, and when they do judges should take them into account. Some of the most important changes of this type relate to substance abuse and relationship status. For example, if alcohol abuse contributed to an offender's previous crimes but he has now been abstinent for years, the predictive power of his previous convictions is no longer the same. Similarly, marriage or a stable long-term relationship may also reduce the probative value of the previous offenses. Other lifestyle changes caused by (or correlated with) a stable relationship include: maintenance of steady employment, less time spent with crime-prone associates, and reduced exposure to drugs or alcohol—all of which are protective factors reducing the likelihood of criminal behavior. Indeed, studies by Ezell (2007) and Kazemian and Farrington (2006) show that lifestyle changes are often better predictors of re-offending than criminal history scores.[3]

One of the key lessons of research on criminal careers and desistance is that these offending patterns are volatile. Current prior record enhancements in U.S. guidelines systems assume a degree of stability in offending over time that is belied by the research (see Kazemian 2010). Again, most life-course and lifestyle changes can be taken into account by use of the expanded departure power we propose. But it may be possible to develop adjustment formulas based on statistical (actuarial) data related to such changes (subject, as always, to departure for case-specific circumstances indicating higher- or lower-than-average risk for this offender).

NOTES

INTRODUCTION

1. For example, this principle is codified in section 718.1 of the Canadian Criminal Code and also in section 8(a) of New Zealand's Sentencing Act 2002 (see Roberts and von Hirsch 1998). A related principle of offense proportionality has also been a key feature of utilitarian sentencing philosophy since the time of Cesare Beccaria and Jeremy Bentham. See generally Frase 2008, 2012.
2. The only jurisdiction of which we are aware that prohibits the use of previous convictions at sentencing is Western Australia, where section 7(2)(b) of the 1995 Sentencing Act notes that "an offence is not aggravated by the fact that . . . the offender has a criminal record."
3. Throughout this book, when sentencing statistics are cited without a specific reference, the statistics are derived from annual data files of sentenced cases, provided by the guidelines commission in the indicated jurisdiction(s) and analyzed by the authors using SPSS software.
4. Likewise, a comparison of German and U.S. sentencing (Frase 2001, table 6) found that German offenders were just as likely to have a prior conviction, and particular numbers of prior convictions, as were offenders in the 75 largest U.S. counties (the latter data series, e.g., BJS 2010, is the only available U.S. national-level data on offender prior records).
5. The highly intuitive relevance of prior convictions is part of the problem. Because it seems so obvious that prior convictions should aggravate sentence, many people fail to consider the issues to any greater depth. While we acknowledge the relevance of prior convictions for sentencing, a central theme of the volume is that the magnitude of the enhancements, and the ways that criminal history should affect the sentence are anything but straightforward. One of our goals is to clarify why, how, and when criminal antecedents should be weighed.
6. Unsurprisingly, defense advocates contest both the theoretical justification for PREs, and the current way that these are implemented (Roberts 2008a, b).

Their skepticism should not be dismissed as mere "adversarialism" at work; defense counsel are likely to have more insight into the origins of current and prior offending, and to see beyond simple schemes that regard recidivists as more culpable and/or higher risk.

7. This research is summarized in chapter 7 of Roberts (2008b). While the offenders interviewed appeared to see previous convictions as a legitimate consideration at sentencing, they also expressed the view that courts should not automatically aggravate the severity to reflect the number and seriousness of prior crimes.
8. These statistics generally suggest that a cumulative sentencing model is followed, in which the probability of a custodial sentence or the length of custody increases in response to the number of prior convictions (see Roberts 2008a, b).
9. Some other jurisdictions (e.g., England and Wales) have also adopted formal sentencing guidelines that clarify the impact of prior convictions (see Roberts 2008a, b). However, these systems do not provide the precise counting rules found in the U.S. guidelines.
10. We define a "sentencing guidelines" system as one in which judges are given a set of recommended sentences, for most types of crime or at least most felonies, that are deemed to be appropriate in typical cases of that type (i.e., cases that do not present aggravating or mitigating factors that might permit departure from the recommendation), and that were developed by a legislatively created sentencing guidelines commission (even if the rules are then embodied in statutes, and even if the commission ceased to exist at some point after the guidelines went into effect). We thus exclude legislatively drafted presumptive sentences such as the ones California and several other states adopted, in the mid- to late 1970s, without input from a sentencing commission. The U.S. state and federal jurisdictions meeting the above definition, and the year when each system's guidelines first became effective, are as follows: Minnesota (1980), Pennsylvania (1982), Maryland (1983), Florida (1983), Washington (1984), Delaware (1987), the U.S. federal courts (1987), Oregon (1989), Tennessee (1989), Kansas (1993), Arkansas (1994), North Carolina (1994), Virginia (1995), Massachusetts (1996), Ohio (1996), Utah (1998), Michigan (1999), District of Columbia (2004), and Alabama (2006) (see Frase 2019, table 1). The primary guidelines document(s) for each system (e.g., Massachusetts Sentencing Commission 2017) are listed under References, infra. However, in Ohio, Oregon, and Tennessee there is no single, official guidelines manual or other document (although Ohio has a "Quick Reference Guide," Ohio Criminal Sentencing Commission 2017, and the Oregon commission publishes a detailed sentencing grid, Oregon Criminal Justice Commission 2018); instead, guidelines rules are contained in a series of statutes or administrative rules. See Ohio Rev. Code, Secs. 2929.11 to 2929.19 (2018); Or. Admin. R. 213-001-0000 to 213-020-0001 (2018); and Tenn. Code Anno., Secs. 40-35-101 to 40-35-122 (2018). For further details on these systems, see Robina Institute 2018 and Frase 2019.

11. This is also the objective of a major research and policy development project of the Robina Institute of Criminal Law and Criminal Justice, located at the University of Minnesota Law School; for further details see: http://www.robinainstitute.org/criminal-history-project/.
12. The classification as "fourth-highest" offense severity level (level 8 in Minnesota; felony class D in North Carolina) does not count extremely serious crimes, such as first-degree murder, carrying mandatory penalties that are not dependent on PRE rules. The lists of crimes classified at this level are very similar in the two states (e.g., armed robbery, first- degree burglary, first-degree arson, and criminal vehicular homicide). See MSGC 2017a, and North Carolina Sentencing and Policy Advisory Commission 2014.
13. The criminal history scale runs higher in North Carolina, topping out at 18 or more points, versus 6 or more points for Minnesota. However, North Carolina's points place offenders into one of six criminal history categories (Minnesota has seven, beginning with zero), and recommended sentences are moderately (but not three times) more severe in North Carolina. The recommended sentence in Minnesota is a single number, although a broader range is provided within which a sentence is not deemed to be a "departure"; in North Carolina a "presumptive range" is provided, so we compare the North Carolina range midpoint to the single-number presumptive sentence provided in Minnesota.
14. It is necessary to convert the maximum prison terms shown on the Minnesota guidelines grid into minimum terms that assume all allowable good-conduct credits, because the recommended prison terms in North Carolina, discussed later on in this Part, are minimum terms that already assume full good-conduct credit.
15. The alternative approach is to leave the determination of the relevance and weight of each prior conviction to the exercise of judicial discretion. This provides greater flexibility and creates a potential safeguard against over-punishment, but it also creates the possibility of disparity of application by sentencing judges.
16. The closest parallel may be found in the English statute cited in Part A, stating that judges may view each prior conviction as an aggravating factor if the court finds that result to be reasonable. However, multivariate research using a new database that draws information directly from the sentencing authority has shown that courts do not strictly apply a cumulative model. Instead, they discount significantly for first offenders and increase only marginally for repeat offenders (see Roberts and Pina Sanchez 2015).
17. See discussion in Roberts 2008a, b.
18. For collections of essays regarding the retributive significance of prior convictions, see Roberts and von Hirsch 2010, and Tamburrini and Ryberg 2012. For exchanges of views, see Roberts and von Hirsch 2009. More recent articles exploring the topic include King 2014, Bagaric 2014a, and Lippke 2015. For reviews of earlier works, see Roberts 1997, 2008b.

19. It is important not to lose sight of the limited predictive power of any single variable, even one, such as criminal history, that in general is strongly correlated with recidivism risk. The decision to reoffend is affected by a wide range of situational, psychological, and social factors. Propensity to reoffend (as measured by the criminal history score) alone will account for only a limited amount of variance in the equation. A sentencing scheme that places heavy reliance on criminal history is likely to suffer from over-prediction of recidivism and hence over-punishment of offenders.
20. As discussed more fully in chapter 4, there is little research support for the argument that prior record enhancements serve to deter this offender or other repeat offenders from committing further crimes.
21. In terms of a criminal conviction, over-punishment is generally regarded as much worse than under-punishment—the requirement of proof beyond reasonable doubt presupposes that convicting the innocent is a more grievous error than acquitting those who are guilty. A similar normative asymmetry is often implicitly assumed by advocates of utilitarian and consequentialist (crime control) punishment goals: the principle of parsimony (also known as necessity, narrow-tailoring, or least restrictive means) lacks a corresponding principle directing sentencing officials to punish *no less severely* than necessary. It has further been argued that retributive theory should likewise view over-punishment as normatively worse than under-punishment (see Frase 2017, for further discussion).
22. USSC 2016a, chap. 4, pt. B, Introductory Commentary. Utah has adopted a similar hybrid approach. On the one hand, the Utah guidelines state that "Risk Management continues to be a legitimate goal of sentencing . . . Risk reduction is addressed through the appropriate identification and reduction of an offender's individual criminal risk factors" (Utah Sentencing Commission 2017, 5–6). On the other hand, "[t]he dominant underlying philosophy of the [Utah] guidelines is that criminal sentences should be proportionate to the seriousness of the [conviction] offense" (Utah Sentencing Commission 2017, 15).
23. Commentary in the current guideline manual notes the subordinate role of criminal history relative to crime seriousness: "Under the Guidelines, the conviction offense is the primary factor, and criminal history is a secondary factor in dispositional decisions" (MSGC 2017a, cmt. 2.B.01).
24. Studies of the extent to which criminal history scores and score components predict recidivism risk have also been conducted for the Pennsylvania and Minnesota guidelines. See Hester (forthcoming) and Laskorunsky (2017, 2018).
25. The Commission did not try to validate the retributive rationale for the recency component, to determine whether offenders who commit a fresh offense within two years of release from a previous sentence are sufficiently more blameworthy to justify the additional punishment associated with two criminal history points. However, the Commission's decision to drop the recency points, based solely on its risk-prediction value and prison costs, implies that the retributive rationale carries little weight (or at least, is not deemed a sufficient justification).

26. Criminal history enhancements have been periodically amended in some guidelines. Amendments to prior record levels to make the intervals between categories more proportionate were introduced in Minnesota (1996 Minn. Laws, chap. 408, art. 3, sec. 39) and in North Carolina (Senate Bill (SB) 488 (2009), "Establishing Proportionate Sentence Lengths" and SB 489 (2009), "Even Out Prior Criminal Record Points"). Similarly, the sixth edition of the Pennsylvania guidelines significantly amended prior record assignments.
27. One possible reason for the relative stability is that many guidelines in the United States and elsewhere are "descriptive" or "historically based on existing judicial norms and practices" (Frase 2005b, 1202), and the underlying sentencing norms are assumed to have not evolved.

CHAPTER 1

1. For example, many people may wish to mitigate punishment for offenders who have made a significant contribution to the community, although there is little room for such considerations within a principled retributive sentencing framework, since they are unrelated to crime seriousness or offender culpability.
2. For example, Section 40k of the Sentencing Law (2012) in Israel identifies a lack of prior convictions as a mitigating factor at sentencing (see Roberts and Gazal-Ayal 2013). So do the Delaware and Ohio guidelines (Delaware Sentencing Accountability Commission 2018, 136; Ohio Revised Code Sec. 2929.12(E)(2)) (2018). See also Wash. Rev. Code sec. 9.94A.650 (2017) (permitting mitigated penalty for most offenders with no prior felony convictions or deferred prosecutions).
3. For discussion of the communicative function of victim impact statements see Roberts and Erez (2009).
4. Statutes often provide a higher penalty range or offense classification for a second and all subsequent violations of the statute. See, e.g., Minn. Stat. Secs. 152.021 subd. 3 and 152.022 subd. 3 (2017) (providing higher penalties for any "subsequent controlled substance conviction" of the first or second degree; a "subsequent" offense is defined in Sec. 152.01, subd. 16a as one committed after the defendant was convicted for a first or second degree controlled substance crime). See also 33 U.S.C.A. § 1319(c) (2017) (second and subsequent violations of federal water pollution law are punishable with up to double the maximum fine and/or prison term provided for first offenders).
5. There are two versions of this argument. In its earliest incarnation, extending some mitigation toward first offenders was justified in terms of their character. In the first edition of his sentencing text Thomas (1970, 197) describes the "progressive loss of credit" approach to offenders with no or few prior convictions. By this term, he refers to the credit accumulated by the offender as a result of his crime-free life up to that point. The credit is progressively lost with each accumulating conviction. Thomas notes: "The fact that a man with previous convictions receives a longer

sentence than a first offender and that a man with five previous convictions receives a longer sentence than a man with two previous convictions, is the result not of progressive aggravation of the basic penalty but a progressive loss of credit for good character until the offender's record is so bad that nothing could be used in his favor in that regard" (1970, 174). This version of the leniency principle has been largely supplanted in the literature by the lapse theory, which justifies the mitigation for first offenders in a quite different way.

6. There is some recognition in the literature of the problematic nature of repeated mitigations. Adler (1991, 171) argues that a moral theory that allows for one lapse or offense is "more plausible than the theory that allows for many."
7. "With repetitions, however, the discount should begin to diminish, and eventually disappear" (Wasik and von Hirsch 1994, 410).
8. This is a practical problem rather than one of principle, but sufficiently important to note.
9. Von Hirsch and Ashworth (2005, 153) also regard the failure to respond to censure as significant when they observe that "Repetition after confrontation with penal censure also suggests a failure on the part of the offender to make the extra effort at self-restraint—the effort which should be the response to being faced with censure."
10. Other factors affecting culpability such as the offender's ability to comply or the existence of external pressure to offend are far more important variables.
11. This point is captured well by Bagaric (2014a, 382) who notes that: "If a recidivist premium is to be conferred, a strong justification is needed. Additional punishment beyond that merited for the instant offense is the logical and moral equivalent of punishing the innocent unless the extra hardship can be accounted for within a strong legal construct." We conclude that no such retributive construct exists to justify the significant and cumulative escalation of severity to reflect prior convictions that is found in U.S. guidelines systems. There is also clearly a need, grounded in offense-based retributive proportionality, to limit the weight that a lengthy prior record carries at sentencing. But sound retributive grounds also exist to mitigate punishment severity for first offenders.
12. See discussion in Roberts (2008, 220–22). The offender should be able to place before the court any actions or experiences that mitigate his culpability notwithstanding his prior record, for example: evidence that he has made efforts, albeit unsuccessful, to address his offending.

CHAPTER 2

1. Even earlier, George Fletcher (1978, 466) wrote that "[t]he contemporary pressure to consider prior convictions in setting the level of . . . [p]unishment reflects a theory of social protection rather than a theory of deserved punishment."
2. One study found that when an offender's most recent conviction is preceded by a conviction-free gap of seven years or greater, the likelihood of further convictions is

substantially lower, albeit not zero, than for offenders with a lesser gap—offenders with a seven- or eight-year gap preceding their current offense had an average remaining active criminal career of about three years, in which time they would commit an average of one further offense (Piquero et al. 2007). Numerous other studies, involving offenders who have one or more earlier convictions but who are *not* facing sentencing for a recent crime, find that after a period of 7 to 10 years with no new convictions an offender's risk of eventually committing a new crime is similar to that of a person who was never convicted (see, e.g., Kurlycheck et al. 2006; Kurlycheck et al. 2007; Soothill and Francis 2009).

3. Gap rules (and to a lesser extent some of the other criminal history factors discussed later on in the chapter, such as custody status) may also be designed to encourage offenders to make greater efforts to remain crime-free; under this rationale, when they have succeeded in doing so for the designated period they are rewarded with lower sentencing severity in order to encourage other offenders to do the same, without regard to whether there is reason to believe the particular offender poses lower risks. However, such an incentive theory suffers from the same defect as the theory of general deterrence—there is little evidence to support the assumption that crime rates are affected by variations in punishment severity, especially small increments to already-severe penalties. For further discussion, see chapter 4.
4. These factors include gender, age, employment history, substance abuse, and antisocial associates. For further discussion, see chapter 3.
5. The U.S. Sentencing Commission also noted the absence of a difference in recidivism rates between offenders in CH categories V and VI. But having suggested that these two categories could therefore be combined without any loss of predictive power, the report then observed that "practitioners and policy makers may identify a culpability difference between offenders in CHC V and CHC VI" (USSC 2004a, 15). Whether policymakers would indeed argue this position, and how one might justify distinguishing between the two categories, is unclear.
6. To compare recidivism rate increases to recommended-sentence increases at a given offense severity level it is necessary to assume that patterns of recidivism by criminal history score are roughly similar across different offense seriousness levels. Published reports do not provide recidivism rates broken down by offense severity and criminal history category (i.e., by grid cell), but one report does show limited variation in recidivism rates by offense severity, with offenders at the lowest and highest severity levels having slightly lower-than-average rearrest rates (USSC 2016b, figure 8).
7. The U.S. Commission's research reports assume that since recidivism rates increase in response to the number of criminal history points, the current architecture of the grid is valid. Our point here is that specific increments in severity need to reflect the degree to which increases in CH points reflect higher risk of re-offending.
8. Even when high-history offenders recidivate with what appears to be a violent crime, it is important to take into account the broad offense-type definitions often

employed in sentencing data. In Minnesota, for example, "person" offenses include many low-severity felonies involving only threats or minor injuries, and no use or display of a weapon (for further discussion, see chapter 6, *infra*).

9. The index was designed to be: (1) consistent with contemporary sentencing and releasing practices, (2) based on objective and accessible records, (3) simple to use, and (4) independent of social status and economic variables (see MSGC 1980, 7).
10. For example, the California Static Risk Assessment (CSRA) scale is heavily based on prior convictions (see Turner et al. 2009). Commissions also assume that prior convictions are a static predictor (see, e.g., Pennsylvania Commission on Sentencing 2011b; Ministry of Justice 2014). Henning et al. (2013) assert that "many [risk-related] items are static—cannot change fact of prior arrest" (13). The arrest cannot be changed, but its significance as a predictor of re-offending or its retributive value can (and does) evolve.
11. On a retributive account the offender who has addressed the cause of her offending has moved away from her prior self: the previous conviction therefore says less about the current individual and accordingly should carry less weight at sentencing. Classifying prior crimes as a static, unchanging risk factor is therefore inappropriate—despite the fact that all common risk scales adopt this approach. For this reason, our model outlined in chapter 11 treats prior crimes as potentially dynamic.
12. This could be achieved in many ways, and we propose several options in chapters 9 and 11. For an earlier proposal along these lines, see Hillier (1997) (suggesting that the federal guidelines should expressly endorse the appropriateness of a downward departure when the prior offense is quite old, and falls just inside the applicable look-back period).
13. The U.S. Sentencing Commission has studied two groups of offenders, one sentenced in fiscal year 1992 (see USSC 2004a, b; 2005, 2010), and the other released on probation or from prison or jail in 2005 (USSC 2016b, 2017a, b, c). See also USSC 2018, providing additional detail on the criminal histories of offenders sentenced in fiscal year 2016. For research examining the risk-predictive accuracy of the Pennsylvania and Minnesota criminal history scores and score components, see Hester (forthcoming) and Laskorunsky (2017, 2018).
14. Similarly, Laskorunsky (2018) found that dropping points for juvenile court adjudications had no effect on the risk-predictive power of Minnesota's criminal history score. In addition, Laskorunsky (2017) and Hester (forthcoming) found that removing the higher weights given to more serious prior felonies did not reduce the predictive power of the Minnesota and Pennsylvania criminal history scores. These results are consistent with the findings, for both states, that higher conviction offense severity is associated with lower recidivism risk. See also USSC (2016b, figure 8) (offenders at the highest federal offense severity levels have slightly lower-than-average re-arrest rates).

    The U.S. Sentencing Commission also identified other limitations of the federal criminal history formula, in particular, the failure to consider two factors clearly associated with lower risk: the offender's older age; and whether the offender was a "true" first offender lacking even a prior arrest record (see USSC 2004a, 2004b, 2005). However, as of this writing the Commission has not made any guidelines changes based on these findings.

CHAPTER 3

1. For illustrative Minnesota case law, see *State v. Park* (1981) (unamenability to probation) and *State v. Trog* (1982) (amenability to probation). For examples of similar departure grounds specified in the guidelines themselves or in statutes, see N.C. Gen. Stat. sec. 15A-1340.16(e) (2013); Utah Sentencing Commission 2015, 22; and Ohio Rev. Stat. sec. 2929.12(D) (2018).
2. To identify low-risk drug offenders, prior juvenile adjudications are also counted, and an explicit recency factor—arrest or confinement within 12 months prior to the current offense—is substituted in lieu of the custody status factor included in the larceny and fraud risk assessments (Virginia Criminal Sentencing Commission 2018a, Sec. D).
3. See, e.g., Virginia Criminal Sentencing Commission 2017, 30–34. The estimated numbers of high-risk enhancements (33) and low-risk mitigations (1,327) are derived by multiplying the reported percentage figures by the total number of cases.
4. Utah Sentencing Commission 2015, 1–6, 8–11. Utah requires such an assessment to be done prior to sentencing in all felony cases.
5. However, in response to criticisms of the use of arrests rather than convictions to measure recidivism, including arrests for technical violations of release conditions, the Commission plans to reanalyze its data to see how the results differ using only reconviction as the outcome measure (Pennsylvania Commission on Sentencing 2018c, 6).
6. The Commission excluded race from the outset, and then assessed the loss of accuracy that would result from removing other contested factors from the scales. It concluded that removing offender age would "dramatically affect the usefulness of the scale," and that removing gender and county of residence would further significantly reduce accuracy. The commission chose to retain gender, but exclude county of residence (Pennsylvania Commission on Sentencing 2015). Race and county were not included in any of the risk scales even though they were found to be significant risk predictors, but they were included in all models so that the weights given to the retained risk factors do not include the indirect effects of the two excluded factors (*Id.*, 2018c, 5; 2018d, 4).
7. See Monahan and Skeem 2014; see also Monahan et al. 2016; Skeem et al. 2016; Monahan et al. 2017 (discussing "promotive" factors such as employment that are associated with desistance from offending, and "protective" factors that moderate the effects of high-risk factors).
8. This instrument was modeled on one that had been developed by the Washington State Institute for Public Policy (WSIPP).

9. As will be noted, none of the 43 scored factors in the LSI-R considers the offender's current age, even though criminal-careers research shows this to be a strong risk-predictor (and one that is included in other well-known risk assessment tools). Perhaps age is omitted from the LSI-R because it adds little predictive value to the large number of other demographic and life-course-related factors that are already included.
10. See, e.g., Hirschi and Gottfredson 1983; Sampson and Laub 1995; Piquero et al. 2007; Monahan et al. 2017. Research by the federal and Pennsylvania sentencing commissions finds that recidivism rates decline with advancing age even for offenders with high criminal history scores at the time of their latest sentencing (USSC 2004a, Exhibit 9; USSC 2017a, Figure 22; Hester forthcoming). And a comparison of the federal criminal history score to the U.S. Parole Commission's risk-validated Salient Factor Score (which factors in offender age) found that, with the addition of a variable estimating the offender's age at the time of the current offense, the criminal history score's recidivism-predictive power was increased to equal that of the Salient Factor Score (USSC 2005, 14). On the other hand, Laskorunsky's (2018) study of Minnesota offenders sentenced in 2003 found that, within the highest criminal history category, recidivism rates were similar across the three oldest of the four age categories examined (25–34, 35–44, and 45 or older). Laskorunky speculates that this pattern may reflect a large number of "life course persistent" or "career" older offenders (citing Moffit 1993 and Piquero et al. 2007), although it is not clear why Minnesota would have more such offenders than either Pennsylvania or the federal courts. Clearly this is an area that requires further research.
11. Evidence of the relative power of aging emerges from multivariate analyses of recidivism predictors reported by the Pennsylvania Commission on Sentencing. For example, the odds of rearrest for offenders with 5–12 prior arrests were approximately three times greater than for offenders with no priors; but for offenders aged 50 or more the odds of re-offending were six times less than for younger offenders (Pennsylvania Commission on Sentencing 2012, Appendix table 1).

CHAPTER 4

1. Evaluation research (empirical validation) of sentencing policies and changes in policy is generally restricted to determining the impact on correctional resources—prison admissions, prison beds, and so forth. A good example is the Minnesota Sentencing Commission's research on the impact of statutory sentencing enhancements. These reports explore the impact of such enhancements on correctional resources but ignore the impact on crime—the justifications for introducing the enhancements. See, e.g., https://mn.gov/sentencing-guidelines/assets/2010%20Impact%20of%20Statutory%20Enhancements_tcm30-31194.pdf (2010).

2. Of course, preventive benefits arising from the use of prior-conviction or other enhancements may well reflect some combination of incapacitation and general and/or special deterrence. There is also the possibility that a longer term of imprisonment may have some rehabilitative effect; the offender may acquire new employment-related skills or may have addressed substance abuse problems while serving time. In light of the literature on the effects of imprisonment, however, we believe that this possibility is remote, and that imprisonment has a net criminogenic effect in all but the small number of therapeutic prisons (research finding that imprisonment is often associated with *higher* recidivism rates is discussed in text at notes 6 and 8–17, *infra*).
3. Of course, case-specific factors can also cause a sentencing formula to *understate* the offender's risk of re-offending. But as discussed below in Part B, enhancements based on findings of case-specific high-risk factors raise both ethical and legal objections. And given the levels of mass incarceration found in most American jurisdictions, it seems likely that over-prediction of risk is much more common than under-prediction.
4. In jurisdictions without detailed presumptively binding guidelines that clearly specify the magnitude of recidivist enhancements, the likelihood of any specific deterrent effect is even more remote, as potential offenders will have little idea of how much additional punishment their past offense will generate at future sentencing decisions.
5. Consistent with previous work this study found that the presence of house alarms and CCTV were the most powerful factors influencing offenders' decisions to re-offend (see Hearnden and Magill 2004, table 4).
6. Limitations on space prevent us from discussing other sources of variation that may moderate the deterrent effect. Research in the United Kingdom has demonstrated that the nature of the penal institution plays a strong role in determining whether ex-prisoners return to crime. A hostile penal climate is associated with higher recidivism rates (e.g., Liebling 2014). This variability also has important consequences for prior record enhancement regimes.
7. As Fazel and Wolf (2015) note, the great variability in definitions, follow-up periods, and other issues prevent these comparisons from being anything but approximate and suggestive.
8. A number of publications have adopted a broader approach to the problem. Rather than comparing recidivism rates of specific sanctions differing in severity, these reviews have compared recidivism rates across jurisdictions (e.g., Fazel and Wolf (2015, 6), finding "no obvious relationship" between a country's incarceration rate and rates of re-offending). The question is whether highly punitive sentencing systems are associated with lower recidivism rates—as would be predicted if increases in punitiveness reduce subsequent offending. We do not review these publications here because they are less well-controlled due to the far greater number of variables in play. However, we note that their conclusions are consistent with the research that compares specific sanctions within a country (e.g., Kury et al. 2003).

9. Including comparisons among the non-prison sentence types, there were a total of 12 comparisons related to each of the two research questions. As to the first question, only four comparisons suggested a deterrent effect, of which two (involving regular versus intensive probation) had a substantively trivial effect size, while eight showed significant *negative* deterrent effects of greater severity; likewise as to the second question, only four comparisons suggested a deterrent effect, while eight showed significant *negative* deterrent effects.
10. These include Champion 1994; Gendreau et al. 2001; Smith et al. 2002; Villettaz et al. 2006; Colorado Division of Criminal Justice 2008; Nagin et al. 2009; Jonson 2010; Kazemian 2010; Cullen et al. 2011; Bales and Piquero 2012; Zara and Farrington 2016; Sentencing Council 2017.
11. Comparisons between prison sentences and suspended sentences of custody yield a similar conclusion, with re-offending rates being lower for the latter sanction (e.g., Ministry of Justice 2015).
12. The adverse effects of having a prison record are in addition to the effects of the criminal conviction record itself; each of these adds to the many barriers to reintegration that offenders confront, ultimately leading to re-offending rather than desistance (e.g., Petersilia 2003; Makarios et al. 2010).
13. Nagin and Snodgrass (2013) note an additional assumption, namely that the deterrent effect of imprisonment has a homogeneous effect upon different categories of offender. We do not review the research relating to this assumption in part because it would be impractical to construct an enhancement regime that adopted a very flexible or bespoke approach depending upon the likely effect upon a specific offender. That said, there seems little a priori reason for accepting the assumption as deterrent effects are likely to be affected by a range of individual variables.
14. Petersilia 1987; Loughran et al. 2009; Anwar and Stephens 2011; Nagin and Snodgrass 2013; Rydberg and Clark 2016.
15. As with any single study, this research cannot provide a definitive answer to the question of whether sentence length correlates negatively with re-offending rates. For example, the follow-up period was relatively brief (six months).
16. One U.S. study did find some support for the hypothesis that imprisonment has a preventive effect—Meade et al. (2013) found that ex-prisoners who had served at least five years in prison were less likely to re-offend. But the researchers acknowledged that they were unable to determine whether a preventive effect associated with the long-term prisoners was a result of incapacitation, deterrence, rehabilitation, or mere aging. Most of the long-term imprisonment offenders had served lengthy periods inside and were accordingly much older at the time of the recidivism follow-up. As was noted in chapter 3, advancing age is one of the strongest predictors of low recidivism risk.
17. This assumes that risk-based enhancements are not ruled out, a priori. As discussed in chapter 1, some proponents of a strictly retributive sentencing model reject all sentence enhancements that are not based on desert, and further argue that prior

record (and thus also, elevated risk) does not increase desert. For these writers, any enhancement based on prior record or on risk is unfair to the offender because it exceeds his or her deserved punishment.

18. See, e.g., Tonry 2014. See also *Miller v. Alabama* (2012) (citing the diminished culpability of juveniles as one reason for limiting their eligibility for the most severe penalties; earlier cases therein support the same proposition).
19. In a national opinion survey, less than half of participants were willing to consider gender at sentencing; however, more than three-quarters would consider advancing age (50 or over) (Scurich et al. 2016, 36–44).
20. Occasionally these factors cut the other way. For example, the low-risk assessment tool applied to larceny offenders in Virginia treats females as posing higher risk than males (see Virginia Criminal Sentencing Commission 2014c, 11). But unless there is some reason to think that this treatment of females reflects actual or implicit bias against them, it is arguably not unfair to deny them low-risk sentence mitigation.
21. Dailey (1993, 774) found that black offenders in Minnesota were less likely than whites to be employed at sentencing, but that, among employed offenders, a higher percent of blacks received a downward dispositional departure (i.e., probation in lieu of the recommended executed prison sentence).
22. Mitigation (or discounting of drug-related priors) should also be permitted if treatment was offered, accepted, and successful—a formerly addicted offender should not continue to be punished for offenses caused by a criminogenic condition that he or she has overcome.
23. Mitchell (2015) has a brief introduction to this important case and its impact on sentencing guidelines systems.
24. However, at least one court has held that facts supporting addition of a custody status point to defendant's criminal history score fall within the *Blakely* exception for the "fact of prior conviction" (*State v. Brooks* (2004)).

CHAPTER 5

1. Of course, the shorter custodial sentences that American offenders serve in a local jail or workhouse are also stigmatizing and represent significant losses of liberty, privacy, and family contact, not to mention the indignity of being locked in a cage like a wild animal. Accordingly, in other common law countries *any custodial sentence* is considered to be a severe penalty, and much attention is paid to questions of whether an offender's case is serious enough to pass the "custody threshold" (see, e.g., Hutton forthcoming).
2. The 12 included guidelines systems are shown in table 5.1. The five excluded non-grid systems are Alabama, Delaware, Florida, Ohio, and Virginia. Several of the included grid systems have one or more specialized grids for certain kinds of crimes, but those systems also have a main grid that is used for the majority of cases. By contrast, all three Maryland grids and all nine Michigan grids are offense-specific, so we excluded those two states.

3. Some grids, including the Minnesota Standard grid shown in figure 5.1, have shaded areas to distinguish their Zone 3 recommended-non-prison cells. But even when a grid does not explicitly identify non-prison cells in this way, Zone 3 can be identified as the group of cells for which the recommended sentence is either probation or an active custody sentence (or midpoint, if a range is given) not exceeding one year (which is the traditional upper limit for sentences to a local jail or workhouse, rather than state prison).
4. Two factors account for the differences between on-paper dispositional magnitude estimates and in-practice estimates based on convictions. First, convicted offenders are distributed unevenly across offense severity levels on the grid and across criminal history categories—more offenders are convicted at lower severity levels and lower criminal history levels than at higher severity and higher history levels (on-paper dispositional magnitude measures essentially assume that a given percentage of grid cells reflects a similar percentage of convicted offenders). Second, in-practice measures based on sentences imposed also take into account judges' decisions about whether to follow or depart from the prison-commit recommendation for Zone 2 offenders.
5. In this and later chapters, whenever state guidelines sentencing data is presented without citation to published reports, the sources are sentencing data files obtained from the sentencing commissions for the indicated states, and analyzed by the authors.
6. On many grids, offenders in the lowest criminal history category convicted of lower-severity crimes are recommended for a non-prison sentence, but in most cases judges have discretion to impose a local jail sentence within a given range, and in some systems a jail sentence is recommended. If we were to exclude all offense severity levels lacking recommended executed-prison terms for low-history offenders, the resulting durational magnitude for that grid would only reflect higher offense-severity levels. We therefore computed durational magnitude measures based on recommended or authorized custody sentences including jail terms—we are comparing, for high-history and low-history offenders, the custody sentence a judge can impose without departing. However, we omitted an offense severity level from the analysis if, for low-history offenders in that level, no executed custody sentence of any kind is permitted without departure.
7. In systems such as Kansas and Oregon that use "border boxes," allowing judges to impose either prison or a non-prison sentence, the top of the custody range for that cell is the recommended prison term or prison-range midpoint and the bottom for that cell is the recommended jail term or the jail-range midpoint.
8. An alternate way to measure the impact of criminal history on recommended prison duration at each offense severity level would be to compare the ceiling of the highest-history cell at that level with the floor of the lowest-history cell; in the example shown in figure 5.2, a severity level 8 offender's recommended prison duration would be deemed to increase from 41 months at zero history to 129 months at the highest history, for a ratio of 3.15 (versus 2.25, using cell midpoints). However,

we chose to use cell midpoints for two reasons: (1) using the highest-history ceiling versus lowest-history floor approach confounds two distinct kinds of variation across guidelines systems—the average increase in recommended-sentence duration from lowest to highest criminal history scores, and the width of grid cell ranges; (2) some jurisdictions and grid cells lack a range, so the single custody-duration numbers provided for these cases are more meaningfully compared to range midpoints.

9. As a test of the robustness of our durational magnitude measure, we analyzed an alternative measure that examines recommended prison durations without regard to the disposition question—that is, we compared highest-history to lowest-history recommended prison durations even if, as is often true for lowest-history offenders at medium or low offense severity, the specified prison term is recommended to be suspended. The results using this alternative measure are fairly similar to those for our main measure, although the size of the durational multiplier is consistently lower than with the main measure (averaging 3.0 across the 12 jurisdictions, ranging from a low of 1.7 in Washington, DC, to a high of 5.5 in Arkansas). Also, the rank order of the systems changes somewhat; nevertheless, four of the six systems in the low-ratio half according to our main measure are still in that half, and four of the six systems in the high-ratio half are still in that half. However, for all systems except Minnesota and Washington, DC, the alternate measure is based on fewer severity levels (since we exclude all levels for which, at the lowest criminal history, not even a suspended prison term is recommended)—for two states, half or fewer than half of the severity levels are represented. We therefore prefer our main measure because in almost all systems it is based on more offense severity levels; also, our main measure captures all custodial sanctions, to jail as well as prison.
10. Unlike Part A, which focused on grid-based guidelines systems, the discussion in this part also includes criminal history components that add to an offender's total point score in some non-grid (worksheet-based) systems. We also occasionally note criminal history factors that are reflected not in criminal history scoring but in lists of aggravating and mitigating circumstances; one example of the latter is Ohio, a guidelines state that uses neither grids nor worksheets.
11. Eleven jurisdictions include custody status in criminal history scoring, six jurisdictions treat such status as an aggravating factor at sentencing, and two jurisdictions have no guidelines provision related to custody status (Roberts 2015a, table 9.1; Ohio Rev. Code Sec. 2929.12(D)(1) (2018)). This topic will be further discussed in chapter 10.
12. In addition, the federal guidelines formerly assigned extra criminal history points for very recent prior crimes (current offense committed within a specified time following the prior crime or sentence) (USSC 2009, sec. 4A1.1(e) (repealed)).
13. For example, in Virginia prior felony sexual assault convictions or adjudications can add up to 12 points out of a maximum of 40 points for criminal history factors, on the Other Sexual Assault Section C worksheet (Virginia Criminal Sentencing Commission 2018e).

14. The underlying aggravated robbery statutes are found in Kan. Stat. Ann. 21-5420 (2018), Minn. Stat. 609.245 (2018), and 18 Pa. C. S. A. 3701 (2018) .

    In Kansas, a prior person offense can take the offender more than halfway across the grid, from criminal history category I (lowest) to category D (fourth highest). The Kansas system counts three Class A and B person misdemeanors as one person felony), but since the hypothetical assumes one serious and three minor misdemeanors, there is no additional premium for misdemeanors (Kansas Sentencing Commission 2014, 37). Adding two juvenile offenses advances the offender from Category D to Category C (Kansas Sentencing Commission 2014, 36). Custody status is not counted, in Kansas.

    In Minnesota, the prior robbery, a severity level 8 offense, accrues 1.5 criminal history points and gives the offender a criminal history score of 1 (partial points are disregarded) (MSGC 2017a, sec. 2.B.02). One point is added because of the four prior misdemeanors, and another point is earned for the two prior juvenile offenses; a point is also added for custody status (MSGC 2017a, sec. 2.B.115). Thus each of the last four hypotheticals adds a point in Minnesota.

    In Pennsylvania, the prior armed robbery gets four prior record points and takes the offender halfway across the grid (to criminal history category 4) (Pennsylvania Commission on Sentencing 2012a, sec. 303.7(a)(1)). Two points are added for every misdemeanor. However, the final two history categories in Pennsylvania, REVOC and RFEL, are reserved for offenders with two or more prior Felony 1 or Felony 2 offenses for REVOC, or 6 or more points from Felony 1s or Felony 2s for RFEL (Pennsylvania Commission on Sentencing 2012a, sec. 303.4(a)(2)). Accordingly, with just one prior serious felony, the hypothetical offender cannot be placed in these final two categories and effectively "tops out" at prior record score 5. This also holds true for the two juvenile offenses, which would add points if the offender were not already in category 5. Custody status, however, does not add additional points in Pennsylvania.
15. In addition, the relative "shapes" of the curves in figure 5.3 depend on the order in which the different score components are entered. For example, if the prior felony were entered as part of the final example ("Hypo E") for each state, instead of as the first with-priors example, Minnesota's curve would remain unchanged but the curves for Pennsylvania and Kansas would be lower than Minnesota's curve until the final example added in the felony priors.
16. The United States is an exception in this regard. For example, in most other common law jurisdictions plea-based sentencing discounts increase in magnitude the earlier that the defendant enters his or her plea (see, e.g., Sentencing Council of England and Wales 2017); across different common law regimes outside of the United States a common approach generally emerges.
17. Offenders convicted of low seriousness crimes with very extensive records could still be committed to custody based on their criminal history if the court departs from the guideline recommendations. In this way "push-in" as we refer to the phenomenon

would be restricted to exceptional cases, and repetitive petty offenders would not routinely be committed to custody (see discussion in Roberts and Harris 2016).

18. In a recent work Michael Tonry has proposed a similar, yet somewhat more restrictive rule. He argues that the premium should be capped at 1.5 (see Tonry 2016, 244).
19. An exception to this rule might be recognized, permitting multiple current offenses to be included in the current criminal history score in lieu of consecutive sentencing of the offenses if that would provide a recommended sentence intermediate in severity between fully concurrent and fully consecutive sentencing. Several guidelines states have taken this approach, including all or some current offenses in the criminal history score or the sentencing grid or worksheet while limiting judicial discretion to sentence consecutively (see Frase 2015c for further discussion).

CHAPTER 6

1. Recommended sentences on guidelines grids or non-grid worksheets assume an ordinary or typical case—offense severity rankings are based on the judgment that, for typical cases of each crime, all offenses ranked at a given severity level are more serious than all offenses ranked one or more severity levels lower, and less serious than all offenses ranked higher. Of course, when aggravating facts are present the principle of offense proportionality permits sanction severity equal to or even exceeding the recommended typical-offense sentences for more serious crimes; similarly, mitigating facts permit a sanction equal to or less than the typical-case recommendations for less serious crimes.
2. The main Minnesota grid does not include offenses subject to sentences of life in prison (without possibility of parole, or with parole eligibility after 30 years). These offenses are excluded from the on-paper proportionality measure discussed in the text because life sentences do not depend on the offender's guidelines criminal history score.
3. See, e.g., MSGC 1984a, 97. Delaware's commission noted their goal of "incapacitation of the violence-prone offender" (Delaware Sentencing Accountability Commission 2015, 22). Kansas's commission listed one goal as "promot[ing] public safety by incarcerating violent offenders (Kansas Sentencing Commission 2009, 2).
4. Guidelines goals in a number of jurisdictions include incapacitation of repeat offenders (Roberts 2015b, 14–16). Frase (2015a) shows how guidelines systems have used criminal history enhancements and other mechanisms to impose more severe penalties on higher-risk offenders. Chapters 2 and 3 of this book discuss the relationship between criminal history scores and various risk factors.
5. See, e.g., Sampson and Laub 1995. See also Moffitt 1993, Piquero et al. 2007.
6. Recidivism rates decline with advancing age, even for offenders with high criminal history scores at the time of their last sentencing (see, e.g., USSC 2004, Exhibit 9; USSC 2017a, figure 22). The relationship between criminal history enhancements and recidivism risk is further examined in chapter 3.

7. However, as discussed more fully in chapter 1, retributive philosophers are in sharp disagreement about whether and to what extent an offender's retributive deserts depend on his or her prior record; indeed, many such writers believe that a prior record should not be considered at all when sentencing a new offense.
8. Here is how we arrived at the particular numbers shown in figure 6.2 (our illustrative, more-offense-proportionate Minnesota grid). We use the existing custody durations for offenders with a criminal history score of 1 as the baseline sentence for each offense severity level—sentences that are neither mitigated (for first offenders) nor enhanced (for offenders with two or more criminal history points). We then shorten some of the recommended durations for criminal history scores of 1, and all of the durations at criminal history 2 or higher, in order to make all cells at history 1 through history 6+ fully proportionate (as defined in the text). As noted in chapters 1 and 2, we believe that only modest sentence enhancements are merited for medium- and high-history offenders, under both retributive and crime-control punishment rationales. As for the first offender (zero-history) recommended durations shown in the table, these mostly equal two-thirds of the recommended duration for criminal history 1 offenders. But at offense severity levels 10 and 11, zero-history durations are 90 percent of history-1 durations (reflecting our view that deserved punishment is not mitigated as much for first offenders committing very serious crimes). Finally, it must be kept in mind that, as with all state and federal guidelines grids, these are recommended sentences for *typical cases* of each type. In an exceptional case justifying departure from the applicable recommendation, the court may impose a longer or shorter custody term, and/or depart from the recommended disposition (prison/no-prison).
9. Minnesota case law has also recognized relaxed proportionality constraints when it comes to permissible dispositional departure grounds: although durational departures must be proportional to crime seriousness, dispositional departures are based on offender amenability or unamenability to probation (Frase 2005a, 2013).
10. Such a rule could be structured so as not to raise issues under *Blakely v. Washington* (2004). For example, the rule could specify a typical-offense recommended sentence or sentence range based on unadjusted criminal history, and allow judges to make downward adjustments according to an age-based formula provided the judge is satisfied that the offender does *not* pose a higher risk than his or her age would otherwise indicate.

CHAPTER 7

1. Nellis 2016, table C. These racial disparities would be even greater if prison inmates—almost all of whom are adults—were compared only to adult populations of each race. Black populations tend to be younger, with a higher proportion of juveniles; thus, if juveniles are included in the population base, this understates the black per capita incarceration rate more than it understates the white rate, thereby

understating the black-to-white disparity ratio and possibly distorting the relative disparity of some states. For example, the black-to-white ratios shown in table 7.2, which are computed using race-specific per capita rates based on adult populations, are higher than the all-ages-based ratios shown for those four states in table 7.1 (although the rank order of these states is the same in both tables). In addition, the all-races per capita prison rates shown in table 7.1 would be higher in every state, if computed relative to state populations excluding juveniles. See BJS 2015b, table 5 (the national incarceration rate per 100,000 adults in 2014 was 30 percent higher than when the rate is computed with juveniles included in the base).

2. Of the 25 states with the highest ratios of black-to-white incarceration rates, 23 states (and seven of the nine guidelines states in this higher-ratio group) had a total (all-races) incarceration rate below the national average. Of the 25 states with the lowest black-to-white ratios, 19 states (and six of the eight guidelines states in this lower-ratio group) had an above-average incarceration rate. This pattern appears to reflect two factors: (1) high-incarceration-rate states tend to imprison large numbers of property offenders, relatively more of whom are white, whereas low-rate states focus on violent and drug-trafficking offenders, relatively more of whom are black; (2) high-incarceration-rate states in the South tend to have white crime rates above the national average for whites and black crime rates below the national average for blacks, whereas the opposite is true for many low-incarceration-rate states in the Northeast and Upper Midwest. For further details, see Frase 2013a, chap. 5; Frase 2009, 223–37.
3. Racial disproportionality in prison populations (the right-hand column in table 7.2) reflects both the frequency and the duration of prison sentences given to offenders of each race, whereas data on recommended and executed prison sentences (the two middle columns) only measures racial differences in the frequency of prison terms. In Section B.2 we present Minnesota data on racial differences in the duration as well as the frequency of prison sentences, and show how each contributes to the bottom line of racially disproportionate prison populations.
4. The methods used here are explained in more detail in Frase (2009).
5. For example, the number of additional blacks recommended for prison due to criminal history is computed by comparing the actual number of blacks in the second zone described in text to the expected number; the latter figure—the number of blacks that would be found in Zone 2 if both races were distributed in the same proportions across all areas of the grid—is derived by multiplying the total number of blacks sentenced by the *percentage of white offenders* found in that zone.
6. Negative values in the right-hand column of this table (and also table 7.5) mean that, for those states, the actual number of blacks recommended for prison from Zone 3 was *lower* than the expected number based on the proportion of whites recommended from this zone.
7. As indicated in the notes to table 7.6, ratios are based on race categories inclusive of Hispanics in order to maintain consistency with arrest and Minnesota prison

data. The ratios reported here for Minnesota are thus slightly different than those reported in table 7.2 where, to permit comparisons across states, the data reported is based on white and black categorizations that excluded individuals with Hispanic origin. Another difference between the data reported in these two tables is that, for table 7.2, the population bases used to compute per capita rates for each race are the Census Bureau's "race alone" counts (respondent chose a single race) whereas, for the reasons explained in the notes to table 7.6, that table's population bases are averages of race-alone and race-alone-or-in-combination counts. As is also explained in those notes, time lags are applied to the population bases used to compute race-specific incarceration rates, from which the race/ethnic disparity ratios shown in table 7.6 are computed.

8. The estimated ratio of Hispanic-to-white year-end prison rates shown in table 7.6 (2.73) is probably higher than the true rate. The Minnesota Department of Corrections reports the total number of Hispanic inmates, but all of the totals by race include Hispanics. Sentencing data indicates that over 90 percent of Hispanics with reported racial identity are white, so the table compares the Hispanic incarceration rate to the estimated non-Hispanic white rate, with the latter computed by subtracting all Hispanic inmates from the white total. Since some Hispanics are nonwhite, subtracting all of them from the white total understates the non-Hispanic white incarceration rate, thus overstating the estimated Hispanic-to-white ratio of incarceration rates.
9. Since only about 15 percent of probation sentences are revoked, recommended stayed-prison durations are not analyzed here.
10. There are 19 severity levels on the two grids, which yields a total of 57 year-levels for the years 2012 to 2014. Nine year-levels are excluded from this comparison because they contain fewer than three recommended-prison offenders of one or both races. Two levels that had equal black and white recommended durations are also excluded. This leaves a total of 46 levels, of which 33 (71.7 percent) had higher average black recommended executed-prison sentences. Some of the higher recommended terms at lower offense levels are due to the application of mandatory-minimum statutes and other special rules; excluding those cases, 69.6 percent (32 of 46) levels had higher average black recommended prison terms.
11. See, e.g., MSGC 2015a, 24. Defendants may also request prison if that sentence would be less onerous than the proposed conditions of probation (Frase 2005a).
12. See Frase 1993 (1987 and 1989 sentencing data); Frase 2005a (2000 and 2001 data); and Frase 2009 (2005 data). The latter study found that race was significant in one model that excluded three districts lacking bivariate racial disparity in downward departure rates).

In more recent years a significant race effect has sometimes appeared for cases sentenced on the main Minnesota grid (the earlier models were for years when all crimes were placed on a single grid; a separate sex-crimes grid was created in 2006, and a drug-crimes grid in 2015). In 2012 to 2014, white downward dispositional departure rates were higher than black rates by 22 percent in 2012 and 19 percent in 2014, but only 13 percent in 2013. For 2012, logistic regression of race and 10 other variables associated with greater or lesser likelihood of an executed-prison sentence found race significant at $p < .027$, but the odds ratio (ExpB = 1.188) was the lowest of the 11 independent variables. For 2014 the same model found a weaker race effect ($p <.064$, ExpB = 1.150). (Every district had bivariate racial disparity in its downward departure rates for one or more of these years, so separate models were not run for selected districts.)

13. This finding at first seems anomalous, given that the white downward dispositional departure rate in 2012–2014 was 18 percent higher than the black rate, and the white upward departure rate was only 1.5 percent higher. But the net effects of upward and downward departures depend on the *numbers of offenders* affected by each departure type; these competing effects balance out because far more offenders are eligible for upward departures (the base used to compute upward departure rates) than are eligible for downward departures, and this is especially true for whites.
14. These figures are based on the sentence for the most serious conviction charge ("CONFINE" variable), but many offenders are sentenced for multiple charges and receive a higher total sentence ("AGGSENTC" variable). Using the latter measure, the average black prison duration was 1.19 times the average white duration (50.2 months for blacks, versus 42.3 months for whites).
15. Non-prison sentences can include a local jail term of up to one year. But in 2012 to 2014 blacks and whites received almost identical average probationary jail terms: 105.7 and 106.7 days, respectively.
16. Excluding one level in which black and white sentence severity was equal yields 56 year-levels, of which 41 (73.2 percent) had higher average black prison months. If we further exclude cases at lower offense severity levels where prison duration within severity levels may be elevated by the application of mandatory-minimum statutes and other special rules (see note 10 to this chapter), then 39 of 55 year levels (70.9 percent) had higher average black prison months (one additional level drops out because of equal black and white sentence severity).
17. The within-severity estimate in text is derived as follows: (1) for each severity level, compute the expected black prison months if there were no racial differences (multiply the number of black offenders convicted at that level by the average months imposed on whites convicted at that level); (2) for each severity level, compute the difference between actual black prison months and expected black months; (3) sum these within-severity differences; (4) compute overall expected black prison months (multiply the number of blacks convicted across all severity levels by the average months imposed on whites); (5) compute the difference between overall expected black months and actual black months (this total difference reflects both within-severity and across-severity racial disparities); and (6) express the sum of within-severity differences (step 3) as a percentage of the total difference (step 5).

CHAPTER 8

1. For Kansas the good time credit is 15 percent or 20 percent depending on the designation of the offense. For North Carolina we do not need to apply a discount because recommended and imposed guidelines sentences are stated in terms of the minimum time that must be served prior to release. Sentencing data for all three states is expressed in months, so we convert these figures to years before multiplying by the number of offenders on which the average is based.
2. The data reported in this section are based on annual sentencing data files obtained from the sentencing guidelines commissions in these three states, and analyzed by the authors.
3. Per capita figures are based on U.S. Census Bureau (2017) population estimates as of July 1, 2015. The 10-year per capita fiscal impact assumes that yearly fiscal impact will remain constant over the 10-year period and calculates the per capita costs using the 2015 census baseline—we do not attempt to adjust for changes in each state's population over time.
4. In 2014, 73.0 percent of severity-level 8 offenders with two criminal history points received an executed prison sentence, whereas the proportion for 3-point offenders was 80.4 percent.
5. However, bed impacts at lower offense severity levels are more difficult to estimate than the one-less-point, durational-impact counterfactual examples discussed in the text. At Minnesota main-grid offense severity levels below level 8 there are grid cells on both sides of the in/out "disposition line." Prosecutors have and often use their power to "target" that line in their charging and plea bargaining decisions (MSGC 1984a), so at these severity levels we cannot assume that one less criminal history point would actually move all "just-over" offenders down to a "just-under" grid cell—in some cases prosecutors might charge or retain additional current offenses in order to keep offenders on the recommended-prison side of the disposition line.
6. This estimate is based on recommended sentences because the actual sentences for lowest-history offenders often involve downward departures that would not be available to high-history offenders. The estimate is also limited to higher-history grid cells where all offenders have recommended executed-prison terms. However, some offenders in cells with recommended non-prison (probation) sentences do receive an executed-prison sentence by means of upward dispositional departure; if all of the latter offenders in 2014 had been recommended for and received a proportionality-capped prison duration (no more severe than the recommended duration for lowest-history offenders one offense level higher), over 70 additional prison beds would not be needed. (In addition, many offenders initially placed on probation are later revoked and sent to prison for the recommended duration in that grid cell.)
7. Many Minnesota Zone 2 offenders are not only convicted of a nonviolent offense, but also lack any prior convictions for violent crimes. For example, in 2016 about

one-third of sentenced Zone 2 offenders had a totally nonviolent record—none of their current or prior convictions was for a person or sex crime. Over 1,000 prison beds were required to house these never-violent, medium- and low-offense-severity offenders, and those prison beds cost the state over $40 million per year to operate (again, these estimates are based only on offenders receiving an initial executed-prison sentence, and do not include offenders later revoked from probation to prison, revoked back to prison, or given less than the maximum good-conduct credit).

CHAPTER 9

1. Arkansas Sentencing Commission 2013, 102–03. Convictions for felonies at severity levels 1 to 5 are no longer counted if a period of 15 years has elapsed "since the date of discharge from or the expiration of the sentence, to the date of the current offense." For prior class A misdemeanors the time limit is 10 years, beginning with the date of commission of that offense.
2. MSGC 2017a, §§ 2.B.1.c and 2.B.3.e. Prior felony convictions are no longer counted "if a period of fifteen years has elapsed since the date of discharge from or expiration of the sentence to the date of the current offense." For prior gross misdemeanors and misdemeanors, the time limit is 10 years, also running from discharge.
3. USSC 2016 a, §§ 4A1.2(d) and 2(e). Three look-back limits are defined: (1) An adult conviction resulting in a sentence of more than 13 months is no longer counted if more than 15 years have elapsed from the date the prior sentence was imposed until the data of commencement of the current offense, but if incarceration resulted from that sentence (including custody imposed upon revocation of probation or post-prison release) the 15-year period begins to run upon final release from custody (this rule also applies to juveniles prosecuted as adults); (2) a prior conviction resulting in a sentence of 13 months or less is no longer counted if more than 10 years have elapsed from the date the prior sentence was imposed until the data of commencement of the current offense; (3) a juvenile adjudication for a crime committed prior to age 18 (or an adult conviction resulting in a sentence of no more than one year and one day imposed for such a crime) is no longer counted if more than five years have elapsed from the date the prior sentence was imposed until the data of commencement of the current offense, but if incarceration of 60 days or more resulted from that offense the period begins to run upon final release from custody.
4. Alaska (which some studies treat as having a "guidelines" system, see, e.g., Kauder and Ostrem 2008) has a 10-year unconditional look-back limit. See Alas. Statutes Sec. 12.55.145(a)(1)(A) (except for unclassified or Class A felonies, prior convictions are not counted if 10 or more years have elapsed between the date of unconditional discharge from that sentence and the date of commission of the current offense).
5. District of Columbia Sentencing Commission 2014, § 2.2.3. A prior felony or misdemeanor conviction is no longer counted if no part of the sentence (incarceration,

probation, parole, supervised release) for that crime or any other crime extended into the 10-year period preceding commission of the current offense.

6. Florida Department of Corrections 2014a, 10. Prior convictions are not counted if the offender was not convicted of any crime in the 10-year period from the most recent date of release from confinement, supervision, or other sanction to the date of the commission of the primary current offense.
7. Maryland State Commission on Sentencing Policy 2013, § 7.1.C.2 (if the offender has lived in the community without "criminal justice system involvement" for at least 10 years prior to commission of the current offense, the "adult criminal record" component of the criminal history score is reduced by one level. The score has a maximum of 7 points, and the adult-record levels and point values are: Major [5 points]; Moderate [3 points]; Minor [1 point]; and None [0 points]).
8. See District of Columbia Sentencing Commission 2014, § 2.2.3, stating that previously lapsed felony convictions (but not misdemeanors) may be revived. The Florida and Maryland rules do not expressly provide for revival of a previously lapsed conviction, but it appears that this can occur given the wording of the relevant statutory provisions (see previous notes).
9. Delaware Sentencing Accountability Commission 2015, 27 (convictions for Felony C or lesser crimes are no longer counted if they preceded a conviction-free period of 10 years, beginning at final release from the most recent incarceration for such crimes, or on the last date of sentencing if only probation at sanction levels I thru IV was ordered).
10. Michigan Judicial Institute 2014 (see Step. 1. D). Prior convictions or adjudications are no longer counted if they predate a period of 10 consecutive years of living in the community after the offender's last date of discharge from any of those sentences, during which the offender was not convicted of any crime.
11. Washington Sentencing Guidelines Commission 2014, 88. Prior convictions or adjudications for Class B non-sex felonies or for repetitive domestic violence are no longer counted if they predate a period of 10 consecutive years of living in the community, after the offender's last release from confinement or from his last sentencing if no confinement was imposed, during which the offender was not convicted of any crime. The required conviction-free period for Class C non-sex felonies and prior serious traffic convictions is five years.
12. Virginia Criminal Sentencing Commission 2014, 27. Priors are selected based on their dates of sentencing or adjudication; adult felonies are scored first, then juvenile felonies, adult misdemeanors (including criminal traffic offenses), and juvenile misdemeanors. Violations of probation or other conditional release are also counted, even if the sentencing date occurred earlier.
13. In addition, nine guidelines jurisdictions have look-back limits or gap rules for some or all juvenile adjudications: Arkansas, Delaware, District of Columbia, Florida, Michigan, Utah, Virginia, Washington, and the U.S. federal courts. See Mitchell 2015a, 36, and Mitchell 2015b, 51–53; see also Utah Sentencing Commission 2015, 14–15 (recently added juvenile look-back limit).

14. MSGC 2017a, 2.B.4(a).
15. Kansas Sentencing Commission 2014, 38; Kan. Stat. Ann. § 21-6810(d)(3) (2014).
16. Maryland State Commission on Sentencing Policy 2013, 22.
17. Pennsylvania Commission on Sentencing 2012a, § 303.6.
18. In Ohio courts are told to take into consideration that an offender "has led a law-abiding life for a significant number of years," Ohio Rev. Code Ann. § 2929.12(E) (2018), but there is no specific direction as to how this factor should affect the court's sentencing decision. Utah has no look-back limits for adult convictions, but in 2015 the state adopted an unconditional look-back limit for some juvenile priors: juvenile court adjudications for "non-person" crimes are only included in criminal history if they were entered within 10 years of the current offense conviction date. Utah Sentencing Commission 2015, 13–16. For discussion of look-back rules in other guidelines systems, see Mitchell 2015a.
19. Adult convictions for felonies at severity levels 6 to 10 are not subject to look-back limits. Arkansas Sentencing Commission 2013, 102–03.
20. Juvenile and adult convictions for Class A and B felonies are not subject to look-back limits. Delaware Sentencing Accountability Commission 2014, 26.
21. Juvenile or adult convictions for Class A felonies and for any felony sex offense are not subject to look-back limits. Washington Sentencing Guidelines Commission 2014, 88.
22. Virginia Criminal Sentencing Commission 2014, 27.
23. The figures in text are overestimates, for those offenders who are granted early discharge from probation. But for other offenders these figures are underestimates, since they exclude additional start-clock delays when the offender, after some period on probation, is revoked and sentenced to serve the previously suspended prison term followed by post-prison supervision.
24. *See* USSC 2005, 8 ("[T]he 'decay' factor of the [criminal history score] is often interpreted as a proxy for age at current offense.").
25. See, e.g., Piquero et al. 2007, at 190–92 (reporting that when an offender's most recent conviction is preceded by a conviction-free gap of seven years or greater, the likelihood of further convictions is substantially lower, albeit not zero, than for offenders with a lesser gap—offenders with a seven- or eight-year gap preceding their current offense had an average remaining active criminal career of about three years, in which time they would commit an average of one further offense). Numerous other studies have found that after a period of 7 to 10 years with no new convictions an offender's risk of eventually committing a new crime is similar to that of a person who was never convicted. See, e.g., Soothill & Francis 2009, 385; Kurlychek et al. 2007, 80; Kurlychek et al. 2006. The latter (often referred to as "redemption" studies), focus on the employment and other collateral consequences of convictions; they are suggestive but not as directly relevant to sentencing as the Piquero et al. study. That study provides data on the future criminality of offenders, given a new conviction as well older convictions; the redemption studies all address

offenders who at the time of inclusion in the study had one or more old convictions, but no new conviction. That low-risk group contains a subset of higher-risk offenders who go on to commit a further offense, and it is these offenders, at the point of their next offense, who correspond directly to defendants facing sentencing—how does the gap since their last offense relate to their risk of future offending?

26. For further discussion of retributive rationales, see chapter 1.
27. This research was co-authored with Rhys Hester and Kelly Mitchell. Further details can be found in Hester et al. (2017); we are grateful to our co-authors for allowing us to include this research in the current volume.
28. Such discretionary departure or adjustment powers are recognized in several guidelines systems. See Frase 2015a for further discussion.
29. This actual or perceived lack of flexibility accounts for the resistance to adopting a numerical sentencing guideline in jurisdictions outside of the United States.

CHAPTER 10

1. See Roper v. Simmons, 543 U.S. 551 (2005); Graham v. Florida, 560 U.S. 48 (2010), and Miller v. Alabama, 132 S. Ct. 2455 (2012).
2. For the crime of burglary there was no severity uplift for the factor "offense committed on bail;" if the offender was on license (post-prison release) at the time of the current crime, the average sentence length increased by eight months (Sentencing Council for England and Wales 2015, figure 4.4).
3. See, e.g., MSGC 1980, 7 (describing prior felony convictions and custody status as the two "core" [i.e., most significant] variables found in pre-guidelines sentencing practices in Minnesota).
4. For example, a court with the discretion to consider custody status may decide not to take this fact into account because the violation occurred as the order was about to expire; we discuss the issue of timing later in this chapter.
5. Alabama, Kansas, Massachusetts, Ohio, and Tennessee treat custody status as an aggravating factor (Roberts 2015a, Table 9.1; Ohio Rev. Code §2929.12(D)(1) (2018)). In the District of Columbia, offenders on custody status are recommended to receive a new sentence consecutive to the sentence that produced the custody status (District of Columbia Sentencing Commission 2014, § 6.1).
6. Florida Department of Corrections 2014a, 25.
7. Washington Sentencing Guidelines Commission 2014, 92.
8. Another source of insight into whether custody status should affect sentence severity is community opinion, yet the empirical research into public perceptions of aggravating factors has overlooked this particular factor. We conclude that custody status is one of a range of factors unrelated to the crime's actual or threatened harm or to offender culpability, and therefore without retributive significance, although there may be other valid justifications.

9. Alternatively, some may advance a deterrence theory—that imposing additional punishment on offenders who violate (through fresh offending) the conditions of a previous sentence encourages compliance with those conditions. At present, however, there is no evidence bearing upon this issue.
10. One widely used risk assessment tool, the Salient Factor Score (SFS), does include commitment or supervision status at the time of the offense. Moreover, some risk assessment tools may exclude custody status either because (as with the LSI-R and the CSRA, discussed in the text) they employ a different but related variable, or because custody-status information was unavailable to the researchers and/or was deemed too often unavailable to users of the assessment tool. The latter limitation may explain why the risk assessment tools developed by the Pennsylvania Commission on Sentencing (2018b) do not include this factor—it was probably not in the commission's database since Pennsylvania is one of two states with no guidelines provision for custody status.
11. The previous version had 10 measures of criminal history, still excluding custody status. Access to the LSI instrument and its validation data is restricted to purchasers of the Users Manual, which is available from Multi-Health Systems at http://www.mhs.com/Safety.aspx.
12. An indication of the relative power of different criminal history components to predict recidivism can be derived from the size of the critical test statistic. The variable reflecting number of prior convictions generated a much higher chi-square than custody status (see USSC 2005, Exhibits 2 and 3).
13. The fact that English courts impose greater punishment on offenders committing an offense while on probation or parole than bail (see text) supports this argument.
14. The timing of offending during a community sentence is considered by courts in other jurisdictions—late breaches are punished less harshly than early breaches. See Sentencing Council of England and Wales 2018.
15. Frase (1993, 310) found that this factor, independently of other criminal history components and other explanatory variables, was one of the strongest predictors of whether offenders recommended for prison would receive a dispositional departure, and be sentenced to probation.
16. This absence of clear and robust patterning premiums is consistent with research into judicial practice in states without guidelines. One such study found a weak patterning premium, and only for person offenses (see Vigorita 2001).
17. In addition to guidelines patterning rules, criminal statutes sometimes provide a higher penalty range or offense classification for a second and all subsequent violations of that or related statutes. See, e.g., Minn. Stat. 152.021 subd. 3 and 152.022 subd. 3 (2018) (providing higher penalties for a repeat controlled substance conviction of the first or second degree); Minn. Stat. 609.2242, subds. 1, 2, and 4 (2018) (domestic assault is a misdemeanor, but a second qualified domestic violence offense in 10 years is a gross misdemeanor, and three or more in 10 years is a felony).

18. One curious feature of American PRE rules is that guidelines systems rarely take account of the trend in the seriousness of offending. One would think that an offender whose current offense is less serious than his or her past crimes would receive a reduced magnitude of PRE. But as noted in text, North Carolina appears to take the opposite approach, enhancing punishment when the current crime is a lesser-included offense of the prior crime.
19. There may also be an intuitive appeal to treating similar prior convictions more harshly. Research in the UK found that members of the public deem a similar prior offense more aggravating than a dissimilar prior conviction. Respondents were provided with a list of potentially aggravating factors and asked whether each one "always," "often," "sometimes," or "never" increases the seriousness of the crime. When told simply that the offender "has prior convictions," two-thirds of the sample responded that this always increased the seriousness. But when it was specified that the prior convictions were unrelated, the percentage declined to 38 percent (Roberts et al. 2009).
20. However, as discussed later on in the chapter, the federal and Minnesota commissions have examined the frequency of *past-to-present*-offense-type patterning. For further discussion of recidivism research conducted by the federal, Minnesota, Pennsylvania, and Virginia sentencing commissions, see chapter 3. See also Florida Department of Corrections 2014b (examining a range of variables related to reoffending, not including offense similarity).
21. The U.S. Sentencing Commission has also examined the relationship between earlier and later offense types, but from a retrospective viewpoint: the current offense type of federal offenders sentenced in fiscal year 2016 was compared to the offense types of these offenders' prior convictions (excluding offenders with no priors) (USSC 2018, 3–6). Evidence of patterning was found for several offense types: 52 percent of previously convicted 2016 offenders convicted of an immigration offense in that year had one or more prior convictions for such an offense, while only 20 percent of all 2016 previously convicted offenders had an immigration prior; for drug trafficking the corresponding figures were 52 and 38 percent; for firearms offenders, 42 and 18 percent; for fraud offenders, 37 and 15 percent. However, these comparisons are not adjusted to control for differences in criminal history; for example, the 2016 firearms offenders were the offense group most likely to have prior convictions, so these offenders had higher-than-average prior conviction rates for all types of crime (*Id.*, 5).
22. Another method for weighting prior felonies is based on the severity of the sentences imposed. Some guidelines systems use more complex category schemes to define prior record seriousness; in these systems the higher prior-record categories usually require a particular number of violent prior felonies, or other combinations of offense type severity and frequency. See generally Hester 2015.

23. For all four components discussed in the text, added points are disregarded if, even without those points, the offender was already in the highest criminal history category (6 or more points).
24. Available Minnesota data does not include the specific weighting of each prior felony, but the net effects of up- and down-weighting (relative to a baseline of 1 point per felony) can be estimated by comparing the number of felony points scored (which includes the effects of all up- and down-weightings) to the number of separate felony crimes shown on the sentencing guidelines worksheet for that case. The data reported in text is only for positive values, for example, 6 scored felony points versus 5 worksheet felonies equals a net upweight value of 1 criminal history point. Since down-weighting (to .5 point) reduces the net upweight value, the degree to which upweighting increases recommended prison durations and prison commitments is greater than the estimates reported in the text.

CHAPTER 11

1. This stipulation reflects the now substantial literature demonstrating that increases in sentence length or the probability of custody have little individual or general deterrent effect. See further discussion in chapter 4.
2. Recommended sentences under guidelines assume a typical case, and our doubling limit likewise applies to typical cases. The limit may be exceeded if a highest-history offender's crime involves case-specific aggravating circumstances, or if a lowest-history offender's crime involves mitigating circumstances.
3. These principles have found widespread application in American, foreign, and international law. See Sullivan and Frase 2009, and Frase 2008 for further discussion.
4. Similar cost-benefit constraints are likewise applied in many fields of law. Sullivan and Frase 2009.
5. American Law Institute 2017, 392 (citing numerous studies).
6. For further discussion of these problematic components, see chapters 5, 7, 9, and 10.
7. See Roper v. Simmons, 543 U.S. 551 (2005); Graham v. Florida, 560 U.S. 48 (2010); and Miller v. Alabama, 567 U.S. 460 (2012).
8. See, e.g., Baxter 2017 and Gilman et al. 2014.
9. If a guidelines system chooses to count juvenile and/or misdemeanor priors, contrary to our recommendations, those offenses should have an even shorter lookback period—no more than five years.
10. We do not separately address the related concept of granting extra points for "recency" of prior offending, since no current guidelines system broadly incorporates such a criminal history component. The federal guidelines formerly did, but that component was eliminated when it was found to require many additional prison

beds without adding very much to the recidivism-prediction accuracy of the federal criminal history score. See U.S. Sentencing Commission 2010.

11. See, e.g., Frase 1993 (table 2), finding that, among offenders with recommended executed-prison sentences, judges were much less likely to order a downward dispositional departure and grant probation if the offender had a custody status point, even controlling for other legal and extralegal predictors of downward departure. An unpublished analysis of more recent (2016) sentencing data by the authors produced very similar findings.
12. Wash. Rev. Code §§ 9.94A.650 (2018). This provision is only available to first offenders who were not convicted of a violent, sex, drug-trafficking, or felony DWI crime. But when it is invoked, the provision is even more favorable than the suspended-sentence treatment recommended in text: only short jail terms and community-based sanctions, not imprisonment, can be used to sanction violations of the conditions of supervision. *Id.* § 9.94A.633(1).
13. Utah recently adopted a version of this approach, and appears to be the only guideline scheme that has done so. Offenders with a recent crime-free gap can earn from one to four negative points, which can be set against positive criminal history points (Utah Sentencing Commission 2017, 18, 26). As noted in chapter 9, Utah is one of the guidelines states that has no general look-back limits or gap rules that exclude older convictions.

APPENDIX A

1. Except where otherwise stated, the sources for this Appendix are Frase et al. 2015 and Robina Institute 2018.

APPENDIX C

1. For further discussion of various options American jurisdictions have used to impose enhanced but not fully consecutive penalties on offenders convicted of multiple crimes, see Frase 2017.
2. We do not, however, support using an offender's youth as an aggravating factor, even though younger offenders are statistically more likely to re-offend. An offender cannot help being young, and should not in effect be punished for something he or she cannot control.

   We also do not support mitigation, at least as a general matter, for another "ascribed" rather than offender-controlled characteristic, gender. Men should not be given more severe punishment simply because they are men. And although women are statistically less likely to ever engage in crime—what criminal careers researchers refer to as the "prevalence" of female crime—criminal history enhancements by definition only apply to offenders who have committed at least one crime; among such offenders, there is less clear evidence of consistent gender differences in crime frequency, criminal career length, or recidivism risk (see, e.g., Piquero et al. 2007; but see Hester forthcoming and Laskorunsky 2018, finding that convicted females were less likely to re-offend even after controlling for other legal and extralegal factors).

3. On a retributive account, the offender who has addressed the cause of his offending has moved away from his prior self: the previous conviction therefore says less about the current individual and accordingly should carry less weight at sentencing. Classifying prior crimes as a static, unchanging risk factor is therefore inappropriate although all common risk scales adopt this approach.

REFERENCES

Aarten, Pauline, Adriaan Denkers, Matthias Borgers, and Peter van der Laan. 2015. "Reconviction Rates after Suspended Sentences: Comparison of the Effects of Different Types of Suspended Sentences on Reconviction in the Netherlands." *International Journal of Offender Therapy and Comparative Criminology* 59(2): 143–58.

Adler, Joseph. 1991. *The Urgings of Conscience: A Theory of Punishment*. Philadelphia: Temple University Press.

Alabama Sentencing Commission. 2016. Presumptive and Voluntary Sentencing Standards Manual. http://sentencingcommission.alacourt.gov/sent_standards.html.

American Law Institute. 2003. *Model Penal Code: Sentencing Report* (April 11, 2003). Philadelphia: American Law Institute.

American Law Institute. 2017. *Model Penal Code: Sentencing, Proposed Final Draft*. Philadelphia: American Law Institute.

Amirault, Joanna, and Patrick Lussier. 2011. "Population Heterogeneity, State Dependence and Sexual Offender Recidivism: The Aging Process and the Lost Predictive Impact of Prior Criminal Charges over Time." *Journal of Criminal Justice* 39: 344–54.

Andrews, Donald A., and James Bonta. 2003. *The Psychology of Criminal Conduct*. 3rd ed. Cincinnati, OH: Anderson.

Andrews, Donald A., James Bonta, and J. Stephen Wormith. 2004. *Level of Service/Case Management Inventory: An Offender Assessment System – Users Manual*. Toronto, Canada: Multi-Health Systems.

Andrews, Donald A., and James Bonta. 2010. *The Psychology of Criminal Conduct*. 5th ed. Cincinnati, OH: Anderson.

Anwar, S., and M. Stephens. 2011. *The Effect of Sentence Length on Recidivism*. Working Paper. Pittsburgh: Carnegie Mellon University.

Arkansas Sentencing Commission. 2013. *Sentencing Standards, Grid Offense Seriousness Rankings and Related Material*. http://cdm16039.contentdm.oclc.org/cdm/ref/collection/p16039coll2/id/514.

Arkansas Sentencing Commission. 2018. *Sentencing Standards, Grid Offense Seriousness Rankings and Related Material*. https://www.arsentencing.com/.

Armstrong, K.G. 1969. "The Retributivist Hits Back." In *The Philosophy of Punishment: A Collection of Papers*, edited by H.B. Acton. London: Macmillan.

Ashworth, Andrew. 1983. *Sentencing and Penal Policy*. London: Weidenfeld and Nicolson.

Ashworth, Andrew. 2005. *Sentencing and Criminal Justice*. 4th ed. Cambridge: Cambridge University Press.

Ashworth, Andrew. 2015. *Sentencing and Criminal Justice*. 6th ed. Cambridge: Cambridge University Press.

Baay, Pieter, Marieke Liem, and Paul Nieuwbeerta. 2012. "Ex-imprisoned Homicide Offenders: Once Bitten, Twice Shy? The Effect of the Length of Imprisonment on Recidivism for Homicide Offenders." *Homicide Studies* 16(3): 259–79.

Bagaric, Mirko. 2000. "Double Punishment and Punishing Character: The Unfairness of Prior Convictions." *Criminal Justice Ethics* 19: 10–28.

Bagaric, Mirko. 2001. *Punishment and Sentencing: A Rational Approach*. Sydney: Cavendish.

Bagaric, Mirko. 2014a. "The Punishment Should Fit the Crime – Not the Prior Convictions of the Person That Committed the Crime: An Argument for Less Impact Being Accorded to Previous Convictions in Sentencing." *San Diego Law Review* 51: 343–415.

Bagaric, Mirko. 2014b. "A Rational Theory of Mitigation and Aggravation in Sentencing: Why Less Is More When It Comes to Punishing Criminals." *Buffalo Law Review* 62: 1159–237.

Bagaric, Mirko, and Theo Alexander. 2014. "First-Time Offender, Productive Offender, Offender with Dependents: Why the Profile of Offenders (Sometimes) Matters in Sentencing." *Albany Law Review* 78(2): 397–446.

Baker, Thomas, Christi Falco Metcalfe, and Alex Piquero. 2015. "Measuring the Intermittency of Criminal Careers." *Crime and Delinquency* 61(8): 1078–103.

Bales, William, and Alex R. Piquero. 2012. "Assessing the Impact of Imprisonment on Recidivism." *Journal of Experimental Criminology* 8: 71–101.

Bartell, Ted, and L. Thomas Winfree. 1977. "Recidivist Impacts of Differential Sentencing Practices for Burglary Offenders." *Criminology* 15(3): 387–96.

Baumer, Eric P. 2013. "Reassessing and Redirecting Research on Race and Sentencing." *Justice Quarterly* 30: 231–61.

Baxter, Emily. 2017. *We Are All Criminals*. https://www.weareallcriminals.org.

Bean, Philip. 1981. *Punishment. A Philosophical and Criminological Inquiry*. Oxford: Martin Robertson.

Bennett, Chris. 2010. "More to Apologize For." In *Previous Convictions at Sentencing: Theoretical and Applied Perspectives*, edited by Julian Roberts and Andrew von Hirsch. Oxford: Hart.

BJS (Bureau of Justice Statistics, U.S. Department of Justice). 1984. *Time Served: Does It Relate to Patterns of Recidivism?* Washington, DC: U.S. Bureau of Justice Statistics.

BJS (Bureau of Justice Statistics, U.S. Department of Justice). 1995. *Felony Defendants in Large Urban Counties, 1992.* Washington, DC: U.S. Bureau of Justice Statistics.

BJS (Bureau of Justice Statistics, U.S. Department of Justice). 2003. *Recidivism of Sex Offenders Released from Prison in 1994.* Washington, DC: U.S. Department of Justice, Bureau of Justice Statistics.

BJS (Bureau of Justice Statistics, U.S. Department of Justice). 2010. *Felony Defendants in Large Urban Counties, 2006.* Washington, DC: U.S. Bureau of Justice Statistics.

BJS (Bureau of Justice Statistics, U.S. Department of Justice). 2013. *State Court Processing Statistics: Felony Defendants in Large Urban Counties, 2009 – Statistical Tables.* Washington, DC: U.S. Department of Justice.

BJS (Bureau of Justice Statistics, U.S. Department of Justice). 2015a. *Multistate Criminal History Patterns of Prisoners Released in 30 States.* Washington, DC: U.S. Department of Justice, Bureau of Justice Statistics.

BJS (Bureau of Justice Statistics, U.S. Department of Justice). 2015b. *Prisoners in 2014.* Washington, DC: U.S. Dept. of Justice.

BJS (Bureau of Justice Statistics, U.S. Department of Justice). 2018. *2018 Update on Prisoner Recidivism: A 9-Year Followup Period (2005–2014).* Washington, DC: U.S. Department of Justice.

Blumstein, Alfred, and Kiminori Nakamura. 2009. "Redemption in the Presence of Widespread Criminal Background Checks." *Criminology* 47: 327–59.

Bottomley, Keith, and Ken Pease. 1986. *Crime and Punishment: Interpreting the Data.* Milton Keynes, UK: Open University Press.

Bouffard, Jeff, Nicole Niebuhr, and M. Lyn Exum. 2016. "Examining Specific Deterrence Effects on DWI among Serious Offenders." *Crime and Delinquency* 63(14): 1923–45.

Bureau of Justice Statistics, U.S. Department of Justice. [See BJS]

California Department of Corrections. 2011. *2011 Adult Institutions Outcome Evaluation Report.* Office of Research, California Department of Corrections. Sacramento: California Department of Corrections.

Champion, Dean. 1994. *Measuring Offender Risk: A Criminal Justice Sourcebook.* Westport, CT: Greenwood.

Chen, Elsa Y. 2008. "Impacts of 'Three Strikes and You're Out' on Crime Trends in California and throughout the United States." *Journal of Contemporary Criminal Justice* 24(4): 345–70.

Cid, José. 2009. "Is Imprisonment Criminogenic? A Comparative Study of Recidivism Rates between Prison and Suspended Prison Sentences." *European Journal of Criminology* 6(6): 459–80.

Clear, Todd R. 2007. *Imprisoning Communities: How Mass Incarceration Makes Disadvantaged Neighborhoods Worse.* New York: Oxford University Press.

Clear, Todd R. 2008. "The Effects of High Imprisonment Rates on Communities." In *Crime & Justice: A Review of Research,* vol. 37, edited by Michael Tonry. Chicago: University of Chicago Press.

Cochran, Joshua, Daniel Mears, and William Bales. 2014. "Assessing the Effectiveness of Correctional Sanctions." *Journal of Quantitative Criminology* 30: 317–47.

Cole, David. 1999. *No Equal Justice.* New York: New Press.

Colorado Division of Criminal Justice. 2008. *What Works: Effective Recidivism Reduction and Risk-Focused Prevention Programs.* RKC Group.

Corlett, J. Angelo. 2012. "Retributivism and Recidivism." In *Recidivist Punishments: The Philosopher's View,* edited by Claudio Tamburrini and Jesper Ryberg. New York: Lexington Books.

Council of State Governments Justice Center. 2012. *States Report Reductions in Recidivism* New York: Council of State Governments Justice Center.

Cullen, Francis, Cheryl Jonson, and Daniel Nagin. 2011. "Prisons Do Not Reduce Recidivism: The High Cost of Ignoring Science." *The Prison Journal* 91 (13): 48S–65S.

D'Alessio, Stewart, and Lisa Stolzenberg. 2017. "Should Repeat Offenders Be Punished More Severely for Their Crimes?" *Criminal Justice Policy Review,* https://journals.sagepub.com/doi/abs/10.1177/0887403417701974.

Dagger, Richard. 2012. "Playing Fair with Recidivists." In *Recidivist Punishments: The Philosopher's view,* edited by Claudio Tamburrini and Jesper Ryberg. New York: Lexington Books.

Dailey, Debra. 1993. "Prison and Race in Minnesota." *University of Colorado Law Review* 64: 761–80.

Davis, Michael. 1985. "Just Deserts for Recidivists." *Criminal Justice Ethics* 4:29–50.

Davis, Michael. 1992. "Just Deserts for Recidivists." In *To Make the Punishment Fit the Crime: Essays in the Theory of Criminal Justice,* edited by Michael Davis. Boulder, CO: Westview Press.

de Keijser, Jan, and Julian Roberts. 2014. "Democratising Punishment: Sentencing, Community Views and Values." *Punishment & Society* 16: 474–98.

Delaware Sentencing Accountability Commission. 2018. *Benchbook 2018.* https://cjc.delaware.gov/sentac/.

Department of Corrective Services. 2014. *Recidivism Trends in Western Australia with Comparisons to National Trends.* Perth: Government of Western Australia, Department of Corrective Services.

District of Columbia Sentencing Commission. 2014. *Voluntary Sentencing Guidelines Manual,* June 12, 2014. https://scdc.dc.gov/sites/default/files/dc/sites/scdc/publication/attachments/2014%20Voluntary%20Sentencing%20Guidelines%20Manual%20_0.pdf.

District of Columbia Sentencing Commission. 2018. *Voluntary Sentencing Guidelines Manual,* July 16, 2018. https://scdc.dc.gov/node/1344086.

Dolovich, Sharon. 2009. "Incarceration American Style." *Harvard Law & Policy Review* 3: 237–59.

Doob, Anthony N., and Cheryl Marie Webster. 2003. "Sentence Severity and Crime: Accepting the Null Hypothesis." In *Crime and Justice: A Review of Research*, vol. 30, edited by Michael Tonry. Chicago: University of Chicago Press.

Dressler, Joshua. 2015. *Understanding Criminal Law.* 7th ed. Newark, NJ: LexisNexis.

Duff, R. Antony. 2001. *Punishment, Communication, and Community*. Oxford: Oxford University Press.

Durham, Alexis. 1987. "Justice in Sentencing: The Role of Prior Record of Criminal Involvement." *Journal of Criminal Law and Criminology* 78: 614–43.

Durlauf, Steven, and Daniel Nagin. 2009. "The Deterrent Effect of Imprisonment." In *Controlling Crime: Strategies and Tradeoffs,* edited by Phillip J. Cook, Jens Ludwig, and Justin McCrary. Chicago: University of Chicago Press.

Ezell, Michael E. 2007. "Examining the Overall and Offense-Specific Criminal Career Lengths of a Sample of Serious Offenders." *Crime & Delinquency* 53: 3–37.

Farrell, Ronald, and Victoria Swigert. 1978. *The Substance of Social Deviance.* New York: Alfred.

Farrington, David. 1998. "Predictors, Causes, and Correlates of Male Youth Violence." In *Crime and Justice: A Review of Research*, vol. 27, edited by Michael Tonry. Chicago: University of Chicago Press.

Farrington, David. 2014. "Encouraging Policy Makers and Practitioners to Make Rational Choices about Programs Based on Scientific Evidence on Developmental Crime Prevention." *Criminology and Public Policy* 12: 295–301.

Fazel, Seena, and Achim Wolf. 2015. "A Systematic Review of Criminal Recidivism Rates Worldwide: Current Difficulties and Recommendations for Best Practice." *PLoS One* 10(6). http://journals.plos.org/plosone/article?id=10.1371/journal.pone.0130390.

Fellner, Jaime, and Patrick Vinck. 2012. *Old Behind Bars: The Aging Prison Population in the United States*. New York: Human Rights Watch. https://www.hrw.org/sites/default/files/reports/usprisons0112webwcover_0.pdf.

Fink, Daniel, and Steve Ducommun-Vaucher. 2014. "Statistical Recidivism Analyses in Switzerland." In *National Reconviction Statistics and Studies in Europe*, edited by Hans-Jörg Albrecht and Jörg-Martin Jehle. Gottingen: University of Gottingen.

Fletcher, George. 1978. *Rethinking Criminal Law*. Boston: Little, Brown.

Fletcher, George. 1982. "The Recidivist Premium." *Criminal Justice Ethics* 1: 54–59.

Florida Department of Corrections. 2014a. *Florida Criminal Punishment Code: Scoresheet Preparation Manual.* http://www.dc.state.fl.us/pub/sen_cpcm/cpc_manual.pdf.

Florida Department of Corrections. 2014b. *Florida Prison Recidivism Report: Releases from 2005 to 2012.* Miami: Florida Department of Corrections, Bureau of Research and Data Analysis.

Fox, Richard. 1994. "The Meaning of Proportionality in Sentencing." *Melbourne Law Review* 19: 489–511.

Frase, Richard S. 1993. "Implementing Commission-Based Sentencing Guidelines: The Lessons of the First Ten Years in Minnesota." *Cornell Journal of Law & Public Policy* 2: 279–337.

Frase, Richard S. 1997. "Sentencing Principles in Theory and Practice." In *Crime & Justice: A Review of Research*, vol. 22, edited by Michael Tonry. Chicago: University of Chicago Press.

Frase, Richard S. 2001. *Sentencing in Germany and the United States: Comparing Äpfel with Apples*. Freiburg: Max Planck Institute. http://www.mpicc.de/shared/data/pdf/frase-endausdruck.pdf.

Frase, Richard S. 2005a. "Sentencing Guidelines in Minnesota, 1978–2003." *Crime and Justice: A Review of Research,* vol. 32, edited by Michael Tonry. Chicago: University of Chicago Press.

Frase, Richard S. 2005b. "State Sentencing Guidelines: Diversity, Consensus, and Unresolved Policy Issues." *Columbia Law Review* 105: 1190–232.

Frase. Richard S. 2008. "Limiting Excessive Prison Sentences under Federal and State Constitutions." *University of Pennsylvania Journal of Constitutional Law* 11:39–72.

Frase, Richard S. 2009. "What Explains Persistent Racial Disproportionality in Minnesota's Prison and Jail Populations?" In *Crime and Justice: A Review of Research*, vol. 38, edited by Michael Tonry. Chicago: University of Chicago Press.

Frase, Richard S. 2010. "Prior-Conviction Sentencing Enhancements: Rationales and Limits Based on Retributive and Utilitarian Proportionality Principles and Social Equality Goals." In *Previous Convictions at Sentencing: Theoretical and Applied Perspectives,* edited by Julian Roberts and Andrew von Hirsch. Oxford: Hart.

Frase, Richard S. 2012. "Theories of Proportionality and Desert." In *Oxford Handbook on Sentencing Corrections*, edited by Joan Petersilia and Kevin Reitz. New York: Oxford University Press.

Frase, Richard S. 2013a. *Just Sentencing: Principles and Procedures for a Workable System*. New York: Oxford University Press.

Frase, Richard S. 2013b. "Research on Race and Sentencing: Goals, Methods, and Topics." *Justice Quarterly* 30(2): 262–69.

Frase, Richard S. 2014. "Recurring Policy Issues of Guidelines (and *non*-Guidelines) Sentencing: Risk Assessments, Criminal History Enhancements, and the Enforcement of Release Conditions." *Federal Sentencing Reporter* 26: 145–57.

Frase, Richard S. 2015a. "The Relationship between Criminal History Scores and Recidivism Risk." In *Criminal History Enhancements Sourcebook*. Minneapolis, MN: Robina Institute of Criminal Law and Criminal Justice. https://robinainstitute.umn.edu/publications/criminal-history-enhancements-sourcebook.

Frase, Richard S. 2015b. "Timing of Current and Prior Crimes: What Counts as a 'Prior' Conviction?" In *Criminal History Enhancements Sourcebook*. Minneapolis, MN: Robina Institute of Criminal Law and Criminal Justice. https://robinainstitute.umn.edu/publications/criminal-history-enhancements-sourcebook.

Frase, Richard S. 2015c. "The Treatment of Multiple Current Offenses." In *Criminal History Enhancements Sourcebook*. Minneapolis, MN: Robina Institute of Criminal Law and Criminal Justice. https://robinainstitute.umn.edu/publications/criminal-history-enhancements-sourcebook.

Frase, Richard S. 2017. "Principles and Procedures for Sentencing of Multiple Current Offenses." In *Sentencing Multiple Crimes*, edited by Jesper Ryberg, Julian V. Roberts, and Jan W. de Keijser. New York: Oxford University Press.

Frase, Richard S. 2019. "Forty Years of American Sentencing Guidelines: What Have We Learned?" In *Crime and Justice: A Review of Research*, vol. 48, edited by Michael Tonry. Chicago: University of Chicago Press.

Frase, Richard S., and Rhys Hester. 2015. "Magnitude of Criminal History Enhancements." In *Criminal History Enhancements Sourcebook*. Minneapolis, MN: Robina Institute of Criminal Law and Criminal Justice. https://robinainstitute.umn.edu/publications/criminal-history-enhancements-sourcebook.

Frase, Richard S., and Kelly Lyn Mitchell. 2017. "Why Are Minnesota's Prison Populations Continuing to Rise in an Era of Decarceration?" *Federal Sentencing Reporter* 30: 114–24.

Frase, Richard S., Julian Roberts, Rhys Hester, and Kelly Mitchell. 2015. *Criminal History Enhancements Sourcebook*. Minneapolis, MN: Robina Institute of Criminal Law and Criminal Justice. https://robinainstitute.umn.edu/publications/criminal-history-enhancements-sourcebook.

Galligan, Denis. 1981. "The Return to Retribution in Penal Theory." In *Crime, Proof and Punishment. Essays in Memory of Sir Rupert Cross,* edited by Colin Tapper. London: Butterworths.

Garland, Brett E., Cassia Spohn, and Eric J. Wardahl. 2008. "Racial Disproportionality in the American Prison Population: Using the Blumstein Model to Address the Critical Race and Justice Issue of the 21st Century." *Justice Policy Journal* 5(2). http://www.cjcj.org/uploads/cjcj/documents/racial_disproportionality.

Gendreau, Paul, Claire Goggin, Francis Cullen, and Donald Andrews. 2001. "The Effects of Community Sanctions and Incarceration on Recidivism." In *Compendium of Effective Correctional Programs*, vol. 1. Ottawa, Ontario: Correctional Service of Canada, Solicitor General of Canada

Gendreau, Paul, Tracy Little, and Claire Goggin. 1996. "A Meta-analysis of the Predictors of Adult Offender Recidivism: What Works!" *Criminology* 34: 575–608.

Gilman, Amanda B., Karl G. Hill, B.K. Elizabeth Kim, Alyssa Nevell, J. David Hawkins, and David P. Farrington. 2014. "Understanding the Relationship between Self-Reported Offending and Official Criminal Charges across Early Adulthood." *Criminal Behaviour and Mental Health* 24(4): 229–40.

Gross, Hyman. 1979. *A Theory of Criminal Justice*. New York: Oxford University Press.

Grunhut, Max. 1948. *Penal Reform: A Comparative Study*. Oxford: Clarendon Press.

Hamilton, Melissa. 2015. "Back to the Future: The Influence of Criminal History on Risk Assessment." *Berkeley Journal of Criminal Law* 20: 75–133.

Hampton, Jean. 1988. "Punishment as Defeat." In *Forgiveness and Mercy*. New York: Cambridge University Press.

Hearnden, Ian, and Christine Magill. 2004. "Decisionmaking by Houseburglars: Offenders' Perspectives." *Home Office Findings 249*. London: Home Office.

Helmus, Leslie, and Trina Forrester. 2017. *Static Factors Assessment (SFA) in the Offender Intake assessment process: Relationship to Release and Community Outcomes*. Ottawa: Correctional Service of Canada.

Henning, Kris, Brian Renauer, and William Feyerherm. 2013. *Risk Assessment and the Public Safety Checklist*. Portland, OR: Portland State University.

Hessick, Carissa Bryne, and F. Andrew Hessick. 2011. "Recognizing Constitutional Rights at Sentencing." *California Law Review* 99: 47–94.

Hester, Rhys. 2015. "Prior Offense Weighting and Special Eligibility Rules for High Criminal History Categories." In *Criminal History Enhancements Sourcebook*. Minneapolis, MN: Robina Institute of Criminal Law and Criminal Justice. https://robinainstitute.umn.edu/publications/criminal-history-enhancements-sourcebook.

Hester, Rhys. Forthcoming. "Prior Record and Recidivism Risk." *American Journal of Criminal Justice* [vol:pages]

Hester, Rhys, Richard S. Frase, Julian V. Roberts, and Kelly Lyn Mitchell. 2018. "Prior Record Enhancements at Sentencing: Unsettled Justifications and Unsettling Consequences." In *Crime and Justice: A Review of Research*, vol. 47, edited by Michael Tonry. Chicago: University of Chicago Press.

Hester, Rhys, Julian V. Roberts, Richard S. Frase, and Kelly Lyn Mitchell. 2017. "A Measure of Tolerance: Public Attitudes on Sentencing Enhancements for Old and Juvenile Prior Records." *Corrections: Policy, Practice and Research*. http://www.tandfonline.com/doi/full/10.1080/23774657.2017.1343105.

Hillier, Thomas. 1997. "Chapter Four: Time for an Overhaul, or a Tune-Up." *Federal Sentencing Reporter*, 9(4): 201–04.

Hirschi, Travis, and Michael Gottfredson. 1983. "Age and the Explanation of Crime." *American Journal of Sociology* 89: 552–84.

Hoffman, Peter B., and James L. Beck. 2004. "The United States Parole Commission's Expedited Revocation Procedure." *US Parole Commission Research Unit Report*. https://www.justice.gov/sites/default/files/uspc/legacy/2004/05/11/expedited_apai1.pdf.

Hsu, Ching, Peter Caputi, and Mitch Byrne. 2009. "The Level of Service Inventory-Revised (LSI-R): A Useful Risk Assessment Measure for Australian Offenders?" *Criminal Justice and Behavior* 36(7): 728–40.

Hutton, Neil. Forthcoming. "Articulating the Custody Threshold." *Law and Contemporary Problems* 82: 1–16.

Jacobs, James B. 2015. *The Eternal Criminal Record*. Cambridge, MA: Harvard University Press.

Jehle, Jörg-Martin. 2014. "Approach, Structures and Outcome of the German Reconviction Study." In *National Reconviction Statistics and Studies in Europe*, edited by Hans-Jörg Albrecht and Jörg-Martin Jehle. Gottingen: University of Gottingen.

Jolliffe, Darrick, and Carol Hedderman. 2015. "Investigating the Impact of Custody on Reoffending Using Propensity Scale Matching." *Crime and Delinquency* 61(8): 1051–77.

Jonson, Cheryl Lero. 2010. *The Impact of Imprisonment on Reoffending: A Meta-analysis.* Cincinnati, OH: Department of Criminology, University of Cincinnati.

Kansas Sentencing Commission. 2009. *Kansas Sentencing Proportionality Recommendation.* Kansas Sentencing Commission. https://sentencing.ks.gov/docs/default-source/publications-reports-and-presentations/2009-kansas-sentencing-proportionality-recommendations.pdf?sfvrsn=0.

Kansas Sentencing Commission. 2014. *Kansas Sentencing Guidelines: Desk Reference Manual, 2014.* https://sentencing.ks.gov/docs/default-source/2014-drm/2014-desk-reference-manual-text.pdf?sfvrsn=0.

Kansas Sentencing Commission. 2017. *Kansas Sentencing Guidelines: Desk Reference Manual, 2017.* https://sentencing.ks.gov/document-center/publications.

Kauder, Neal B., and Brian J. Ostrom. 2008. *State Sentencing Guidelines: Profiles and Continuum.* Williamsburg, VA: National Center for State Courts.

Kazemian, Leila. 2010. "Assessing the Impact of a Recidivist Sentencing Premium on Crime and Recidivism Rates." In *Previous Convictions at Sentencing: Theoretical and Applied Perspectives*, edited by Julian V. Roberts and Andrew von Hirsch. Oxford: Hart.

Kazemian, Leila, and David Farrington. 2006. "Exploring Residual Career Length and Residual Number of Offenses for Two Generations of Repeat Offenders." *Journal of Research in Crime and Delinquency* 43(1): 89–113.

King, Nancy. 2014. "Sentencing and Prior Convictions: The Past, the Future, and the End of the Prior Conviction Exception to Apprendi." *Marquette University Law Review* 97: 523–98.

Kleck, Gary, and J.C. Barnes. 2008. "Deterrence and Macro-level Perceptions of Punishment Risks: Is There a 'Collective Wisdom'?" *Crime and Delinquency* 59(7): 1006–35.

Kleck, Gary, Brion Sever, Spencer Li, and Marc Gertz. 2005. "The Missing Link in General Deterrence Research." *Criminology* 43: 623–60.

Kovandzic, Tomislav, John J. Sloan, and Lynn M. Vieraitis. 2004. "'Striking Out' as Crime Reduction Policy: The Impact of 'Three Strikes' Laws on Crime Rates in U.S. Cities." *Justice Quarterly 21*(2): 207–39.

Kurlycheck, Megan C., Robert Brame, and Shawn D. Bushway. 2006. "Scarlet Letters and Recidivism: Does an Old Criminal Record Predict Future Offending?" *Criminology & Public Policy* 5: 483–504.

Kurlycheck, Megan C., Robert Brame, and Shawn D. Bushway. 2007. "Enduring Risk? Old Criminal Records and Predictions of Future Criminal Involvement." *Crime & Delinquency* 53: 64–83.

Kury, Helmut, Theodore N. Ferdinand, and Joachim Obergfell-Fuchs. 2003. "Does Severe Punishment Mean Less Criminality?" *International Criminal Justice Review* 13: 110–48.

Kutateladze, Besiki L., Nancy R. Andiloro, Brian D. Johnson, and Cassia C. Spohn. 2014. "Cumulative Disadvantage: Examining Racial and Ethnic Disparity in Prosecution and Sentencing." *Criminology* 52(3): 514–51.

Langan, Patrick A., and David J. Levin. 2002. "Recidivism of Prisoners Released in 1994." *Federal Sentencing Reporter.* 15.1: 58–65.

Laskorunsky, Julia. 2013. "Offense Specialization and Versatility as Predictors of Recidivism." Masters Thesis, Penn State University. https://etda.libraries.psu.edu/catalog/19936.

Laskorunsky, Julia. 2017. *The Predictive Validity of the Minnesota Sentencing Guidelines Criminal History Score*. Minneapolis, MN: Robina Institute of Criminal Law and Criminal Justice.

Laskorunsky, Julia. 2018. *Minnesota Criminal History Recidivism Project*. Minneapolis, MN: Robina Institute of Criminal Law and Criminal Justice.

Lee, Youngjae. 2009. "Recidivism as Omission: A Relational Account." *Texas Law Review* 87: 571–622.

Lee, Youngjae. 2010. "Repeat Offenders and the Question of Desert." In *The Role of Previous Convictions at Sentencing: Theoretical and Applied Perspective*, edited by Julian Roberts and Andrew von Hirsch, 49–71. Oxford: Hart.

Lippke, Richard. 2015. "Elaborating Negative Retribution." *Philosophy and Public Issues* 5: 57–71.

Lippke, Richard. 2016. "The Ethics of Recidivist Premiums." In *The Routledge Handbook of Criminal Justice Ethics,* edited by Jonathan Jacobs and Jonathan Jackson. London: Routledge.

Loughran, Thomas A., Edward P. Mulvey, Carol A. Schubert, Jeffrey Fagan, Alex R. Piquero, and Sandra H. Losoyo. 2009. "Examining a Dose-Response Relationship between Length of Stay and Future Recidivism in Serious Juvenile Offenders." *Criminology* 47: 699–740.

MacPherson, Darcy. 2002. "The Relevance of Prior Record in the Criminal Law: A Response to the Theory of Professor von Hirsch." *Queen's Law Journal* 28: 177–219.

Mai, Chris, and Ram Subramanian. 2017. *The Price of Prisons: Examining State Spending Trends, 2010–2015.* New York: Vera Institute of Justice. https://www.vera.org/publications/price-of-prisons-2015-state-spending-trends.

Makarios, Matthew, Benjamin Steiner, and Lawrence F. Travis. 2010. "Examining the Predictors of Recidivism among Men and Women Released from Prison in Ohio." *Criminal Justice and Behavior* 37(12): 1377–91.

Manson, Alan. 2001. *The Law of Sentencing*. Toronto: Irwin Law.

Maryland State Commission on Sentencing Policy. 2013. *Maryland Sentencing Guideline Manual, Version 6.1.,* http://msccsp.org/Files/Guidelines/MSGM/Version_6.1.pdf.

Massachusetts Sentencing Commission. 2002. *Comprehensive Recidivism Study*. Boston: Massachusetts Sentencing Commission.

Massachusetts Sentencing Commission. 2017. *Advisory Sentencing Guidelines*. https://www.mass.gov/doc/advisory-sentencing-guidelines.

Matravers, Matt. 2000. *Justice and Punishment. The Rationale of Coercion*. Oxford: Oxford University Press.

Mauer, Marc. 1999. *Race to Incarcerate*. New York: The New Press.

Meade, Benjamin, Benjamin Steiner, Matthew Makarios, and Lawrence Travis. 2013. "Estimating a Dose-Response Relationship between Time Served in Prison and Recidivism." *Journal of Research in Crime and Delinquency* 50(4): 525–50.

Mears, Daniel P., and Joshua C. Cochran. 2018. "Progressively Tougher Sanctioning and Recidivism: Assessing the Effects of Different Types of Sanctions." *Journal of Research in Crime and Delinquency* 55: 194–241.

Michigan Judicial Institute. 2014. *State of Michigan Sentencing Guidelines Manual, May 2014*. https://mjieducation.mi.gov/documents/sgm-files/94-sgm.

Ministry of Justice. 2010. *Reoffending of Adults: Results from the 2008 Cohort*. Ministry of Justice Statistics Bulletin. London: Ministry of Justice.

Ministry of Justice. 2014. *Transforming Rehabilitation: A Summary of Evidence on Reducing Reoffending (Second Edition)*. London: Ministry of Justice.

Ministry of Justice. 2015. *The Impact of Short Custodial Sentences, Community Orders and Suspended Sentence Orders on Re-offending*. London: Ministry of Justice.

Ministry of Justice. 2016. *Proven Reoffending Statistics Quarterly Bulletin, July 2013 to June 2014*. England and Wales. London: Ministry of Justice.

Minnesota Bureau of Criminal Apprehension. 2016. *Minnesota Uniform Crime Reports*. https://dps.mn.gov/divisions/bca/bca-divisions/mnjis/Pages/uniform-crime-reports.aspx.

Minnesota Department of Corrections. 2018a. *Adult Inmate Profile as of January 1, 2015*. St. Paul: Minnesota Department of Corrections. https://mn.gov/doc/assets/Minnesota_Department_of_Corrections_Adult_Inmate_Profile__01_01_2015_Revised_tcm1089-300101.pdf.

Minnesota Department of Corrections. 2018b. *Historical Offender Population Summary Reports*. Minnesota Department of Public Safety. https://mn.gov/doc/data-publications/offender-statistics/historical-population-summary-reports.

Minnesota Sentencing Guidelines Commission. [see MSGC]

Missouri Sentencing Advisory Commission. 2013. *User Guide 2012–2013*. http://www.mosac.mo.gov/file.jsp?id=45394

Mitchell, Kelly Lyn. 2015a. "Decay and Gap Policies." In *Criminal History Enhancements Sourcebook*. Minneapolis, MN: Robina Institute of Criminal Law and Criminal Justice. https://robinainstitute.umn.edu/publications/criminal-history-enhancements-sourcebook.

Mitchell, Kelly Lyn. 2015b. "Prior Juvenile Adjudications." In *Criminal History Enhancements Sourcebook*. Minneapolis, MN: Robina Institute of Criminal

Law and Criminal Justice. https://robinainstitute.umn.edu/publications/criminal-history-enhancements-sourcebook.

Mitchell, Kelly Lyn. 2015c. "Prior Misdemeanor Convictions." In *Criminal History Enhancements Sourcebook*. Minneapolis, MN: Robina Institute of Criminal Law and Criminal Justice. https://robinainstitute.umn.edu/publications/criminal-history-enhancements-sourcebook.

Mitchell, Kelly Lyn. 2015d. "What Is *Blakely* and Why Is It So Important?" *Sentencing Guidelines Resource Center*. http://sentencing.umn.edu/content/what-blakely-and-why-it-so-important.

Moffitt, Terrie E. 1993. "'Life-Course-Persistent' and 'Adolescence-Limited' Antisocial Behavior: A Developmental Taxonomy." *Psychological Review* 100: 674–701.

Monahan, John, and Jennifer L. Skeem. 2014. "Risk Redux: The Resurgence of Risk Assessment in Criminal Sentencing." *Federal Sentencing Reporter* 26: 158–66.

Monahan, John, and Jennifer L. Skeem. 2016. "Risk Assessment in Criminal Sentencing." *Annual Review of Clinical Psychology* 12:489–513.

Monahan, John, Jenifer L. Skeem, and Christopher Lowenkamp. 2017. "Age, Risk Assessment, and Sanctioning: Overestimating the Old, Underestimating the Young." *Law and Human Behavior* 40: 191–201.

Morris, Norval. 1974. *The Future of Imprisonment*. Chicago: University of Chicago Press.

Morris, Norval. 1982. *Madness and the Criminal Law*. Chicago: University of Chicago Press.

Morris, Norval, and Michael Tonry. 1990. *Between Prison and Probation: Intermediate Punishments in a Rational Sentencing System*. New York: Oxford University Press.

MSGC (Minnesota Sentencing Guidelines Commission). 1980. *Report to the Legislature, January 1, 1980*. St. Paul: Minnesota Sentencing Guidelines Commission.

MSGC (Minnesota Sentencing Guidelines Commission). 1984. *The Impact of the Minnesota Sentencing Guidelines: Three Year Evaluation*. St. Paul: Minnesota Sentencing Guidelines Commission.

MSGC (Minnesota Sentencing Guidelines Commission). 1989. *Report to the Legislature, January 1989*. St. Paul: Minnesota Sentencing Guidelines Commission. https://mn.gov/sentencing-guidelines/assets/1989%20Report%20to%20the%20Legislature_tcm30-81504.pdf.

MSGC (Minnesota Sentencing Guidelines Commission). 2015a. *2014 Sentencing Practices*. St. Paul: Minnesota Sentencing Guidelines Commission. https://mn.gov/sentencing-guidelines/reports/.

MSGC (Minnesota Sentencing Guidelines Commission). 2015b. *Drug Sentencing in Minnesota*. St. Paul: Minnesota Sentencing Guidelines Commission. https://mn.gov/sentencing-guidelines/assets/Drug%20Discussion_tcm30-60098.pdf

MSGC (Minnesota Sentencing Guidelines Commission). 2017a. *Minnesota Sentencing Guidelines and Commentary*. St. Paul: Minnesota Sentencing Guidelines Commission. https://mn.gov/sentencing-guidelines/guidelines/currentguidelines.jsp.

MSGC (Minnesota Sentencing Guidelines Commission). 2017b. *Report to the Legislature. January 13, 2017*. St. Paul: Minnesota Sentencing Guidelines Commission.

MSGC (Minnesota Sentencing Guidelines Commission). 2017c. *2016 Sentencing Practices: Annual Summary Statistics for Felony Offenders*. St. Paul: Minnesota Sentencing Guidelines Commission. https://mn.gov/sentencing-guidelines/reports/.

Nagin, Daniel. 2013. "Deterrence in the Twenty-First Century." In *Crime and Justice: A Review of Research*, vol. 42, edited by Michael Tonry. Chicago: University of Chicago Press.

Nagin, Daniel, and Matthew Snodgrass. 2013. "The Effect of Incarceration on Re-Offending: Evidence from a Natural Experiment in Pennsylvania." *Journal of Quantitative Criminology* 29: 601–42.

Nagin, Daniel, Francis T. Cullen, and Cheryl Lero Jonson. 2009. "Imprisonment and Reoffending." In *Crime and Justice: A Review of the Research*, vol. 38, edited by Michael Tonry. Chicago: University of Chicago Press.

Nellis, Ashley. 2016. *The Color of Justice: Racial and Ethnic Disparity in State Prisons*. Washington, DC: The Sentencing Project.

North Carolina Sentencing and Policy Advisory Commission. 2013. *Structured Sentencing Statistical Report for Felonies and Misdemeanors*. Raleigh: North Carolina Sentencing and Policy Advisory Commission.

North Carolina Sentencing and Policy Advisory Commission. 2014. *Structured Sentencing Training and Reference Manual*. http://www.nccourts.org/Courts/CRS/Councils/spac/Sentencing/Training/Manuals.asp.

O'Hear, Michael. 2009. "Rethinking Drug Courts: Restorative Justice as a Response to Racial Injustice." *Stanford Law & Policy Review* 20: 463–99.

Ohio Criminal Sentencing Commission. 2017. *Felony Sentencing Quick Reference Guide*. http://www.supremecourt.ohio.gov/Boards/Sentencing/resources/jud-Practitioner/default.asp.

O'Neill, Michael, Linda Maxfield, and Miles Harer. 2004. "Past as Prologue: Reconciling Recidivism and Culpability." *Fordham Law Review* 73: 245–95.

Oregon Criminal Justice Commission. 2018. *Oregon Sentencing Guidelines Grid*. https://www.oregon.gov/CJC/pages/index.aspx.

Owen, Natalie, and Christine Cooper. 2013. *The Start of a Criminal Career: Does the Type Of Debut Offence Predict Future Offending?* London: Home Office.

Parent, Dale G. 1988. *Structuring Criminal Sentences: The Evolution of Minnesota's Sentencing Guidelines*. Stoneham, MA: Butterworth Legal Publishers.

Pennsylvania Commission on Sentencing. 1988. *Sentencing Guidelines Implementation Manual*. 3rd ed. State College: Pennsylvania Commission on Sentencing.

Pennsylvania Commission on Sentencing. 2011. *Recidivism Study: Initial Recidivism Information. Risk/ Needs Assessment Project*. Interim Report No. 2. State College: Pennsylvania Commission on Sentencing.

Pennsylvania Commission on Sentencing. 2012a. *Pennsylvania Guidelines Implementation Manual, 7th Edition*. Harrisburg, PA: Pennsylvania Commission on Sentencing. https://sentencing.umn.edu/sites/sentencing.umn.edu/files/Pennsylvania%20Sentencing%20Guidelines%20Manual%207th%20Edition.pdf.

Pennsylvania Commission on Sentencing. 2012b. *Risk/Needs Assessment Project, Interim Report 4: Development of Risk Assessment Scale*. http://pcs.la.psu.edu/publications-and-research/risk-assessment.

Pennsylvania Commission on Sentencing. 2015. *Special Report: The Impact of Removing Age, Gender, and County from the Risk Assessment Scale, March 2015*. Pennsylvania Commission on Sentencing. http://pcs.la.psu.edu/publications-and-research/research-and-evaluation-reports/risk-assessment/phase-ii-reports/special-report-impact-of-removing-demographic-factors/view

Pennsylvania Commission on Sentencing. 2018a. *Policy Overview of the Sentence Risk Assessment Instrument*. http://pcs.la.psu.edu/news/guidelines/proposed-risk-assessment-instrument.

Pennsylvania Commission on Sentencing. 2018b. *Proposed Risk Assessment Instrument*. http://pcs.la.psu.edu/news/guidelines/proposed-risk-assessment-instrument.

Pennsylvania Commission on Sentencing. 2018c. *Proposed Risk Assessment Instrument: Responses to Public Comments; Requests for Proposals*. http://pcs.la.psu.edu/news/guidelines/proposed-risk-assessment-instrument.

Pennsylvania Commission on Sentencing. 2018d. *Research Overview of the Sentence Risk Assessment Instrument*. http://pcs.la.psu.edu/news/guidelines/proposed-risk-assessment-instrument.

Pennsylvania Commission on Sentencing. 2018e. *Risk Assessment Project Phase III: The Development and Validation of the Proposed Risk Assessment Scales*. http://pcs.la.psu.edu/news/guidelines/proposed-risk-assessment-instrument.

Pennsylvania Commission on Sentencing. 2018f. *Risk Assessment Project Phase III: Racial Impact Analysis of the Proposed Risk Assessment Scales*. http://pcs.la.psu edu/news/guidelines/proposed-risk-assessment-instrument.

Petersilia, Joan. 1987. *The Influence of Criminal Justice Research*. Santa Monica, CA: Rand.

Petersilia, Joan. 2003. *When Prisoners Come Home: Parole and Prisoner Reentry*. New York: Oxford University Press.

Pew Center Review. 2012. *Time Served. The High Cost, Low Return of Longer Prison Terms*. Washington, DC: The Pew Center on the States.

Pew Charitable Trusts. 2015. Utah's 2015 Criminal Justice Reforms. https://www.pewtrusts.org/-/media/assets/2015/10/utahs2015criminaljusticereforms-(1).pdf.

Piquero, Alex R. 2000. "Frequency, Specialization, and Violence in Offending Careers." *Journal of Research in Crime and Delinquency* 37(4): 392–418.

Piquero, Alex R., David P. Farrington, and Alfred Blumstein. 2007. *Key Issues in Criminal Career Research: New Analyses of the Cambridge Study in Delinquent Development*. Cambridge: Cambridge University Press.

Piquero, Alex R., and Greg Pogarsky. 2002. "Beyond Stafford and Warr's Reconceptualization of Deterrence: Personal and Vicarious Experiences, Impulsivity, and Offending Behavior." *Journal of Research in Crime and Delinquency* 39: 153–86.

Ramakers, Anke, Paul Nieuwbeerta, Johan Van Wilsem, Robert Apel, and Anja Dirkzwager. 2017. "The Past and Future Labor Market Careers of Dutch Prisoners." In *The Routledge International Handbook of Life-Course Criminology*, edited by A.A.J. Blokland and V. van der Geest, 377–96. London: Taylor & Francis.

Rehavi, Marit M., and Sonja B. Starr. 2014. "Racial Disparity in Federal Criminal Sentences." *Journal of Political Economy* 122(6): 1320–54.

Roberts, Julian V. 1997. "The Role of Criminal Record in the Sentencing Process." In *Crime and Justice: A Review of Research,* vol. 22, edited by Michael Tonry. Chicago: University of Chicago Press.

Roberts, Julian V. 2008a. "Punishing Persistence: Explaining the Enduring Appeal of the Recidivist Sentencing Premium." *British Journal of Criminology* 48: 468–81.

Roberts, Julian V. 2008b. *Punishing Persistent Offenders*. Oxford: Oxford University Press.

Roberts, Julian V. 2010. "First Offender Sentencing Discounts: Exploring the Justifications." In *Previous Convictions at Sentencing: Theoretical and Applied Perspectives*, edited by Julian V. Roberts and Andrew von Hirsch. Oxford: Hart Publishing.

Roberts, Julian V. 2015a. "Custody Status as a Criminal History Enhancement." In *Criminal History Enhancements Sourcebook*. Minneapolis, MN: Robina Institute of Criminal Law and Criminal Justice. https://robinainstitute.umn.edu/publications/criminal-history-enhancements-sourcebook.

Roberts, Julian V. 2015b. "Justifying Criminal History Enhancements at Sentencing." In *Criminal History Enhancements Sourcebook*. Minneapolis, MN: Robina Institute of Criminal Law and Criminal Justice. https://robinainstitute.umn.edu/publications/criminal-history-enhancements-sourcebook.

Roberts, Julian V. 2015c. "Severity Premium for Similar Prior Offending: Patterning Rules." In *Criminal History Enhancements Sourcebook*. Minneapolis, MN: Robina Institute of Criminal Law and Criminal Justice. https://robinainstitute.umn.edu/publications/criminal-history-enhancements-sourcebook.

Roberts, Julian V. 2019. "From Grids to Guidance: Comparing Sentencing Guidelines in Minnesota and England and Wales." In *Crime and Justice: A Review of Research*, vol. 48, edited by Michael Tonry. Chicago: University of Chicago Press.

Roberts, Julian V., and Edna Erez. 2009. "Victim Impact Statements at Sentencing: Expressive and Instrumental Purposes." In *Hearing the Victim: Adversarial Justice, Crime Victims, and the State*. Cullompton, UK: Willan.

Roberts, Julian V., and Oren Gazal-Ayal. 2013. "Statutory Sentencing Reform in Israel: Exploring the Sentencing Law of 2012." *Israel Law Review* 46: 455–79.

Roberts, Julian V., and Stefan Harrendorf. 2019. "The Role of Prior Convictions at Sentencing in Anglo-Saxon jurisdictions and Germany." In *Core Issues in Criminal*

Law and Criminal Justice, vol. 1, edited by Kai Ambos et al. Cambridge: Cambridge University Press.

Roberts, Julian V., and Lyndon Harris. 2016. 'The Use of Imprisonment as a Sanction: Lessons from the Academy," in Mary Bosworth, Carolyn Hoyle, and Lucia Zedner (eds), *The Changing Contours of Criminal Justice*. Oxford: Oxford University Press.

Roberts, Julian V., Mike Hough, Jessica Jacobson, and Nick Moon. 2009. "Public Attitudes to Sentencing Purposes and Sentencing Factors: An Empirical Analysis." *Criminal Law Review* 11: 771–82.

Roberts, Julian V., and Mike Hough. 2011. "Custody or Community? Exploring the Boundaries of Public Punitiveness in England and Wales." *Criminology and Criminal Justice* 11: 185–202.

Roberts, Julian V., and Jose Pina-Sanchez. 2014. "Previous Convictions at Sentencing: Exploring Empirical Trends in the Crown Court." *Criminal Law Review* 8: 575–88.

Roberts, Julian V., and Jose Pina Sanchez. 2015. "Paying for the Past: The Role of Previous Convictions at Sentencing in the Crown Court. In *Exploring Sentencing Practice in England and Wales*, edited by Julian V. Roberts. Basingstoke, UK: Palgrave Macmillan.

Roberts, Julian V., and Andrew von Hirsch. 1998. "Conditional Sentencing and the Fundamental Principle of Proportionality in Sentencing." *Criminal Reports* 10: 222–31.

Roberts, Julian V., and Andrew von Hirsch. 2009. "The Recidivist Sentencing Premium: For and Against." In *Principled Sentencing. Readings on Theory and Policy,* 3rd ed., edited by Andrew von Hirsch et al. Oxford: Hart.

Roberts, Julian V., and Andrew von Hirsch, eds. 2010. *Previous Convictions at Sentencing: Theoretical and Applied Perspectives*. Oxford: Hart.

Roberts, Julian V., and Orhun Yalinchak. 2014. "Revisiting Prior Record Enhancement Provisions in State Sentencing Guidelines." *Federal Sentencing Reporter* 26: 177-90.

Robina Institute of Criminal Law and Criminal Justice. 2018. *Sentencing Guidelines Resource Center*. http://sentencing.umn.edu/.

Robinson, Paul. 2013. *Intuitions of Justice and the Utility of Desert*. New York: Oxford University Press.

Robinson, Paul. 2014. "The Proper Role of Community in Determining Criminal Liability and Punishment." In *Popular Punishment: The Normative Significance of Public Opinion for Sentencing Theory and Practice*, edited by Jesper Ryberg and Julian V. Roberts. New York: Oxford University Press.

Rossi, Peter, Richard Berk, and Alec Campbell. 1997. "Just Punishments, Guideline Sentences and Normative Consensus." *Journal of Quantitative Criminology* 13(3): 267–90.

Ryberg, Jesper. 2004. *The Ethics of Proportionate Punishment: A Critical Investigation*. London: Kluwer.

Ryberg, Jesper. 2010. "Recidivism, Retributivism, and the Lapse Theory of Previous Convictions." In *Previous Convictions at Sentencing: Theoretical and Applied Perspectives,* edited by Julian Roberts and Andrew von Hirsch. Oxford: Hart.

Rydberg, Jason, and Kyleigh Clark. 2016. "Variation in the Incarceration Length-Recidivism Dose-Response Relationship." *Journal of Criminal Justice* 46: 118–28.

Ryberg, Jesper, and Julian V. Roberts, eds. 2014. *Popular Punishment. The Normative Significance of Public Opinion for Sentencing Theory and Practice*. New York: Oxford University Press.

Sampson, Robert J., and John H. Laub. 1995. *Crime in the Making: Pathways and Turning Points through Life*. Cambridge, MA: Harvard University Press.

Sampson, Robert J., and Janet L. Lauritsen. 1997. "Racial and Ethnic Disparities in Crime and Criminal Justice in the United States." *Crime & Justice: A Review of Research*, vol. 21, edited by Michael Tonry, 311–74. Chicago: University of Chicago Press.

Scurich, Nicholas, and John Monahan. 2016. "Evidence-Based Sentencing: Public Openness and Opposition to Using Gender, Age, and Race as Risk Factors for Recidivism." *Law & Human Behavior* 40: 36–41.

Sentencing Council for England and Wales. 2015. *Crown Court Sentencing Survey. Annual Publication*. London: Sentencing Council for England and Wales.

Sentencing Council for England and Wales. 2017. *Reduction in Sentence for a Guilty Plea*. London: Sentencing Council for England and Wales. https://www.sentencingcouncil.org.uk/wp-content/uploads/Guilty-plea-research-report_final.pdf.

Sentencing Council for England and Wales. 2018. *Definitive Guideline. Sentencing for Breach*. London: Sentencing Council for England and Wales.

Sentencing Guidelines Council. 2004. *Overarching Principles: Seriousness: Definitive Guideline*. https://www.sentencingcouncil.org.uk/publications/item/overarching-principles-seriousness-definitive-guideline/.

Sentencing Project. 2008. *Reducing Racial Disparity in the Criminal Justice System: A Manual for Practitioners and Policymakers*. Washington, DC: The Sentencing Project. http://www.sentencingproject.org/publications/reducing-racial-disparity-in-the-criminal-justice-system-a-manual-for-practitioners-and-policymakers/.

Simon, L.M. 1997. "Do Offenders Specialize in Crime Types?" *Applied and Preventive Psychology* 6: 35–53.

Singer, Richard G. 1979. *Just Deserts: Sentencing Based on Equality and Desert*. Cambridge MA: Ballinger.

Skeem, Jennifer L., John Monahan, and Christopher Lowenkamp. 2016. "Gender, Risk Assessment, and Sanctioning: The Cost of Treating Women Like Men." *Law and Human Behavior* 40: 580–93.

Smith, Paula, and Paul Gendreau. 2010. "A Longitudinal Examination of Inmate Behavior and Program Activities on Institutional Adjustment and Recidivism." *Criminology and Public Policy* 8: 1601–26.

Smith, Paula, Claire Goggin, and Paul Gendreau. 2002. *The Effects of Prison Sentences and Intermediate Sanctions on Recidivism: General Effects and Individual Differences*. Ottawa: Solicitor General Canada.

Soothill, Keith, and Brian Francis. 2009. "When Do Ex-offenders Become Like Non-offenders?" *The Howard Journal* 48(4): 373–87.

Starr, Sonja B. 2015. "The New Profiling: Why Punishment Based on Poverty and Identity Is Unconstitutional and Wrong." *Federal Sentencing Reporter* 27: 229–36.

Steffensmeier, Darrell, and Stephen Demuth. 2006. "Does Gender Modify the Effects of Race-Ethnicity on Criminal Sanctioning? Sentences for Male and Female White, Black, and Hispanic Defendants." *Journal of Quantitative Criminology* 22(3): 241–61.

Stolzenberg, Lisa, Stewart J. D'Alessio, and David Eitle. 2013. "Race and Cumulative Discrimination in the Prosecution of Criminal Defendants." *Race and Justice* 3(4): 275–99.

Sullivan, E. Thomas, and Richard S. Frase. 2009. *Proportionality Principles in American Law: Controlling Excessive Government Actions*. New York: Oxford University Press.

Tamburrini, Claudio. 2012. "What's Wrong with Recidivist Punishments?" In *Recidivist Punishments: The Philosopher's View*, edited by Claudio Tamburrini and Jesper Ryberg. Lantham, MD: Lexington Books.

Tamburrini, Claudio, and Jesper Ryberg, eds. 2012. *Recidivist Punishments: The Philosopher's View*. New York: Lexington Books.

Tennessee Sentencing Commission. 1989. *Summary of Criminal Code Revision, Criminal Sentencing Reform Act of 1989, Classification of Criminal Offenses*. https://www.ncjrs.gov/App/publications/Abstract.aspx?id=118867.

Thomas, David. 1970. *Principles of Sentencing*. 1st ed. London: Heinemann.

Tonry, Michael. 1995. *Malign Neglect: Race, Crime and Punishment in America*. New York: Oxford University Press.

Tonry, Michael. 2010. "The Questionable Relevance of Previous Convictions to Punishments for Later Crimes." In *Previous Convictions at Sentencing: Theoretical and Applied Perspectives*, edited by Julian V. Roberts and Andrew von Hirsch. Oxford: Hart.

Tonry, Michael. 2011. *Punishing Race: A Continuing American Dilemma*. New York: Oxford University Press.

Tonry, Michael. 2014. "Legal and Ethical Issues in the Prediction of Recidivism." *Federal Sentencing Reporter* 26: 167–76.

Tonry, Michael. 2016. *Sentencing Fragments: Penal Reform in America, 1975-2025*. New York: Oxford University Press.

Tonry, Michael, and Matthew Melewski. 2008. "The Malign Effects of Drug and Crime Control Policies on Black Americans." In *Crime & Justice: A Review of Research*, vol. 37, edited by Michael Tonry. Chicago: University of Chicago Press.

Travis, Jeremy, Bruce Western, and Steve Redburn. 2014. *The Growth of Incarceration in the United States: Exploring Causes and Consequences*. National Research Council Committee on Law and Justice. Washington, DC: National Academies Press.

Turner, Susan, James Hess, and Jesse Jannetta. 2009. "Development of the California Static Risk Assessment Instrument." *Center for Evidence-Based Corrections*. Irvine: The University of California, Irvine. http://ucicorrections.seweb.uci.edu/files/2009/11/CSRA-Working-Paper.pdf.

Tyler, Tom. 2006. *Why People Obey the Law*. Princeton, NJ: Princeton University Press.

U.S. Census Bureau. 2016. Washington, DC: U.S. Department of Commerce. factfinder.census.gov.

U.S. Census Bureau. 2017. *Annual Estimates of the Resident Population: April 1, 2010 to July 1, 2016.* Washington, DC: U.S. Department of Commerce. https://factfinder.census.gov/faces/tableservices/jsf/pages/productview.xhtml?pid=PEP_2016_PEPANNRES&src=pt.

USSC (U.S. Sentencing Commission). 1986. *Preliminary Draft*. Washington DC: U.S. Sentencing Commission.

USSC (U.S. Sentencing Commission). 2004a. *Measuring Recidivism: The Criminal History Computation of the Federal Sentencing Guidelines*. http://www.ussc.gov/Research/ Research_Publications/Recidivism/200405_Recidivism_Criminal_History.pdf.

USSC (U.S. Sentencing Commission). 2004b. *Recidivism and the "First Offender."* Research Series on the Recidivism of Federal Guideline Offenders. Washington, DC: U.S. Sentencing Commission.

USSC (U.S. Sentencing Commission). 2005. *A Comparison of the Federal Sentencing Guidelines Criminal History Category and the U.S. Parole Commission Salient Factor Score.* http://www.ussc.gov/sites/default/files/pdf/research-and-publications/research-publications/2005/20050104_Recidivism_Salient_Factor_Computation.pdf.

USSC (U.S. Sentencing Commission). 2009. *Federal Sentencing Guidelines Manual.* Washington, DC: United States Sentencing Commission. https://www.ussc.gov/guidelines/archive/2009-federal-sentencing-guidelines-manual.

USSC (U.S. Sentencing Commission). 2010. *Computation of "Recency" Criminal History Points under USSG §4A1.1(e).* http://www.ussc.gov/sites/default/files/pdf/research-and-publications/research-publications/2010/20100818_Recency_Report.pdf.

USSC (U.S. Sentencing Commission). 2014. *Federal Sentencing Guidelines Manual.* http://www.ussc.gov/sites/default/files/pdf/guidelines-manual/2014/GLMFull.pdf.

USSC (U.S. Sentencing Commission). 2016a. *Federal Sentencing Guidelines Manual.* http://www.ussc.gov/sites/default/files/pdf/guidelines-manual/2016/GLMFull.pdf

USSC (U.S. Sentencing Commission). 2016b. *Recidivism among Federal Offenders: A Comprehensive Overview.* Washington, DC: U.S. Sentencing Commission.

USSC (United States Sentencing Commission). 2017a. *The Effects of Aging on Recidivism among Federal Offenders*, https://www.ussc.gov/research/research-reports/effects-aging-recidivism-among-federal-offenders.

USSC (U.S. Sentencing Commission). 2017b. *The Past Predicts the Future: Criminal History and Recidivism of Federal Offenders.* Washington, DC: U.S. Sentencing Commission.

USSC (U.S. Sentencing Commission). 2017c. *2016 Sourcebook of Federal Sentencing Statistics*. https://www.ussc.gov/research/sourcebook-2016.

USSC (United States Sentencing Commission). 2018. *The Criminal History of Federal Offenders*, https://www.ussc.gov/research/research-reports/criminal-history-federal-offenders.

U.S. Sentencing Commission. [see USSC]

Utah Sentencing Commission. 2015. *2015 Adult Sentencing & Release Guidelines*. https://www.utah.gov/pmn/files/172049.pdf

Utah Sentencing Commission. 2017. *2017 Adult Sentencing & Release Guidelines*. https://justice.utah.gov/Sentencing/.

Vigorita, Michael S. 2001. "Prior Offense Type and the Probability of Incarceration." *Journal of Contemporary Criminal Justice* 17(2): 167–93.

Villettaz, Patrice, Gwladys Gillieron, and Martin Killias. 2015. *The Effects on Re-offending of Custodial vs Non-custodial Sanctions*. Philadelphia: Campbell Collaboration Crime and Justice Group.

Villettaz, Patrice, Martin Killias, and Isabel Zoder. 2006. *The Effects of Custodial vs. Non-custodial Sentences on Re-offending: A Systematic Review of the State of Knowledge*. Philadelphia: Campbell Collaboration Crime and Justice Group.

Virginia Criminal Sentencing Commission. 2014. *Virginia Sentencing Guidelines, 17th Edition (effective July 1, 2014)*. https://sentencing.umn.edu/repository?title=&field_document_type_tid=All&field_document_jurisdiction_orig_tid=126.

Virginia Criminal Sentencing Commission. 2017. *Annual Report*. http://www.vcsc.virginia.gov/reports.html.

Virginia Criminal Sentencing Commission. 2018a. "Nonviolent Risk Assessment, Drug/Schedule I/II." http://www.vcsc.virginia.gov/worksheets.html.

Virginia Criminal Sentencing Commission. 2018b. "Nonviolent Risk Assessment, Fraud." http://www.vcsc.virginia.gov/worksheets.html.

Virginia Criminal Sentencing Commission. 2018c. "Nonviolent Risk Assessment, Larceny." http://www.vcsc.virginia.gov/worksheets.html.

Virginia Criminal Sentencing Commission. 2018d. "Nonviolent Risk Assessment, Other Sexual Assault Worksheet." http://www.vcsc.virginia.gov/worksheets.html.

Virginia Criminal Sentencing Commission. 2018e. "Other Sexual Assault Worksheet." http://www.vcsc.virginia.gov/worksheets.html.

von Hirsch, Andrew. 1981. "Desert and Previous Convictions in Sentencing." *Minnesota Law Review* 65: 591–634.

von Hirsch, Andrew. 1985. *Past or Future Crimes: Deservedness and Dangerousness in the Sentencing of Criminals*. New Brunswick, NJ: Rutgers: University Press.

von Hirsch, Andrew. 1993. *Censure and Sanctions*. Oxford: Clarendon Press.

von Hirsch, Andrew. 2010. "Proportionality and the Progressive Loss of Mitigation: Some Further Reflections." In *Previous Convictions at Sentencing: Theoretical and Applied Perspectives*, edited by Julian V. Roberts and Andrew von Hirsch. Oxford: Hart.

von Hirsch, Andreas. 2017. *Deserved Criminal Sentences*. Oxford: Hart.

von Hirsch, Andrew, and Andrew Ashworth. 2005. *Proportionate Sentencing. Exploring the Principles*. Oxford: Oxford University Press.

von Hirsch, Andrew, Anthony E. Bottoms, Elizabeth Burney, and P-O Wikstrom. 1999. *Criminal Deterrence and Sentence Severity. An Analysis of Recent Research*. Oxford: Hart.

Walker, Nigel. 1985. *Sentencing: Theory, Law, and Practice*. London: Butterworths.

Walker, Samuel, Cassia Spohn, and Miriam DeLone. 2007. *The Color of Justice: Race, Ethnicity, and Crime in America*. 4th ed. Belmont, CA: Thompson.

Wang, Xia, Daniel P. Mears, Cassia Spohn, and Lisa Dario. 2009. "Assessing the Differential Effects of Race and Ethnicity on Sentence Outcomes under Different Sentencing Systems." *Crime & Delinquency* 59(1): 87–114.

Washington State Sentencing Guidelines Commission. 1992. *A Statistical Summary of Adult Felony Sentencing: Fiscal Year 1992*. Olympia: Washington State Sentencing Guidelines Commission.

Washington Sentencing Guidelines Commission. 2014. *2014 State Adult Sentencing Guidelines Manual*. http://www.cfc.wa.gov/PublicationSentencing/Sentencing-Manual/Adult_Sentencing_Manual_2014.pdf.

Wasik, Martin M. 1987. "Guidance, Guidelines, and Criminal Record." In *Sentencing Reform in England: Guidance or Guidelines?*, edited by Martin M. Wasik and Ken Pease. Manchester, UK: Manchester University Press.

Wasik, Martin M. 2010. "Dimensions of Criminal History: Reflections on Theory and Practice." In *Previous Convictions at Sentencing: Theoretical and Applied Perspectives*, edited by Julian V. Roberts and Andrew von Hirsch. Oxford: Hart.

Wasik, Martin M., and Richard Taylor. 1991. *Blackstone's Guide to the Criminal Justice Act 1991*. London: Blackstone Press.

Wasik, Martin M., and Andrew von Hirsch. 1994. "Section 29 Revised: Previous Convictions in Sentencing." *Criminal Law Review* 409–18.

Weatherburn, Don. 2010. "The Effect of Prison on Adult Re-offending." *Crime and Justice Bulletin*: 1–11.

Weidner, Robert R., Richard S. Frase, and Jennifer S. Schultz. 2005. "The Impact of Contextual Factors on the Decision to Imprison in Large Urban Jurisdictions: A Multilevel Analysis." *Crime & Delinquency* 51(3): 400–24.

Wermink, Hilde, Paul Nieuwbeerta, Anke Ramakers, Jan W. de Keijser, and Anja Dirkzwager. 2017. "Short-Term Effects of Imprisonment Length on Recidivism in the Netherlands." *Crime and Delinquency*: 64: 1057–1093.

Western, Bruce. 2006. *Punishment and Inequality in America*. New York: Sage.

Wolff, Michael A. 2008. "Evidence-Based Judicial Discretion: Promoting Public Safety through State Sentencing Reform." *New York University Law Review* 83: 1389–419.

Zara, Georgia, and David Farrington. 2016. *Criminal Recidivism. Explanation, Prediction and Prevention*. London: Routledge.

TABLE OF CASES

Blakely v. Washington, 542 U.S. 961 (2004).
Graham v. Florida, 560 U.S. 48 (2010).
Miller v. Alabama, 567 U.S. 460 (2012).
Roper v. Simmons, 543 U.S. 551 (2005).
State v. Brooks, 690 N.W.2d 160 (Minn. App. 2004).
State v. Park, 305 N.W.2d 775 (Minn. 1981).
State v. Soto, 855 N.W.2d 303, 310 (Minn. 2014).
State v. Trog, 323 N.W.2d 28 (Minn. 1982).
Witte v. United States, 515 U.S. 389 (1995).

INDEX

Tables and figures are denoted by "t" and "f" following the page numbers.

www.ingramcontent.com/pod-product-compliance
Ingram Content Group UK Ltd.
Pitfield, Milton Keynes, MK11 3LW, UK
UKHW020849150926
475595UK00003B/85

9 780190 254001